Nick Asbury

White Hart Red Lion

THE ENGLAND OF
Shakespeare's Histories

OBERON BOOKS

LONDON

WWW.OBERONBOOKS.COM

First published in 2013 by Oberon Books Ltd
521 Caledonian Road, London N7 9RH
Tel: +44 (0) 20 7607 3637 / Fax: +44 (0) 20 7607 3629
e-mail: info@oberonbooks.com
www.oberonbooks.com

A catalogue record for this book is available from the British Library.

PB ISBN: 978-1-84943-241-2
E ISBN: 978-1-84943-932-9

Cover photograph © Chris McLoughlin

Printed, bound and converted
by CPI Group (UK) Ltd, Croydon, CR0 4YY.

To all my fellow travellers in body and spirit.

Contents

Acknowledgements

This book would not have been completed if I had not received The Michael Meyer Award from the Society of Authors and The Author's Foundation in 2011. The financial help it gave me, and the confidence it instilled, was immense. Thank you.

Huge and immeasurable thanks should go to all who have been so supportive in bringing this book to fruition. Julian Kemp for cracking the whip and initially talking of a journey. Sir Michael Boyd for his thoughts and encouragement. Those who read first offerings and suggested, cajoled and encouraged are Steve Sarossy, Jackie Williamson, Katie Forsyth, the Rev. Dr. Jonathan Arnold, Professor Anita Hagerman, Peter Kiddle, Dugald Bruce-Lockhart, Geoffrey Streatfeild and Clive Wood. Special thanks and love to Mikka Styles. This book would not have been possible without her.

My editors at Oberon, Andrew Walby,
Melina Theocharidou, George Spender and Emily Tinker have been tireless in bringing the book to life. Many thanks.

Toby Colver, for the map and his time.

Above all, thanks to the actors that pop up from time to time on this journey – Clive Wood, David Warner, Geoffrey Streatfeild and Miles Richardson – who went along with the spirit of it and helped me on my way and in my thoughts.
A couple of them even foolishly agreed to spend a lot of time with me in a camper van.

And above all watch with glittering eyes the world around you because the greatest secrets are always hidden in the most unlikely places. Those who don't believe in magic will never find it.

Roald Dahl

The earth hath bubbles as the water hath.

William Shakespeare

N
W   E
S

PERCY & NEVILLE COUNTRY

ENGLAND

WALES

FOREST OF ARDEN

ARCADIA

R. Trent
R. Nene
R. Severn
R. Lugg
R. Wye
R. Avon
Watling Street
R. Thames
R. Somme

London

FRANCE

1. Windsor
2. Coventry
3. Berkeley Castle
4. Bristol
5. Harlech
6. Conwy
7. Flint
8. King's Langley
9. Pontefract
10. Gad's Hill
11. Alnwick
12. The Marches
13. Shrewsbury
14. York
15. Dover's Hill
16. Southampton
17. Harfleur
18. Azincourt
19. Rouen
20. Stratford-upon-Avon
21. Meon Hill
22. Bury St. Edmunds
23. St. Albans
24. Wakefield
25. Mortimer's Cross
26. Towton Moor
27. Berwick-upon-Tweed
28. Barnet
29. Tewkesbury
30. Salisbury and Wilton
31. Bosworth
32. Leicester
33. Fotheringhay
34. Naseby

King Edward III. m. Philippa of Hainault

Edward
The Black Prince

Richard II

Lionel
Duke of Clarence

Philippa
m. Edmund Mortimer

Roger Mortimer

Edmund Mortimer
Earl of March

Anne m. Richard
Earl of Cambridge

Richard Plantagenet
Duke of York   m. Cecily Neville

Edmund,
Earl of Rutland

Richard

Edward IV

George
Duke of Clarence

Richard III

Elizabeth
of York

Edward V

John of Gaunt m. *first* Blanche of Lancaster
Duke of Lancaster m. *third* Katherine Swynford

Henry Bolingbroke

Henry V

Henry VI
m. Margaret of Anjou

Prince Edward

John Beaufort
Earl of Somerset

Henry Beaufort
Bishop of Winchester

John Beaufort
1ˢᵗ Duke of Somerset

Margaret Beaufort

Edmund Beaufort
2ⁿᵈ Duke of Somerset

Henry Beaufort
3ʳᵈ Duke of Somerset

Edmund Beaufort
4ᵗʰ Duke of Somerset

Henry VII

Edmund Langley
Duke of York

Edward,
Duke of Aumerle

Richard,
Earl of Cambridge

Thomas of Woodstock
Duke of Goucester

Henry VIII

Mary I

Elizabeth I

Edward VI

Mary Tudor

Frances Grey

Eleanor Clifford

Lady Jane Grey

Margaret Clifford

Ferdinando Stanley
5ᵗʰ Earl of Derby

**James IV
of Scotland** m. Margaret Tudor

**James V
of Scotland**

**Mary Stuart,
Queen of Scots**

**James VI of Scotland
also James I**

Timeline

1393	King Richard II issues a decree that all Inns, Taverns and Public Houses should place a sign outside their premises. The landlords grudgingly put up a 'White Hart', Richard's insignia, and it becomes a generic term for a 'pub'.
1399	John of Gaunt, Duke of Lancaster, dies. King Richard II is deposed by Henry Bolingbroke, John of Gaunt's son. Bolingbroke is crowned King Henry IV and speaks English at his coronation.
1400	Richard II dies of starvation in Pontefract Castle.
1403	Battle of Shrewsbury. Hotspur, rebelling against Henry IV, is killed.
1405	Tripartite Indenture between Edmund Mortimer; the Earl of Northumberland; and Owain Glendower. Archbishop of York is executed.
1409	Harlech Castle finally falls. Owain Glendower goes on the run.
1413	Henry IV dies. His son, Prince Hal, is crowned King Henry V.
1414	Sir John Oldcastle leads a Lollard rebellion against Henry V.
1415	Henry V leads the French campaign to Harfleur and Agincourt.
1420	Treaty of Troyes acknowledges Henry V as heir to the throne of France.
1422	Henry V dies, aged 35. His son, Henry, is nine months old.
1423	Regency Council established in England.
1429	Joan of Arc inspires the French to victory at Orleans. The Dauphin (the eldest son of the French King) is crowned in Rheims. Henry VI crowned King of England.
1431	Joan of Arc burnt in Rouen. Henry VI crowned King of France in Paris.
1435	The Duke of Bedford dies in Rouen. The duc of Burgundy turns to the French.
1437	Henry VI comes 'of age'.
1445	Henry VI marries Margaret of Anjou.
1447	The Duke of Gloucester dies at Bury St. Edmunds. The Bishop of Winchester dies. The Duke of Somerset grows in power alongside Queen Margaret.
1450	Normandy lost. The Duke of Suffolk exiled and murdered. Jack Cade rebellion.
1455	First Battle of St. Albans. The Duke of York, fighting to rid the King of corrupt advisors such as Somerset, is victorious against the forces of 'Lancastrian' Henry VI. Somerset is killed.
1460	York named as Henry's successor. Henry's six-year old son, Edward, is disinherited. York and his son, Rutland, killed at Battle of Wakefield by the Lancastrian army.

1461	Jasper Tudor, half-brother to Henry VI, is routed by York's son, Edward, at Mortimer's Cross. Owen Tudor executed. Edward is proclaimed King in London. Lancastrian forces defeated at the Battle of Towton. Henry and Margaret flee. King Edward IV is crowned in June.
1464	Lancastrians finally mopped up at the Battle of Hexham. King Edward IV marries Elizabeth Woodville.
1465	Henry VI captured and imprisoned in the Tower. Margaret and their son, Edward, are in exile in France.
1470	The Earl of Warwick, having fought for the 'Yorkists' and laboured to place them on the throne, reconciles with Margaret and invades England alongside another Yorkist: the Duke of Clarence, King Edward's brother. King Edward IV flees with his other brother, Richard, Duke of Gloucester. Henry VI restored as King.
1471	Edward and Richard invade England. Their brother, Clarence, is reconciled to them. At the Battle of Barnet, Warwick is killed. Queen Margaret's forces are smashed at Tewkesbury and her only child, Edward, is killed. Henry VI 'dies' in the Tower. Edward restored as King.
1478	Clarence executed in the Tower.
1483	King Edward dies suddenly. His brother, Richard, aided by the Duke of Buckingham, sweeps to power by declaring Edward's sons illegitimate. Even though the eldest boy is proclaimed Edward V, the 'Princes in the Tower' are never seen again. Richard is crowned King Richard III. Buckingham stages a failed rebellion against him.
1485	Henry Tudor, great-great grandson of John of Gaunt, lands in Wales and kills Richard III at the Battle of Bosworth. He is crowned on the battlefield and later becomes King Henry VII and marries King Edward IV's daughter, Elizabeth of York, ostensibly uniting the houses of York and Lancaster. Lord Stanley is created Earl of Derby in gratitude for his deeds at Bosworth.
1502	Henry VII's eldest son and heir, Prince Arthur, dies after a twenty-week marriage to Catherine of Aragon.
1509	Henry VII dies. His second son is crowned King Henry VIII having married his late brother's wife, Catherine of Aragon.
1516	Princess Mary is born.
1532/34	The Protestant Reformation. Henry VIII's marriage to Catherine of Aragon is annulled. He marries Anne Boleyn. Princess Elizabeth is born. Henry is excommunicated by the Pope. The Act of Supremacy declares Henry the Supreme Head of the Church of England. All relations with Rome are cut off.
1535	Sir Thomas More executed for refusing to take the Oath of Supremacy.
1536/42	The Dissolution of the Monasteries.
1536	Anne Boleyn executed. Henry is married to Jane Seymour. Princess Mary and Princess Elizabeth both declared illegitimate.
1537	Prince Edward born. His mother, Jane Seymour, dies as a result.
1544	Mary and Elizabeth declared in line for the succession after Prince Edward.

1547	Henry VIII dies. His nine-year old Protestant son, Edward, is crowned King Edward VI. Edward Seymour, the King's uncle, is in charge of the Regency Council which furthers Protestant reform under Thomas Cranmer, Archbishop of Canterbury.
1549	The Book of Common Prayer, edited by Cranmer, is introduced. The 'Prayer Book Rebellion' requires military intervention.
1553	King Edward VI dies. To secure a Protestant succession, Lady Jane Grey is pronounced Queen. Nine days later Edward's half-sister, Princess Mary, is declared Queen instead, and Lady Grey is later executed. Roman Catholicism is re-established. Over 300 religious dissenters are burnt at the stake during her reign.
1554	Queen Mary marries Philip II of Spain.
1556	Cranmer is executed.
1558	Calais, the last English foothold in France, is lost. Queen Mary dies. Cranmer's Catholic successor as Archbishop of Canterbury, Reginald Pole, dies on the same day. The Protestant Elizabeth, daughter of Anne Boleyn, is proclaimed Queen.
1559	The Elizabethan Religious Settlement re-establishes the Act of Supremacy and the Act of Uniformity which makes attendance at church and the use of the Book of Common Prayer compulsory. Her motto is 'video et taceo' (I see but say nothing). Systemic persecution is avoided and fines for not going to Protestant Church, recusancy, are lenient.
1564	William Shakespeare is born to parents John and Mary, née Arden, in Stratford-upon-Avon, Warwickshire.
1568	The Catholic Mary Stuart, Queen of Scots, flees Scotland to England and is detained indefinitely by Elizabeth.
1569	The Rising of the North seeks to place Mary, Queen of Scots on the throne of England. Elizabeth executes over 800 in reprisals.
1570	To aid the rebellion, Pope Pius V issues a Papal Bull declaring Elizabeth a heretic, threatening to excommunicate any Catholics who obey her. Parliamentary legislation against Catholics is swift in response, although Elizabeth mitigates the worst effects.
1571	The failed Ridolfi Plot to assassinate Elizabeth further increases tension on both Elizabeth and Mary, Queen of Scots.
1579	The Coventry Mystery Plays banned.
1583	Sir Francis Throckmorton, of Warwickshire, confesses under torture to a massive Plot involving mobilization of Catholics all over Europe and invasion by the Duke of Guise – all to place Mary, Queen of Scots on the throne. John Somerville, of Warwickshire, is found dead in his cell in London having been arrested for bragging that he was going to kill the Queen. Edward Arden of Warwickshire, Somerville's father-in-law, is implicated and executed.
1584	William Cecil and Francis Walsingham, the Queen's architects of power, devise the 'Bond of Association' enabling the execution of Catholics who plot against the Queen.

1586	The Babington Plot fails. Mary, Queen of Scots is implicated and is put on trial for plotting against Elizabeth. Sir Philip Sidney dies from wounds sustained at the Battle of Zutphen. Sir William Stanley, having fought at the same battle, later defects to the Spanish.
1587	Mary, Queen of Scots is executed at Fotheringhay Castle.
1588	The Spanish Armada is defeated by the English. The Earl of Leicester dies.
1590	George Talbot, 6th Earl of Shrewsbury dies. So too does Sir Francis Walsingham who is succeeded by William Cecil's son, Robert.
1591	Sir Christopher Hatton dies. Leicester's step son, the Earl of Essex – part of the new wave of courtiers – leads a failed expedition to Rouen to aid Protestant Henry IV of France, but nevertheless rises in the Queen's favour and is opposed to the Cecils, thereby factionalising the Court. William Shakespeare's *Henry VI* plays are written/performed by Lord Strange's Men.
1592	William Cecil suffers a stroke or heart attack. Robert Cecil assumes more power.
1594 (*approx*)	*Richard III* is written/performed. England engages in the 'Nine Years' War' with Ireland. Ferdinando Stanley, Lord Strange and 5th Earl of Derby, potential heir to Elizabeth through Henry VIII's will, dies in mysterious circumstances.
1595 (*approx*)	*Richard II* is written/performed.
1596/7 (*approx*)	*Henry IV Parts 1* and *2* are written/performed. Lord Hunsdon, the Lord Chamberlain, dies and is replaced by Lord Cobham. The Lord Chamberlain's Men cannot perform. He dies a year later enabling them to return to the public stage.
1598/9 (*approx*)	*Henry V* is written/performed. William Cecil dies.
1599	On publication of his *Henry IV* plays, Shakespeare changes the character of Sir John Oldcastle's name to that of Falstaff. The Earl of Essex fails in his expedition to Ireland and is placed under house arrest as a consequence. Robert Cecil's faction at Court is all the more powerful.
1601	Essex leads a failed rebellion against Elizabeth and, chiefly, her courtiers. He is executed for treason.
1603	Robert Cecil oversees the smooth transition of power when Elizabeth dies and the Protestant James VI of Scotland – Mary, Queen of Scots' son – is crowned King James I. He is descended from Margaret Tudor, Henry VIII's elder sister, and not Mary Tudor, as Henry had willed. James decrees that his Red Lion insignia should be stamped on all public buildings – including Public Houses.
1605	The Gunpowder Plot, based in Warwickshire, fails against King James I and the new aristocracy.
1606 (*approx*)	*Macbeth* is written/performed.
1616	Shakespeare dies.
1623	*The First Folio*, comprising most of his works, is published.

Preface

White and Red.

An apple's red skin, white tasty flesh.
Blood.
Bone.

Roses, ambulances, strawberries and cream. Blossom, toadstools, sticks of rock. A festering boil. Poppies and the Cenotaph. The setting sun and the rising moon.
Boiling rage and pale-faced fear. Blushing shame, cold disbelief. Rude health and wan sickness. Blood and bone.
Red rags and white flags. Danger, appeasement. Red mist. The white dove of peace.
Virgin. Whore.
Semen. Womb.

Red is nature's colour of warning. Its own 'do not consume' sign or 'leave me alone, I kill, you don't want to fight me' – holly berries and foxes, say. We use it ourselves to portray a threat of danger and also a hint of sex. From brake lights and stop signs to Ferraris and the lady in red.
White is the blank canvas, the neutral, the antidote to the red. The partner of red, the setting. Pure. Unblemished. From the driven snow to white horses, wedding dresses and priestly collars.
More ambiguous than black and white, red and white seem to affirm life – the present – in all its flesh and bloody gloriousness, filth and delight. It's sex. It's procreation. A woman bleeds red. A man ejaculates white. It's lifeblood. Red and white corpuscles. It's wine – red and white. It's food – red meats, white meats. It's flesh and blood. It's love. It's hate. It's living. In the pink. It's life. It's NOW. It's US.
It's also THEN.
Red and white are the colours that separated a nation for nearly a hundred years and, 600 years on, still combine to create its national flag and emblem. We are the product of a schism that ripped the body of England apart in 1399, which was seemingly bandaged together in 1485, yet hacked and bloodied anew in the Reformation by the longer-lasting pain of Catholicism and Protestantism with which these islands still wrestle today.

It was into this fresh wound of division that William Shakespeare was born and raised. Perhaps then it is no surprise that he chose division as the central plot around which all his plays revolved. Through the prism of History and what we now term the 'Wars of the Roses' he looked at, and commented on, his own cleft world. Later in his career he returned to write about the genesis of the battle between White Rose and Red, when Henry Bolingbroke deposed and killed his cousin, Richard II – the great Cain and Abel moment of this other Eden. Richard's insignia was a White Hart, Bolingbroke's was, among other symbols, a Red Lion.

This was a tapestry of history, religion and life that Shakespeare could unpick and re-weave into an exploration of his own time and the deep division at the heart of his world. He was born on the banks of the River Avon that separates the South and the North of England. He straddled town and country and rode the fresh path of the Northern Renaissance. He was in the middle of the hourglass between Mediaeval and Modern and thus his work has lasted through Time, shining as brightly as fresh ink, by the crossing of divides.

It also gives me some fantastic pubs to go in.

In 1393 Richard II issued a decree that all Inns and Public Houses which sold ale or wine should place a sign outside their premises so the Ale Taster could more easily identify where he was going, presumably amidst the fog of drunkenness, and supposedly keep the brewing standards high. Innkeepers grudgingly stuck up a sign of Richard's insignia, the White Hart. To the Arthurian Britons this was a fabled deer that ironically could never be caught and thus signified man's quest for knowledge. To other Celts that followed it was a living symbol, if spotted, that some taboo had been crossed or a moral law had been broken. In the twelfth century, a White Hart is said to have charged at King David I of Scotland, and when he prayed to God for release the White Hart's antlers turned into a cross and the beast disappeared in a cloud of smoke. At the site he built the Palace of Holyrood. By the time Richard II ascended to the throne two hundred years later the White Hart was a symbol of purity and luck. For others though, if killed, it remained a harbinger of doom, depending on your point of view.

The 'White Hart' sign outside a tavern became so ubiquitous that it was used almost entirely to refer to a pub and became a generic term. Then Henry Bolingbroke, crowned by the name of Henry IV, took over the throne. His Red Lion insignia, among other ermine and fleur-de-lys, began to spring up on pub signs and walls all over the country. In the feudal world of a tottering country, it made sense to keep in with your ruling Lord's master. However, Sir John Swinton, riding through London wearing the livery collar of Bolingbroke's father, John of Gaunt, was lynched for his pains. So if your ruling Lord didn't approve of the 'usurpation', as they saw it, then the White Hart sign could stay fixed firmly outside the local pubs, and thus still in the people's minds.

A lot of the Red Lion pubs that are named today come from the few consolidating years just after the slobbering King James I succeeded Queen Elizabeth I in 1603. In an act of supreme insecurity, James decreed that almost every building and certainly every pub should be imprinted with his own insignia, the Red Lion, just to remind all those peasants who couldn't read who was boss. History had come full circle.

'The Crown' is still the most common pub name in the country according to a survey carried out by the 'Campaign for Real Ale' in 2007. The Red Lion is second. The White Hart is fifth. (The Swan, the emblem of Stratford-upon-Avon and royal property is fourth, and The Royal Oak, the signature of England and royal insecurity, is third).

It is easy to underestimate the schism that tore apart England when Henry Bolingbroke usurped the throne from his cousin Richard II and left him for dead in prison – an act of fratricide that ripped through the nation like the red hot poker that mythically dispatched their great-grandfather. All were faced with the question of whether to follow the King with a divine right, or the man most equipped to rule the country best.

The Reformation is perhaps easier to understand. The tensions and terrors that led to Catholic fathers pitted against newly Protestant sons, one Lord's estate barricaded against another's and families hating families are sadly all too real for us. By the time Shakespeare was twenty-three, the Protestant monarch Elizabeth had been forced to kill her own Catholic cousin Mary Stuart, Queen of Scots, for her own political survival. In the early 1590s Shakespeare wrote, in the final speech by the newly victorious Henry VII, in his play *Richard III*:

> *England hath long been mad, and scarr'd herself;*
> *The brother blindly shed the brother's blood,*
> *The father rashly slaughter'd his own son,*
> *The son, compell'd, been butcher to the sire:*
> *All this divided York and Lancaster,*
> *Divided in their dire division...*
>
> (*Richard III Act 5 Sc. 5*)

To the audience that heard these words it must have seemed a pyrrhic victory by Elizabeth's grandfather. History had indeed repeated itself – revolved with death at its centre like a barrel of blood – and 'this fair land's peace' that Henry VII talked of in the play was nothing but an illusion. The bloodletting was no longer on the battlefield but in the doctrinal arguments of Henry VIII and Sir Thomas More, Protestant King Edward VI and his Catholic sister, Queen Mary I. For the feudal commoners of England, losing your life for your Lord had been replaced by losing your life for *the* Lord.

From the flames and passions of this Tudor time our world today has been forged. The English are still fascinated with Elizabeth I and talk as if the Virgin Queen, the white face with the red hair, gave birth to us all. She is Eve in this other Eden.

She is a white goddess in a sea of blood. Britannia.

For two and a half years from 2006 to 2008 I was an actor in The Histories at the Royal Shakespeare Company – performing all Shakespeare's History Plays from *Richard II*, *Henry IV Part 1* and *2*, *Henry V*, *Henry VI Parts 1, 2 and 3*, ending with *Richard III*. It was a massive success and won the RSC multiple awards across the theatrical spectrum. It will remain long in the hearts not just of the people that saw it but for anybody who worked on such a life-changing project. As we performed them every night, I began to find resonances that seemed to chime with my own experience. Scenes took place in locations that I knew and seemed to mean so much, but famous events roared by with the hazy familiarity of a schoolboy's knowledge. Talking to the cast, crew and the audience I could sense the same. On some level these Histories touched us all.

So I want to go on a journey to find out why they seemed to touch something within us, actors and audience alike, when we played them. What was it? What is the England that now watches these plays? And does the life of the White Hart and the Red Lion still run through this old place like the colours in a stick of rock?

I want to see where Richard II died. I want to feel the thrill of Eastcheap where Falstaff and Prince Hal worked their magic. I want to walk the route of the anointed Kings as they lie where they were crowned in Westminster Abbey, and I want to explore the battlefields of England where the bandages of a wounded nation lie beneath the soil. In the Yorkshire village of Towton, for example, the locals play golf over the killing fields of the largest single loss of blood on English soil.

Little do they know that with their nine-irons and their niblicks they are chipping away at the skulls of their ancestors.

I'm going to take with me some of the actors who played the parts relevant to the story to see what the man who played Bolingbroke thinks of Shrewsbury, what Falstaff thinks of Eastcheap and what Henry V makes of Agincourt. John Shakespeare, William's father, was an Ale Taster before he was a glover and luminary of Stratford-upon-Avon, so in his footsteps I and my travelling players will be exploring the hostelries and byways of an England forged on the battlefields, triumphs and betrayals of The Histories: on the one hand, Red – be it a pub or bloody Rose. On the other hand, White – be it the alabaster tombs of broken Princes or the quill of a playwright from Stratford-upon-Avon.

*

O ne

I'm standing backstage shaking like a leaf before my first entrance. Except backstage isn't backstage as such. I'm behind the ornate wall that is the altar of Westminster Abbey which protects the shrine of Edward the Confessor, King of England. In fact I'm IN the shrine. Next to me is Richard II and there are two of them. The first, in the shape of fellow actor Jon Slinger, is about to play Richard II in a few minutes, and the other is actually Richard II who's lying there in his tomb next to us.

The tiered black and gold casket of Edward rises behind us. King of England until 1066 he was martyred in a ceremony presided over by Thomas á Becket in 1161. According to the Catholic Church, Edward is the patron saint of 'Kings, difficult marriages and separated spouses' which in one stroke set the tone of the English monarchy for the next 900 years. As the Norman occupation grafted with the root stock of Anglo-Saxon culture, so Edward's reputation as the saintly tree of England grew and his antecedents wished to be directly allied to his legacy. So the Abbey he founded in 1065 became the focal point of Kings and Queens for their Coronation and death. This holy little island of Thorney upon which the Abbey stands just to the west of the City of London thus became the centre of English government and power – and so it remains. Across the road is the Palace of Westminster that churns out its laws and buffoonery to this day.

From the altar where I stand I might be able to see Westminster Hall if it weren't for the Lady Chapel that so magnificently holds the tombs of Henry VII and his wife Elizabeth of York. Their two granddaughters Mary I and Elizabeth I lie a few yards away close to their cousin, Mary, Queen of Scots and her son, King James I. Closer to me, within the shrine, is Henry V's tomb placed at the apogee of a horseshoe of Kings and Queens that surround Edward in a glorious roll-call of history. This is the centre of England. Richard II, Edward III and his wife Philippa of Hainault, Henry III, Edward I and his wife Eleanor of Castile make up the high-powered group that shimmer quietly in the setting sun streaming through the west windows far, far away.

I can see the shoe-shaped shallows as they wind from the foot of Richard's tomb to the tiny chantry chapel above Henry's own resting place. Grooves forged by thousands of monks' footsteps praying daily for their souls.

We are restaging, in Westminster Abbey, a few scenes from The Histories, which we last performed two years before, to see these famous characters brought to life in the very place they knew so well. Jon had played both Richard II and Richard III; Clive Wood, shifting nervously at my other side, had played Henry IV. All three Kings were anointed just the other side of this ancient altar screen. Tonight, for one night only, I am playing an extremely jittery and nervous Earl of Northumberland who doesn't know his lines.

The maudlin plainsong of three *vicars chorale* plait their way through the hearts of the audience as Jon steps through the door of the altar and stands at exactly the place where Kings and Queens have been crowned for the last 1,000 years and speaks to the audience as Richard II:

> *For God's sake, let us sit upon the ground*
> *And tell sad stories of the death of kings;*

Very well, I will.

Windsor

When I was twenty-one I used to drink tremendous and revealing amounts of whisky in Windsor Castle. My best friend was a singer in the choir at St George's Chapel and lived in the Cloisters nestled high within the castle walls looking out over Albion. I would visit every few months or so and even at such a swaggering age I could appreciate the vast privilege of having free rein to wander around such a place. Shakespeare too would get to come here as an actor and cavort around the grounds: another boy, like me, from the provinces – an outsider crossing the boundaries. Standing in Windsor Castle now amongst the tourists and tiaras it seems precisely nothing has changed since I would drink into the night and go for walks amongst the ghosts.

The castle stands like a toothy grin in the sky and can be seen from miles around standing guard on the banks of the Thames. First built by William the Conqueror, it is the longest-occupied palace in Europe, having been the preferred home, and occasional refuge, of most of the subsequent monarchs for nearly a thousand years. Each has put their own stamp on the place, but it was Edward III in the 1300s who turned it into the heart of the monarchy by taking the existing Chapel of St.

Edward the Confessor and rebuilding it to spearhead his new Order of the Garter. The renamed St George's Chapel became the centre of his movement to create an England separate from France based on the mythical fountain of Arthurian legend and the flower of mediaeval chivalry. His grandson, Richard II, carried out extensive works to enlarge the chapel but it was Edward IV who really created what we see now. He lies buried under the altar and close by is the body of Henry VI – the man whom Edward had to dethrone twice in order to become King himself.

The person who entombed the two warring Kings in an eternal bid for attention was the man who has grabbed all the limelight ever since – Richard III. He had the murdered body of Henry VI moved to St. George's during his brief reign. His successor, Henry Tudor, turned the grave into a shrine in preparation for Henry VI's spiritual ascent to sainthood.

The trouble is that Henry VI never became a saint and the shrine was never finished. His case for martyrdom was eclipsed by the subsequent travails of Sir Thomas More and the English Reformation led by Henry VIII who had his corpulent grave constructed at St. George's alongside Jane Seymour in 1547. Just over a century later the headless body of Charles I was laid in the same vault in a jumble of division scarcely rivalled.

Today the heraldic banners of all the members of the Order of the Garter still hang on the rarified walls. If the Chapel is no longer a shrine to Henry VI, it is now a shrine to England. The high, delicate walls are cast in yellow sandstone that seem to cascade like a waterfall to the floor. The Quire stalls peer at each other in close proximity and it almost seems wrong to walk over the chessboard squares that lead past the vault of Henry VIII and Charles I to the altar under which Edward IV and Henry VI lie in perpetual mistrust. Yet it is the Stall Plates of the Knights of the Garter that take the breath away. Each plate is given to a Knight or Lady that enters the Order whereupon it stays in perpetuity. As a consequence around each seat there is a jigsaw of dragons, lions and bears that are a pictorial journey back in time to the 1300s. Quietly opaque under the perfect wood carvings that turn almost to lace, they are a unique testament to the ruling powers of England over 700 years. Perhaps because it feels more like a mausoleum than most cathedrals or chapels, the respectful hush that descends on the visitors when they walk through the door seems more complete.

Doubtless a similar hush would descend when walking into the Court of Elizabeth I. She used Windsor Castle almost as a refuge from the plots on her life that so riddled her reign. It was here, she said, that she could plausibly be safe 'knowing it could stand a siege if need be'. She was high on the hit list of Catholic forces in Europe and was also the target for numerous internal plots against her that wove through the fabric of society.

The 'Throckmorton' plot of 1583, like so many others in Elizabethan England, aimed to place Mary, Queen of Scots on the throne in order to restore the old religion. Sir Francis Throckmorton, whose family seat was fifteen miles from Stratford-upon-Avon, was found to be acting as a spy. Under torture he confessed to a plot involving an invasion by the Duke of Guise and an organised uprising of Catholics within England.

At the same time a Warwickshire man called John Somerville was arrested in London insanely bragging of his mission to shoot the Queen. He was put to the rack and confessed all, implicating his father-in-law Edward Arden – the *paterfamilias* to Shakespeare's mother's family. Arden was strung up at Tyburn and his head placed on London Bridge in the age-old manner of traitors, whilst Somerville was described as insane and ended up being strangled in his cell either by a long-suffering fellow prisoner or by his fellow Catholics who stopped him singing like a canary.

The Warwickshire plots ushered in a fresh era of hostility from the authorities towards Catholics and in 1584 the 'Bond of Association' was created by the Queen's architects of power, William Cecil and Sir Francis Walsingham, that required all signatories to execute anyone attempting to usurp the throne or kill the Queen. All of which led not only to the tightening of the Protestant grip around the Catholic throat but ultimately to the 'legal' execution of Mary, Queen of Scots in 1587 when more evidence of plotting emerged.

It was soon after these plots, in 1585, that another young Warwickshire man, William Shakespeare, disappeared from the radar of history only to turn up in the early 1590s in London writing plays that had at their heart the division of Mediaeval England a century before, yet performed in front of an audience more experienced in social division than ever.

Elizabeth was still very much alive and her earlier sparkling reign of peace and tolerance to the Catholics on one side and the 'godly' Puritans on the other was a thing of distant memory. Two generations had lived under her rule, and her miraculous longevity combined with a furious indisposition to name a successor had seen once lustrous leaves grow limp and dull upon the tree. England was not only between one crown and another, it lay between one idea and another. It was not yet Protestant but neither was it Catholic. It stood on the *limen* of two religions and two worlds, the Old and the New. The longer she lived, the more dangerous England became.

By the time Shakespeare was writing *Richard II* around 1595, he had proved himself capable of treading the line with jail-dodging ease. His *Romeo and Juliet* neatly exposed the two sides of society when he showed that love and passion can fall in between. *Richard III* pleased the Tudors with its depiction of a nasty, deformed Plantagenet but under that disguise subtly turned the Elizabethan world on its head. Other not so nimble-footed playwrights were imprisoned for much less. John Hayward found himself in the Tower in 1600 when his play *The First Part of the Life and Reign of King Henry IV* featured a 'sympathetic' version of Richard II's abdication. It was the line between thesis and antithesis that kept the brilliant Shakespeare from jail.

Richard II is a prequel that goes back to the beginning – to the moment the garden of England fell from grace. It starts in Windsor with a murder having been committed and a banishment. Raising Cain. Thomas of Woodstock, Duke of Gloucester and uncle to Richard II, has been murdered and no one is quite sure who did it. The King's cousin, Henry Bolingbroke, Earl of March, has pointed the finger at the Duke of Norfolk, Thomas Mowbray, and now the King sits before the two and hears their case at Windsor.

It is Bolingbroke that wants blood. He was the son of John of Gaunt, Duke of Lancaster, who was by this time the most powerful man in the country and certainly the richest. Richard was only eleven years old when he became King and his uncle, Gaunt, had maintained peace through sharp politics and brutal force. Importantly, when the young Richard came of age Gaunt had been prepared to be ruled by his rightful sovereign. Yet in running the country for so long Gaunt's roots extended deep underground – a fact which began to irk the increasingly irrepressible Richard the longer he ruled.

Gradually Richard took to his side various courtiers from the lower echelons of nobility untainted by alliance with Gaunt and thus two factions began to emerge in Court – the new, increasingly louche favourites of the King, and the old dynastic world of Gaunt and his son, Henry Bolingbroke.

Through all the machinations of the first scenes of *Richard II* it is the chasm between the two cousins, Richard and Bolingbroke, that takes centre stage. Richard was the first King to insist on being called 'Majesty' and the haughty rhetoric of Richard compared to the bullish musings of Bolingbroke set the scene for the two to clash irretrievably before long.

Even though it's a cold morning in January, Windsor is heaving with tourists when I stand outside St George's Chapel imagining the fractious Court meeting in the turreted Royal apartments beyond. I've left the cosy, yellowing confines of the Chapel and I'm yards away from where I would sit and drink whisky long into the night amongst the Tudor timbers of the Cloisters. My mind full of Kings, Princes and Plots, I am disturbed from my nostalgia by an American who asks, 'Excuse me, are you Prince Edward?'

'Which one?' I say.

'Are there two?'

Pause.

'No. I'm not Prince Edward.'

'Gee, I didn't think he'd be out here, but you never know.'

Yes, you do.

'No. I suppose you don't,' I say.

I leave through the gates and get on the train to London.

The odd trip to Windsor aside, I spent a large part of my twenties under the Strand where John of Gaunt's Palace stood in the 1300s. The 'Green Room Club' played host to all the crews manning the West End shows and all the penniless actors scraping around London. You couldn't see for the smoke yet it was a place in which I found lasting friendships amongst the subterranean arches. It had a liberty all of its own and wrapped its sweaty arm around a scared country boy who returned the favour by playing the honky-tonk piano long into the night.

It has long been replaced by the swank and marble of an exclusive club and when I go in to take a peek through the foyer I note with joy that behind the veneer the place still stinks of mould and sewage. Maybe they just hadn't warmed it up for the day but the smell is unmistakable. The river is just too close, and the bricks too rotten, to wipe away the past. I turn and walk away with a smile.

Gaunt's palace was the most impressive building in London and from one end to the other almost connected the City of London in the

East with the Minster to the West. Through various marriages Gaunt had become the Duc de Sauvoy in France hence the Savoy Hotel stands now on the spot just along from 'Lancaster Place' and the house of his descendants from his third marriage – Somerset House.

Evidence of just how deep the division went between the King and Gaunt's Lancastrian estates can be found in the Savoy itself: as late as the nineteenth century the land was subject to different laws than the rest of the country as it was owned by the Duchy of Lancaster and governed by the Lancashire county 'palatine' – an ancient administrative area that like much of the North West of England in the Middle Ages pretty much governed itself. Known as the *liberty of the Savoy*, debtors could reside there and not be subject to the normal laws of the rest of London. The 'Manor of the Savoy' would famously go 'beating the bounds' – an ancient ritual that reinforced the boundaries of the parish, renewing the land and community within it. It only stopped in the 1960s and attempts have been made to reintroduce the ceremony once again since 2010. Its uniqueness in the heart of London stretches back 700 years. This land is Lancastrian, not London. Red not White.

I think about going into The Savoy yet one of the things I learnt when I was out of work as an actor and playing piano in these hotels is that the poshness of a place is only as deep as the swing door that separates the art deco lounge from the staff canteen. Down there in the kitchens the true heart of London beats: the vast multicultural swirl that has always been the best of London exists in complete harmony. Shakespeare lived and worked in the *liberty of the Clink* – land owned by the Bishops of Winchester on the South Bank and therefore, like the Savoy, not subject to most common laws of the land. It was similarly filled with the incoming tide of the world. Today, behind the doors at the Savoy, the chambermaids, waiters, and doormen all pile the same cheap apple crumbles on to their plates. The top hat towers of the hotels above are resting on their foundation. It's exhilarating. But it means I will never pay £18 for a pot of tea and some cake merely for a slice of gentrification. I'd rather be down the 'Green Room Club' but, like Gaunt's Palace, that isn't there any more either.

By the time of the events in Shakespeare's play the Palace had been all but destroyed in the Peasants' Revolt of 1381 and Gaunt was renting the Bishop of Ely's London house in what is now Holborn. The upshot of the divisions and accusations at Windsor was that Gaunt's son, Henry Bolingbroke, was to fight Mowbray to the death in order to prove the other wrong.

But Gaunt was well aware of the political situation: he knew, for example, that it had been Richard himself who gave the word for the Duke of Gloucester to be killed in order to curb the power of his uncles and thus set in motion an inevitable family conflict that would rip England apart.

Coventry

Bolingbroke's fight was to take place in the Warwickshire city of Coventry, which by the Middle Ages had become the beating heart of England – its huge cathedral spire pointing wealthily to the sky. Close to the meeting point of the Roman roads of Watling Street and the Fosse Way (still major roads to this day), and thus to the old Danelaw line which followed Watling Street marking the border between Viking and Saxon Britain, Coventry had been an important trading post for 600 years by the time Bolingbroke and Mowbray were due to fight to the death. It was still thriving 165 years later when Shakespeare was born twenty miles away in Stratford-upon-Avon.

The city played host to a set of Mystery Plays that reaffirmed the community as much as beating the bounds or any ale-fuelled festivals of antiquity. Since the 1100s the clergy had been forbidden to appear on a public stage so the telling of bible stories had fallen to the townspeople. The respective Guilds took it upon themselves to provide all the different materials needed for the Plays and by the time of the Reformation the performances of these stories from the Bible were as woven into society as the Church itself. Most scholars seem to agree that the young William would have seen the Coventry Mystery Plays until they were banned in 1579 when he was fifteen. The stage was set, literally, for the shifting of the 'Plays' from the streets into the secular boundaries of a new performance space – the theatre.

Despite the best efforts of the Reformation, Coventry thrived. Even in the twentieth century it was still one of the finest, most beautiful mediaeval cities anywhere in Europe. It also contained a distillation of skilled mechanics: after centuries of trade and cloth manufacturing, the workings of the loom had matured into clock- and watch-making which in turn became bicycle and then automotive engineering. Jaguar still has a factory here.

Because of its beauty and talent Hitler flattened it in 1940.

Over 500 people died on 14th November of that year and more than 4,000 homes and three-quarters of the factories on which it relied were obliterated. It is now 'twinned' with Dresden in an act of hand-holding so poignant, hopeful and horrible, I think a lot of people just look away.

What Hitler didn't finish, the planners of the 1950s and 1960s managed to complete. They proceeded to get rid of most of the mediaeval buildings left standing and sweep through the new city rising from the flames with an architectural broom that was startling in its zeal and ignorance. They even paved over the river.

There is a map of England by Robert Morden drawn in 1695 which shows Coventry in the dead centre of the country. All roads lead through it. Now all roads lead around it. From the M6 to the Inner Ring Road, driving into Coventry seems designed to keep you out rather than welcome you in. Spon Street, however, still survives in the centre having miraculously avoided the hands of evil and naivety. It has beautiful little red sandstone houses, half-timbered doorways and windows, and is the one place I can begin to imagine the two great knights of the realm, Bolingbroke and Mowbray, as they square up to each other for their fight.

Today the low, easy buildings on Spon Street glow in the evening sun. They're filled with kebab shops and it smells of greasy chicken but it is beautifully picturesque until the Inner Ring Road cuts off the street like a torn needle from a record. I walk back to the other end of the street and the huge blue square of an Ikea store refurnishes the sky.

I love the thrill of new architecture. In the 1950s this was the largest piece of urban planning in Europe. In 1962, when Britten's War Requiem was commissioned for the opening of the magnificent new cathedral built next to the bombed-out shell of the old one, it must have seemed like the Phoenix was rising from the ashes and the hope of the New World would conquer the sins of the Old. Fresh, exciting, and alive.

However, like the Catholics of Elizabethan England who adopted the Phoenix as their own motto, things never quite turned out the way they wanted it to be. As I stand seeking the cathedral in the turmoil of the city centre, I feel similarly lost.

I am totally confused amongst the 'pedestrian pathways' lined with pound shops and chain stores. Coventry retains the boundaries of the old city walls but they built a fortress of shops inside it so all you get from the outside is walls. Earlier, I had stood next to The Belgrade

Theatre and had no idea that I was about 200 yards from the main centre of the town. All I could see from there was decaying concrete and the ceaseless mist of air-conditioning units.

Having found my way in – no mean feat to the stranger in town – I'm encouraged to spend, but not to live. I try to find a postcard and ask a woman at the till in a card shop where I can find one. She looks at me with disinterest and says 'There aren't any. Why would you want a postcard of Coventry?'

I find the cathedral but it turns out to be another shopping centre, the Cathedral Plaza. But then I round a corner and there is the actual cathedral, burning red in the setting sun. The earthy sandstone so different from the white of Westminster, brooding and somehow exultant that it is still here.

This is a magnificent place. The broken walls of the nave survived the bombs and the ensuing all-consuming fire. So, too, the spire which remains the third tallest in England. You can walk straight through the old doors and stand in the empty, roofless middle that was once one of the mightiest cathedrals in Europe. It is somehow terribly greater than had it been left untouched by the bombs. There are little memorials dotted amongst the red stone and tiny reminders of its glorious past – a gargoyle here, an exquisite sculptured cross over there, but mostly it sits in harrowing starkness.

Next to this shell is the new cathedral. Hugely of its time, large once-white walls crease and fold in squares and diamonds like concrete origami. Glass doors on its front open it up to the world in a welcoming embrace so I peer in and Evensong is being sung. Seven people are at the service. The massive space leading to the central Cross stretches away forever in staggering modern beauty yet lined with empty pews.

Outside, across the square, teenagers skateboard loudly. Ten people are watching. I stand for a long while, transfixed. They're really good. I look back and see the old spire and all it represents bleeding into the evening. It is extraordinary that the imagination existed to keep it still standing and as such is one of the most important and eloquent War Memorials in the country.

When Richard II, Bolingbroke and Mowbray thrashed out their differences here, the city was in its pomp: important, historic even then, pregnant with the future it so readily delivered. Now Coventry is sadly a symbol of the twentieth century – how it was torn apart by evil, idealism and goodwill. The old cathedral stands like a toothless Grandmother over a world changed beyond belief. Her skateboarding progeny are lost to her in another world she cannot understand. But she struggles on and as with every Grandmother she should be paid more respect and learnt from.

Round the back of the cathedral there still remain a good few of the old buildings that made this glorious city, and tucked away in their centre is St. Mary's Guildhall where Richard II convened many Parliaments and great councils throughout his reign. The Guildhall itself is a vaulted stone hall, long and ancient. The great North Window has nine panels on it, each depicting a King, and is dominated by two huge tapestries either side of it – one woven in the 1500s. High up in the wooden arched roof studded all over the beams are many White Harts that seem as prevalent as the security cameras that hover next to them. Both stare at me impassively.

Richard convened a Council here at St. Mary's Guildhall in January 1399 with knights, barons and prelates summoned from all over the country. He had spent Christmas further up Watling Street in Lichfield, where his celebrations were long and legendary. A month before that, a huge comet had been observed across Britain and Europe and for eight nights it burned brightly in the sky, 'its tail turned towards the west'. Monks in Paris noted that astrologers held it portended the death of kings or impending revolutions. The New Year heralded more bad omens – the laurel trees everywhere withered, and then revived. A river in Bedford suddenly changed its course signifying division within the land.

Richard had high Christian aspirations. He reinforced the 'Divine' right to rule and introduced the concept of the crown itself being almost worshipped: the man with the direct link to God. He wanted to be Holy Roman Emperor and had given considerable support to the Byzantine Emperor, beleaguered in Constantinople, whose son-in-law was at Lichfield for the Christmas celebrations, one reason perhaps why they were so impressive. The Church at the time was itself riven by schism, and Richard had become an important pawn in the war within it. It has even been suggested that had he become Holy Roman Emperor he may have abdicated anyway. There was, too, a prophecy linking the conquest of Ireland to a vaunted destiny in Christendom and Richard believed it was his.

To this end, at the Council in Coventry, Richard asked for money to go to Ireland and conquer the rebels that had risen up there, which goes some way to explaining why he opted to leave the country just as he had made a serious enemy of Bolingbroke.

Standing in the middle of the division of his nobles, Richard was only pushing them apart rather than holding them together. So he called off the fight at Coventry as it was about to start and promptly banished Mowbray for life and Bolingbroke for ten years – later reduced to six on account of Gaunt. Nothing like clearing the desk. Yet he was only building up more resentment from an already fractious nobility.

Ely House

The men whom Richard chose to surround himself with in Court were by no means friends of Bolingbroke's either. Bushy, Bagot and Green – the 'caterpillars of the commonwealth' as Bolingbroke later calls them in Shakespeare's play – were low-lying aristocrats that had grown up through the gaps in the nobility left by the Black Death. The Duke of Aumerle, however, was a cousin of both Richard and Bolingbroke and the eldest son of Edmund Langley, Duke of York. After Richard and Bolingbroke, Aumerle was the next senior of all the grandsons of Edward III and he was an important ally to Richard in his battles with the old guard. It is highly probable that Aumerle was involved in the murder of the Duke of Gloucester, and it is to Aumerle and his father York – a man pulled apart by the widening divisions in his world – that Shakespeare reaches to tell his story.

Gaunt is dying in Ely House and York is looking after him. Ely House is still there – tucked around the back of the jewellery shops of Hatton Gardens in London. St Etheldreda's Church was part of the original house and grounds that covered this whole site and still stands as one of the oldest Catholic Churches in Britain, built in the time of Edward I. It must have smelt quite bad as the Fleet River, sludging past where Farringdon Road is now forming a boundary of the City, had by that time become the main sewer of London. Yet it was owned by the Bishops of Ely who rented out this near-palace so handily situated by the old City walls.

As a consequence, the Old Mitre Tavern still stands guard on the corner. To walk along the alleyway in which it sits, surrounded by the uniform administrations of modern-day office blocks, is to slip gently back in time as it feels instantly Dickensian and quiet. The pub itself is a wonder of an older time and feels snug, hidden in a tiny eddy of history and the city outside. Browned beams frame the patches of well-worn carpet and the two bars connected by pitted wooden doors seem to wait to be found rather than be on display. I order a frothing pint of beer and sit in the wooden armchairs surrounded by pictures on the wall of Richard II and scenes from the play.

In one corner there is a small picture of the man who in Tudor times gave his name to the Gardens outside. In 1576, some of the house and lands surrounding the chapel were granted by the Bishop of Ely to Sir Christopher Hatton, a particular favourite of Elizabeth I. It was his money that had sent Francis Drake around the world – Hatton's coat of arms was a Golden Hind – and like Shakespeare, Hatton is a conundrum. Born in Northamptonshire in 1540, he was training at the Inner Temple when he famously caught the eye of the visiting Queen Elizabeth through his excellent dancing and 'tall stature.' He excelled himself at Court even though he was said to be Roman Catholic in all but name, and in religious matters he promoted moderation and tolerance on both sides. However he was accused by the figurehead of Catholicism at the time, Mary, Queen of Scots, of having an affair with the Queen and in 1584 he stood in front of the House of Commons and got 400 members to chant their allegiance to a politically damaged Elizabeth. He was on the commission that found Mary guilty of treason and sent her to her death, yet he had constantly reassured Mary that he would fetch her to London if Elizabeth died.

An infatuated and grateful Elizabeth applied much pressure to the Bishop of Ely to let Ely House to Hatton at a reduced rent: ten pounds, ten loads of hay and one red rose per year.

The area was under the jurisdiction of the Bishops of Ely and was therefore a *liberty*, so as long as the Bishops were kept happy and the rent kept coming in, the laws of the land could be bypassed. As a consequence, during Hatton's tolerant tenancy the crypt of the church was used as a tavern where Catholics would gather. There is no doubt that Shakespeare knew his way around the 'liberties' of London, and the audience are told twice that the death scene of John of Gaunt is at Ely House (even though he actually died at Leicester), so as I sit in the Old Mitre it is easy, however fanciful, to think of Shakespeare dreaming up his famous paean to a lost world in the very same place it was set.

The 'Sceptered Isle' speech is tattooed on the body of England, yet what is rarely noted is that it is all one sentence that ends with a negative. It is a challenge for any actor – both technically and also burdened by the fact that he has to wade through the sands of nationalism.

Gaunt

This royal throne of kings, this scepter'd isle,
This earth of majesty, this seat of Mars,
This other Eden, demi-paradise,
This fortress built by Nature for herself
Against infection and the hand of war,
This happy breed of men, this little world,
This precious stone set in the silver sea,
Which serves it in the office of a wall,
Or as a moat defensive to a house,
Against the envy of less happier lands,
This blessed plot, this earth, this realm, this England,
This nurse, this teeming womb of royal kings,
Fear'd by their breed and famous by their birth,
Renowned for their deeds as far from home,
For Christian service and true chivalry,
As is the sepulchre in stubborn Jewry,
Of the world's ransom, blessed Mary's Son,
This land of such dear souls, this dear dear land,
Dear for her reputation through the world,
Is now leased out, I die pronouncing it,
Like to a tenement or pelting farm:
England, bound in with the triumphant sea
Whose rocky shore beats back the envious siege
Of watery Neptune, is now bound in with shame,
With inky blots and rotten parchment bonds:
That England, that was wont to conquer others
Hath made a shameful conquest of itself
Ah, would the scandal vanish with my life,
How happy then were my ensuing death.

(Richard II Act 2, Sc. 1)

And, breathe.

It is a whinge. A lament. England is leased out. Bound in with shame. Made a shameful conquest of itself.

19

Nowadays it is almost impossible to play it properly as an actor. Most audiences never listen but just hear the words. I was in the audience waiting to enter onto the stage every night for a year when that speech was being said. I could hear them sit up in their seats and stop coughing. Even now, on finishing it, the audience on occasion will applaud. Are they applauding the back-slapping figurehead of words or the fact that the country is leased out and bound in with shame? At the foundation and height of Empire it was as important a speech as any in the English language, and people would go to performances of *Richard II* just to hear that speech done by Garrick or Kean. They just conveniently forgot to finish the sentence.

By the time Elizabeth I was midway through her long reign, the disparate jigsaw of England had gradually coalesced and come into a focus, a perspective. Before this time, each feudal estate, each personal fiefdom, certainly each County, was like a mini-state in itself. There had been a loyalty to the King, but the Church was the real unifying power within the country. However, with each unresolved feud and disputed inheritance passing to the monarch, the king began to assume more power and control. It was a slow process that took hundreds of years. Then all at once Henry VIII dissolved the monasteries in the Reformation and placed the land that had been in the power of the church into the power of the Crown and the new mercantile landowners. The land – England's wealth, power and soul – began to form into a shape, an idea. The idea of the 'State', secular and running alongside that of the Church of England, came into being towards the end of Elizabeth's reign.

The Virgin Elizabeth gave birth to the idea of Britannia and nothing was more helpful as a midwife than this speech. Yet it is a conundrum, like Sir Christopher Hatton being a Catholic and condemning his Mary, that the speech is a defiant swipe at the selling of England's soul: Elizabeth, and Protestantism, had dodged so many bullets that they had taken root. The people who bled for England's Catholic soul had failed. With every botched Catholic plot, every Protestant victory in war, with the death of the Queen of Scots, according to the Catholics of England the snake had wound itself around the tree.

In describing England's fall Shakespeare has fed the genesis, the myth, the cuckoo in the nest of a new Britain to which we still adhere. This glorification is perhaps what kept this 'Warwickshire upstart young crow' out of jail. His creations have defined the very thing he was satirising. No wonder, at the end of his career, he came up with Prospero.

Brought up on the banks of the Avon that marked the boundary of the Forest of Arden to the north and the broad plains of the Feldon that stretch to the south-east, Shakespeare followed the path to London. He was born into a time and place that witnessed the increasing difference between rural and urban which largely meant Catholic and Protestant respectively. Like most things, he spanned the divide. The mythical sceptered isle he was writing of had no division but grew from nature, the divine hand of any God. It was Eden.

I sit in The Old Mitre and I look out of the window and see nothing but slabs of concrete. The pavements, the buildings. No green at all. No colour. Nothing but a very hard layer between us and the land. Down the street I see a glimmer of red and realise it's a McDonalds. Leased out and bound in with shame.

With Gaunt's death Richard ironically had lost his chief defender. However vexed Gaunt had been with Richard he still upheld the sanctity of the crown and would under no circumstances rise up against it. His son was not so coy. As soon as Richard stripped Bolingbroke of his inheritance in order to fund his campaign in Ireland, he lit the touchpaper for rebellion.

With Richard having set off for Ireland, Bolingbroke promptly landed at Ravenspurgh in Yorkshire in order to reclaim his inheritance. What is more, many powerful lords including the Earl of Northumberland and his son, young Harry Percy (nicknamed Hotspur), quietly flocked to him. The favourites of Richard immediately scattered. Aumerle chose to flee to Richard's side in Ireland, so too Bagot who followed the king through Wales to the coast. Heading west, Bushy and Green holed up in Bristol Castle.

In this widening gap of loyalty, his arms pulled wider than an apostate, the Duke of York desperately tried to cling to his country. After Gaunt's death, Richard had given him the powers of a Regent whilst away in Ireland. So now Shakespeare brings him centre stage partly clothed in armour, all at sixes and sevens, barking off orders and receiving bad news. Fearful of civil war and weakened by age he can do nothing to stop the tide of Red sweeping across his land.

Berkeley Castle

Berkeley Castle is sandwiched between the Cotswold Hills to the East and the Severn Estuary to the West. As such it was one of the most important and strategic castles in the country as it lay precisely on the easiest western route to the north. Bristol, guarding the Channel twenty miles further south is most definitely a 'West Country' city but Berkeley lies on the line between the South and the Midlands.

It doesn't tower over its surroundings like its Welsh counterparts but then it doesn't have to – it was secure of its place geographically, so simply being there was enough. After Windsor Castle and the Tower of London it is the oldest continuously occupied castle in the country – and certainly the oldest lived in by the same family. They've been present at almost every important staging post along the road of English and British history, quietly influencing behind the scenes and a Berkeley still lives there now.

However, the place is shut when I get there. I had been told so by a man with a pitchfork and a glint in his eye, so I find myself scrabbling about in the fringes of a churchyard trying to catch a glimpse. I suddenly find a path which leads me to a massive gatehouse and from there I get uninterrupted views to the castle, nestling in the folds of the Gloucestershire countryside. The dark brown stone is dull and broody on this January day, and as usual with a castle that still remains lived in, there's the normal awful Victorian amendments that make a castle look like a pastiche of itself – all fake castellation and Gothic arches. But the old Norman keep remains, circular and threatening, and the rest of the building snaking away is discreet and demure. Simply sitting in the environment it rests easy on its bed of History.

It was here that Edward II – Richard, Bolingbroke and Aumerle's great-grandfather – was allegedly murdered and it was to this castle that their uncle York decamped once Bolingbroke swept across the country garnering nobles, men and popular support. To travel further South, Bolingbroke would have to negotiate with York at Berkeley. Likewise, York was in a strategically important place for Richard when he chose to return from Ireland.

In theory, the banished Bolingbroke was claiming his dukedom not the throne. In so doing he was committing treason, yet he could not simply march in and seize the throne – he had to be seen to be wanted by the people. Under the yoke of miserable taxes and almost non-existent government the people were ready to follow whoever put their hand up, and this glorious Knight, one of the finest in Europe, was a better option than the weak Richard who had never fought in battle – the man who wrung their purses dry and sued for *peace* with France. But Henry's right was not Divine. It may have been popular, but it was not Divine and as such his actions thrust a sword deep into the body of England.

It is at the gatehouse where I am standing that Shakespeare sweeps York out from the castle to meet his offending nephew:

York
Show me thy humble heart and not thy knee
Whose duty is deceivable and false…

(Richard II Act 2 Sc. 3)

But Henry and his followers proclaim their case. Some say it was weakness on York's part, others that he threw in his lot with the man more likely to prove a better king, or that it was the last play of the dice to keep his country from tearing apart, but York, still proclaiming they are traitors, nevertheless invites them in for the night.

In 1570 and again in 1588, a Papal Bull was issued declaring Queen Elizabeth I a heretic: it released her subjects from allegiance to her, excommunicating any that obeyed her orders. In other words, Catholics who had been quietly going about their worship under a system of tolerance in the first fifteen years of Elizabeth's reign, were now traitors in their own land. It was disastrous for them. They were as English as their neighbour but were held to be treasonous. Thought was now a crime.

At the gates of Berkeley the Duke of York is placed in a similarly awful situation. He is damned if he does and damned if he doesn't. His allegiance was to his country, his belief was that Bolingbroke would be the better king to run it. As such he was an unwilling traitor in his own land.

I walk back through the undergrowth to the magnificent church standing proudly beside the castle, hugely out of proportion with the surrounding town. On the walls of the nave are extraordinary mediaeval religious paintings untouched by the whitewashing desire of Protestantism, which makes me think that the Berkeleys might have had a vested interest in keeping them up there: they had enough power and influence to stop the Puritan wave of white. At the start of Elizabeth's reign the country had changed religion so many times in the previous twenty years that some churches simply put boards up in front of the altar walls so that if there was another reversal they wouldn't have harmed the paintings so frowned upon by the Protestants. Here in Berkeley Church, however, the paintings are deeply coloured and untouched. Yet high up on the Southern transept wall is the biggest Tudor Rose – the red and the white rose – I have ever seen. It celebrates King Edward VI, Henry VIII's ill-fated and zealously Protestant son – Elizabeth's half brother. It seems this castle and this church, this family, are very adept at sitting on the fence. No wonder, like Shakespeare, it has lasted so long.

There are only three such families that exist in Britain with such an unbroken male lineage through to Saxon times. One of the other two families is the Swinton family (as in Tilda, white face, red hair and famous actress) who come from Berwickshire, the *limen* between Scotland and England.

The third family is the Ardens. Shakespeare's mother, Mary Arden, and her family were hewn from the oaks of the Forest they were named after.

Derived from the Saxon word *Ârdu* meaning 'high land', the Forest of Arden stretched from the River Avon at Stratford-upon-Avon and covered what is now the ugly spread of Birmingham and its environs. It went as far north as Tamworth, where Sherwood Forest spread south from Nottinghamshire. Not even the Romans could cut a road through and the edges of the forest can roughly be defined by the great roads they built around it: The Fosse Way, Watling Street, Ickfield Street and the Salt Road. It is also defined by the particular soil upon which it lies – a thick layer of Warwickshire mudstone and then, a few inches down, deep clay hated by farmers, loved by oaks.

Here in the centre of the country the Forest grew, the oaks lay on guard, and the magic lay like mist in the morning sun. The makings of England stirred in it. Loxley is a few miles from Stratford-upon-Avon and the Forest stretched from here north to Nottingham. In Bearley, the village beyond Mary Arden's birthplace of Wilmcote near Stratford, one of the Arden oaks still stands huge and protecting in the hedgerow. The Green Man of moss, myth and magic still seems to sigh in its branches. Robin Hood lives within it.

Thorkill of Arden, grandson of the Earl of Mercia, was one of the few significant Saxon landowners to retain their lands after the Norman Conquest. It is his lineage that still exists today. Down the line, Robert Arden, Shakespeare's great-great-great grandfather was executed by Henry VI for supporting Richard Plantagenet, Duke of York in the Wars of the Roses. Shakespeare's mother, Mary Arden, was second cousin to the Edward Arden executed for plotting against Elizabeth.

The Church that the Berkeleys built remains a testament to longevity and a desire to survive. The axe marks and musket balls from a Civil War siege still adorn the huge oak doors on the West front and the proud graves of a thousand years nestle among the paintings and the pews. Shakespeare was hewn from an equally old tree over which he now towers. The forest of oaks that formed his Church is gone but remains in his work. He is the deer in the forest.

From Berkeley, Bolingbroke sped the few miles to Bristol and took the castle with ease. Bushy and Green were no match for this warring Knight and the weight of public opinion behind him. He immediately had them beheaded for leading the King astray. It was an act of regal judgement that was the first sign of his boats being burnt and also served to let everyone know how dangerous he could be.

Bristol Castle is now a deeply unimpressive exposed pile of stones on 'Castle Green' looking out to sea and the vast Channel that flows like a needle into England. Here Bristol stands guard along with Cardiff – the capital of Wales twinkling even at this time on the opposite shore almost over the horizon. Like many of the border castles Bristol was flattened in the Civil War. A few high-raised buildings dot the area around the green and the wind hits me like a pick-axe. The castle used to be as impregnable and mighty as any in England, befitting its place as guardian of the West, but now the crisp packets and fag ends of a public park in England mark it out as just another place on the hill. I think of Bushy and Green dying publicly, accused of turning a King from his Queen and a Prince from his King. Whether they felt shame or not I feel it now.

It is a hard place in which to linger, so I follow the Severn upstream to Tewkesbury where it meets the Avon. Follow the Avon upstream and it is like a story going back in time to the heart of England past Stratford-upon-Avon and Arden. Alternatively, follow the Severn to its source and the heart of a different beast of magic and wonder can be found.

Wales

Clive Wood and I are heading West. Flame-haired and formidable, Clive played Bolingbroke in The Histories and he's coming with me on this trip to Wales. We first worked together in 2000 when we staged Michael Boyd's original *Henry VI* and *Richard III* tetralogy at the RSC and we have been great friends ever since. We're in a camper van called a Bongo which has a roof that rises at the touch of a button to create a whole new room and there's a fridge in the back that I have stuffed with as much Pinot Grigio and pork pies as I could find.

We cross the Severn at Shrewsbury and the Welsh mountains begin to appear in the distance clean and bright in the spring sunshine, and the Bongo starts to sweat a little as we pull uphill from the valley floor. We take a right to Dolgellau and we're going up. And up.

This was lawless country. Sandwiched between the near autonomous rule of the Marcher Lords to the east and the Welsh rulers of Meirionnydd to the west it was no-man's-land – a place of highwaymen and brigands.

The Bongo ascends and we're deep behind enemy lines here. From being a stunning, warm day the clouds close in and rain patterns the windscreen. The almost sheer slopes of the mountains press upon us and loom up to the clouds. Faces appear to us in the walls, etched into the stone. Wind buffets the Bongo as she gasps the last few yards to the gap that is the Bwlch Oerddrws – a pass through the mountains used by armies, thieves and travellers through history.

To give the Bongo a rest and calm our fevered nerves we stop at the top. I open the door and it is immediately blown back into my face – the wind rips through here like a bolting horse. There is a darkness that descends on the spirit in places like this and we are both astonished by the change in the weather, landscape and light within the space of ten minutes. God, it's miserable here. And wonderful. Its craggy skree is littered with the weight of weather and history, its toughness lined with a beauty that is hard to resist.

In need of cheering up we head to the seaside. Within a minute the sky has cleared and the broad sweep of sandy beaches leading to yet more mountains beyond is staggeringly beautiful. Today the tops of

Snowdonia are simply flecked with cotton wool clouds which appear and then vanish as ghosts. Shakespeare sets the belated arrival of Richard from Ireland at 'Barkloughly Castle.' It is a respelling of what his main historical source, Raphael Holinshed, called 'Barclowlie' and is a complete confusion with the Berkeley Castle of the previous scenes. The correct spelling was Hertlowlie, which is now modern Harlech in North Wales. The Castle is perched on the slopes running to the sea. Built by Edward I to keep the troublesome Welsh in order, it rises from the cliff and sits in the landscape like a bull in a field. The mountains rise behind Harlech, the atmosphere so clear in the winter-washed spring that in this sun they come closer as if under a lens.

Richard, according to Holinshed, meant to return to England to take issue with Bolingbroke immediately but through bad weather and '*through persuasion*', writes Holinshed, '*of the duke of Aumarle (as was thought) he staied, till he might haue all is ships, and other prouision, full readie for his passage.*'

He did however send the Earl of Salisbury post-haste over to Wales '*to gather a power togither, by help of the kings freends in Wales, and Cheshire, with all speed possible.*' This, Salisbury did very well indeed. He landed at Conwy and within four days assembled 40,000 willing and able Welshmen and Cheshire bowmen, who all hoped to find the King at Conwy. But Richard never came and within two weeks they had either dispersed or, believing that Richard was dead, gone over to Bolingbroke's side.

Richard actually landed in Milford Haven in South Wales in order to sweep through into the south of England raising support in both places as he went. But the moment Bolingbroke took Bristol, Richard was in a useless position so he had to go North to find the troops willing to fight that Salisbury had raised, thus doing what he should have done two weeks earlier. Leaving what small forces he had with Aumerle and the Earl of Worcester in Milford Haven, he stole away at night with a small company of attendant Lords. He himself allegedly dressed as a Franciscan Friar to evade capture. At Harlech he found forces that were still loyal to him and he pressed on to Conwy Castle on the North coast where the Earl of Salisbury broke the news to him that most had gone over to the rebels' side.

The army he'd left in South Wales then deserted him too. On their passage across Wales to join up with Bolingbroke – who was now sitting pretty at Shrewsbury – they were taken apart by the bandits who inhabited the lawless centre and the mountain passes similar to the one Clive and I drove through. They turned up at Shrewsbury, nobles and peasants alike, with nothing but rags on their backs.

Even Richard's greyhound defected. It found Henry in the Abbey at Shrewsbury and according to the Chronicle of Adam Usk '*crouched obediently… with a look a purest pleasure on his face*'.

Shakespeare simply places Richard on the coast near Harlech and gives him wave after wave of bad news – first the seeping away of the Welsh; second the almost total defection of England to Bolingbroke; and then the deaths of Bushy and Green. Richard is spent:

Richard II

… of comfort no man speak:
Let's talk of graves, of worms, and epitaphs;
Make dust our paper and with rainy eyes
Write sorrow on the bosom of the earth,
Let's choose executors and talk of wills:
And yet not so, for what can we bequeath
Save our deposed bodies to the ground?
Our lands, our lives and all are Bolingbroke's,
And nothing can we call our own but death
And that small model of the barren earth
Which serves as paste and cover to our bones.
For God's sake, let us sit upon the ground
And tell sad stories of the death of kings;
How some have been deposed; some slain in war,
Some haunted by the ghosts they have deposed;
Some poison'd by their wives: some sleeping kill'd;
All murder'd: for within the hollow crown
That rounds the mortal temples of a king
Keeps Death his court and there the antic sits,
Scoffing his state and grinning at his pomp,
Allowing him a breath, a little scene,
To monarchize, be fear'd and kill with looks,
Infusing him with self and vain conceit,
As if this flesh which walls about our life,

Were brass impregnable, and humour'd thus
Comes at the last and with a little pin
Bores through his castle wall, and farewell king!
Cover your heads and mock not flesh and blood
With solemn reverence: throw away respect,
Tradition, form and ceremonious duty,
For you have but mistook me all this while:
I live with bread like you, feel want,
Taste grief, need friends: subjected thus,
How can you say to me, I am a king?

(Richard II Act 3 Sc. 2)

If the experience of the previous sixty years had proved anything to Shakespeare – where the Tudors had played with religion like a toy – it was that monarchs are mortal and they live with bread like us, feel want, taste grief, need friends. This play may well have been performed for Elizabeth and sometime later she is quoted as saying '*I am Richard II, know ye not that?*'

Clive and I are standing on the beach by Harlech. The tourists have gone, the sun is setting and the sea lies heavy and quiet in the late afternoon. We watch the colours spread across the sky and turn the limpid waves to wine.

'Thank God that Bongo's got a fridge for the Pinot,' says Clive and walks fifty yards to one of the most idyllic campsites I've ever seen. The mountains swing up sturdy behind us and the clouds which top them like toupees begin to clear. The red sky streaks yellow and the waves whisper on the wind. The landscape holds us in a bowl.

The woman who owns the campsite potters from her distant farmhouse, stick in hand, and says it would be better to collect our money this evening because she had the dentist's in the morning. It is twelve pounds for the night, but then we get talking about why we are here and how her husband would like the Bongo:

'But where would we go in it?' she says, 'I suppose we could go round the bay, but then we'd only be seeing us from the other side.'

She and her husband farm the land around here. 'We did dairy for about ten years, but it gets very hard. The supermarkets did for us. Sheep and campers are easier,' she says, 'O, go on then, just give me ten pounds.'

29

Off she totters to her wonderful windblown farmhouse laughing at the sight of these two grown men hopelessly ill-fitted to the trials of a Bongo by night. Clive is laughing himself. He just loves the melting pot, he says, of this silly little island.

With the Saxon invasion forcing some of the Celts to the edges, the Danish squashing the Anglo-Saxons, the French grafting on top of the Anglo-Saxons, perhaps this furious island has managed to survive through laughing at each other as well as tearing ourselves apart. Comedy and tragedy. It is what has made us a nation of such good actors. We are forever on the border; the job always ends.

The friendships will always last. Clive hasn't spent a night outside since he went camping with his Croyden school and one of the boys shat himself in his tent whilst weeping with misery, so it's an interesting flashback for him. However, he is busying himself with the wine and laying out our feast. We eat pies and drink an awful lot of wine, then I try to blow up my air mattress. I sleep on the floor.

The next morning there is nothing on the road except lorries carrying spoil from the mines which we finally see when scaling the pass at Blaenau Ffestiniog. Richard II must have taken this route to Conwy too and it is pretty bleak. The mines have shattered the landscape. Old chapels and roads crumble back into the rock they were built with as if being reclaimed. All is grey. The road, the rock, the houses, the sky. Then once again we drop into a green and luscious valley, the sun comes out and we meander with the river which leads to Conwy.

The first thing you notice about Conwy Castle is that someone has built a socking great railway through it. It turns out to be Robert Stephenson, the inventor of the steam train, so it becomes almost a palimpsest of architecture. The railway tracks curl along the town walls from the mountains in the distance, bringing slate down and taking tourists up. It slices through the front of the castle and heads off over the estuary into the hills, now suburbs, the other side. The road comes back alongside the railway but sweeps the other side of the castle so it is besieged by modern-day transport.

All tumbledown castles look pretty much the same. It is the landscape you put them in and their story that gives them their power. For example, 'Men of Harlech' was written about a siege in the Wars of the Roses where Harlech castle held out for seven months. Like the Aboriginal songlines, it can be sung into existence. The Elizabethans recognised this and called it 'Chorography' – where the combining threads of history and geography would describe a place. To tell a story about somewhere was to map it and make it real. From the top of the tower at Conwy Castle the mountains speckle, the sea sparkles and you are lifted through time and place from the present to the past in an exhilarating swoop of chorography.

Richard had no choice but to negotiate with the rebels. Bolingbroke was in total control. At Conwy the Earl of Northumberland picked Richard up and persuaded him to come and see Bolingbroke at Flint. Richard hoped to flee Northumberland's clutches and raise an army for a later day but the canny Earl had hidden a massive force in a valley just beyond Conwy, and as Richard set off so he discovered that he was trapped. He knew that all was lost. A feeling many may feel along the same stretch of road to this day.

Wales changes in an instant. I love it. When you've been up in the mountains it's a cruel blow to drive through Rhyl and Prestatyn. The beach is somewhere to our left hidden by flashing arcades and burger joints. Further on, what passes for the centre of Rhyl comprises of decaying buildings and boarded-up hotels, the ground floors selling sparkly things. Rhyl was once, like all great seaside towns, a fantastic place crammed with holiday makers from the mountains or the dockers from Liverpool and Salford. The happiness that each person brought I yearn for on these streets. Now, the reason seems to have gone.

Prestatyn is nothing but a sea of bungalows and then we wind, speechless, through a Dantean world of broken pubs and bland, corporate car parks. The only thing of note is a massive ocean-going liner on the horizon moored up for breaking, crying with rust. It towers over its surroundings like a castle.

Flint Castle cost twenty times more than Conwy Castle. Whereas Conwy is still proud, Flint Castle is twenty times diminished. Castles may be one of the first examples of brutalism, but the land was all – where it was, what it said, and who it could see coming were the reasons they were built. The beauty is inherent. The castle must have been an extraordinary sight as it dominated the Dee Estuary, yet now the land is overtaken by some office blocks and a housing estate. The castle stands between them and the sea, forgotten and unwanted.

No one has even had the courage finally to get rid of it like they have done elsewhere in the country. There are a few bits of it left: half a tower and just the outline of the keep. Standing at the wall looking out over the estuary is beautiful until the eye sweeps past the rugby club to the pylons and chimneys of a huge industrial mire in the distance.

Perhaps the dourness is because one of the most important points in the history of these isles – the arrest of a monarch – took place here in August, 1399. When Northumberland sent news that Richard was at Flint, Henry was in Chester and overjoyed. He gathered his now vast army, took them en masse over the River Dee and marched up the beach to Flint. John Creton, author of *The Metrical History of the Deposition of Richard II*, who had been with Richard in Ireland and was alongside him in Flint, claimed he had never seen so many people. He estimated 'many knights and squires at upwards of 100,000 men'. That was around three percent of the population. As statements go it was pretty categorical from Henry. He entered the castle 'armed at all points' but bowed deeply to Richard, who promptly returned the compliment.

This is a situation almost made for Shakespeare's imagination. To twist the knife he places a weeping York beside Bolingbroke:

> **Richard II**
> *Uncle, give me your hands: nay, dry your eyes;*
> *Tears show their love, but want their remedies.*
> *Cousin, I am too young to be your father,*
> *Though you are old enough to be my heir.*
> *What you will have, I'll give, and willing too;*
> *For do we must what force will have us do.*
> *Set on towards London, cousin, is it so?*
> **Henry Bolingbroke**
> *Yea, my good lord.*
> **Richard II**
> *Then I must not say no.*
>
> (Richard II Act 3 Sc. 4)

According to John Creton, Henry gave his ultimatum: Richard had governed the people badly and he would offer to help 'govern them better than they have been governed in the past'. Richard's answer was simple: 'Fair cousin, since it pleaseth you, it pleaseth us well.'

'Bring out the king's horses', said Henry. Richard left Flint on a tired old nag and stumbled all the way to London.

I peer down into the well at the castle – plastic bottles fill its surface deep below. I look around once more at where we are and what we've just driven through from Conwy, and I fancy I can hear Richard saying out of the side of his mouth, paraphrasing Dylan Thomas as he stumbled away on his pathetic steed: 'Good luck, mate, you can have it.'

King's Langley

The Duke of York's tears were fulsome and fruitless: his betrayal was only confirmed by his inaction. England, this other Eden, was falling so Shakespeare simply puts his play into the hand-wringing Duke of York's garden:

Gardener

> Bolingbroke
>
> *Hath seized the wasteful king. O, what pity is it*
> *That he had not so trimm'd and dress'd his land*
> *As we this garden! We at time of year*
> *Do wound the bark, the skin of our fruit-trees,*
> *Lest, being over-proud in sap and blood,*
> *With too much riches it confound itself:*
> *Had he done so to great and growing men,*
> *They might have lived to bear and he to taste*
> *Their fruits of duty: superfluous branches*
> *We lop away, that bearing boughs may live:*
> *Had he done so, himself had borne the crown,*
> *Which waste of idle hours hath quite thrown down.*

Queen

> *Thou, old Adam's likeness...*
>
> *What Eve, what serpent, hath suggested thee*
> *To make a second fall of cursed man?*

(Richard II Act 3 Sc. 4)

Today, the main problem is that the Duke of York's garden is round the back of a Primary School in King's Langley. I'm trying to find the one thing that remains of the Duke of York's palace but it is dusk and far too late to be rooting around playing fields for a fourteenth century pillar. There is a Priory, which was built next to the palace that still survives, but I'm furtively looking into bushes and then trying to look normal as four healthy-looking adults bearing squash racquets come sauntering out to their cars.

King's Langley is a rather beautiful small town on the southern edge of the Chiltern Hills near the foot of Watling Street as it approaches London. York was born here at the Manor occupied by his father Edward III in times of plague and he is buried in what has become the All Saints' Church nearby. Now a commuter town for London it has suffered because of its travel connections to other places – you only ever go through there to get somewhere else. It is located in the armpit of the M1, the A41 and the M25. The Grand Union Canal and the West Coast Main Train Line barge past as well.

It's a still, warm, spring night and the heady scent of blossom tingling in the air is somewhat diminished by the relentless roar of speeding traffic, unseen but everywhere. I couldn't live here – it's like having tinnitus. I'd arranged to see the Headmaster who was going to show me the pillar of the old Palace which is built into one of the school buildings. In the past, the kids have even done a little exhibition of finds from their playing fields where the Palace had been, and he was keen to show me. But I'd sat in a traffic jam on the M25 for an hour and a half, I was hideously late and the Headmaster had gone so I had decided on a furtive approach but still couldn't find the pillar. More and more adults come sprightly past with their racquets and healthy-looking shoes. I give up and just look at the sports field mown freshly green in the spring air. Here is Eden – with a soundtrack of cars and squash balls.

So I walk to the other end of the school car park to find the Priory. Founded by Edward II it became the burial place of his beloved Piers Gaveston and was fussed over with much care by both him and, surprisingly, his son Edward III who continually paid to keep the Priory going. Gaveston's grave has long since been lost and the Priory was disbanded in the Dissolution only to be reinstated by Catholic Queen Mary I and her husband Philip of Spain in 1553. Queen Elizabeth took it over once she got into power and the place remained in possession of the crown whilst the Palace next to it fell into disrepair.

The trouble is I can't find the Priory either. I stop a woman to ask her if she knows where it is and once she gets over the fact that I'm not going to kill her in the half-light, she points to the building right beside us and says that's it. 'It's very old. There are probably lots of ghosts there.'

I climb over a little chain put across the drive and discover from a small picture board that a Christian Community still lives here. Built in an L-shape around a courtyard of bushes and paths it is wonderfully incongruous with the present. There is nothing at all to indicate that the last two hundred years has ever happened. The buildings tumble over each other as they rise high on thick stone walls. Steps lead to thatched porches. It is most definitely not of this time. All I can think of is that it feels like visiting a very old maiden aunt. The air breathes in and out of this place. It feels older than most churches. If ever there is a place to believe in ghosts it is here in this little backwater of history.

Brooding in the dusk I realise I am trespassing and above the buildings the moon slivers new as a thin blade. I freeze as two eyes glint in the darkness. Then two more. And more. My body checks and I breathe a little tighter. As if appearing from nowhere the fattest cat I have ever seen is sitting on the path looking at me. There's another in the bushes eyeing me impassively. After a swift count I think I see ten sets of eyes hunting me down. I start to retreat, heart racing, legs arching backwards as if pulled by a string. I turn and flee over the chain-link fence and skid over the loose gravel of the car park. At the car I fiddle madly with the keys looking anxiously back to see if I'm being pursued by a vicious horde of waddling cats. I fling open the door and the bloody thing won't start. I let out a whimper, firing it up again, and I'm off – leaving Eden in a cloud of dust.

Around the corner there is a village green surrounded by trees. Kids are playing football in what is left of the light. A couple are snogging on a bench and the red and white cherry blossoms droop over them like confetti. A set of sightscreens are laid out, ready to be painted, as it is the first day of the cricket season. Maybe I have just driven into Eden. It is if you want it to be, I suppose.

A train rams past – I hear it but don't see it. I get back on the M25 and drive into London past the high rises and the expressways. Albion never pretended to be equal.

Westminster

If the heart of England is elsewhere then Westminster Hall may well be the brain. Between Westminster Abbey and the river, the Hall lies within the Palace complex that holds the House of Commons and the House of Lords and has survived the ravages of Cromwell, Victorian architects and Hitler's bombs. The sun streams in through the massive South window far in the distance and the roof surges away into the sky, held aloft by carved angels bearing shields with Richard II's coat-of-arms upon them. White Harts and mitres are studded around the entire mantle of the roof but below it the Red Lion broods on the wall. Although built by William II, Richard had this place completely redone. He raised the roof and inserted huge windows so it became the largest unsupported mediaeval roof span in Europe. It is mightily impressive for a secular building and was designed to inspire the same awe of cathedrals, only this time for a King.

The white walls on either side would have formed the backdrop to large galleried seats filled with the English Parliament bearing down on whoever entered. Richard placed sculptures of all the previous English Kings upon the South and East sides so they too would tower above whoever was brought before the King. Unfortunately what was designed by Richard to create awe in his subjects had its first use upon himself.

It was reported in the official Parliament Roll that Richard was quite jolly when he entered here and renounced his crown. But they would say that. In fact, Adam of Usk, who was present, portrays a picture of him being anything but jovial. In front of the Parliament gathered to fill the Hall (along with some tasty hostile Londoners brought in to make sure things went to plan), Richard stood before his empty throne, placed his crown upon the ground, and underneath the very carved angels holding his banner he 'resigned his right to God.'

After making a short speech in which he hoped Bolingbroke would treat him well, a list of accusations were read aloud to him. He was not allowed to say anything in his defence and was escorted back to the Tower. Once he had gone the Bishop of Carlisle stood up to say he should have been allowed to answer his case but the one lone voice was ignored.

Another Bishop of Carlisle once again took centre stage 150 years later, as he was the only Bishop that could be found to crown Elizabeth after five years of her half-sister Mary's Catholic rule. Firstly, he refused to take the Oath of Supremacy that acknowledged the King or Queen to be Head of the Church of England. Then he disobeyed Elizabeth when she specifically asked for various Catholic elements of the ceremony to be withdrawn. She promptly walked out of her own coronation service when he elevated the host, and afterwards denied him from office. He died in the same year.

Perhaps it is no surprise that Shakespeare gives Carlisle the longest and most prophetic speech in a scene that comprises an entire Act of the play:

Carlisle
…The blood of English shall manure the ground
And future ages groan for this foul act…

(Richard II Act 4 Sc. 1)

However, it seems this whole deposition scene which takes place in Westminster Hall was left out of performances until after Elizabeth died, as the notion that Divine rule could be cut off if not good enough was simply too contentious. The play was performed fully intact, however, in front of the Earl of Essex and his supporters the night before their inept rebellion against Elizabeth in 1601. As a consequence Shakespeare and his troupe of players were told to leave London for a while, which seems a small punishment since Essex lost his head.

But the fact remains that in the play a ruling monarch removes their crown to give to another:

Richard II
Give me the crown.
Here, cousin, seize the crown; Here cousin:
On this side my hand, and on that side yours.
Now is this golden crown like a deep well
That owes two buckets, filling one another,
The emptier ever dancing in the air,
The other down, unseen and full of water:
That bucket down and full of tears am I,
Drinking my griefs, whilst you mount up on high.

Bolingbroke
I thought you had been willing to resign.

Richard II
My crown I am; but still my griefs are mine:
You may my glories and my state depose,
But not my griefs; still am I king of those.

(Richard II Act 4 Sc. 1)

Every time we performed this play I sighed at the terrible beauty of the language. For Elizabethan England, to lose a monarch in such a way could lead to civil war – at the unsure end of Elizabeth's reign it was the terrifying threat that hung over them all.

To get into the Hall today you first have to go through the fleecing security of a similarly terrified nation. Cameras track you as you head down past Cromwell's statue (how envious he must be of all this control) and then you are made to stand in front of a camera which snaps you and the image put on a chain around your neck – presumably the picture goes flying off to some central database where they check every image taken of anyone ever and then decide I'm not going to kill the Prime Minister. My bag is put through the X-ray machine, as am I, and then I'm shown the door to the Palace Yard. It is all done with immense cheer and smiles by the policemen and security people that have to stand there day in, day out. It's rather alarming when someone smiles at you with a gun.

With Richard gone, Bolingbroke found it slightly easier to enter this great chamber of England. Flanked by his four sons he sat in his father's old seat as the Duke of Lancaster but was led by the Archbishops of York and Canterbury over to the King's throne. He had to be seen to rule with the consent of the ruled. His was not a Divine right. He promptly tried to assert exactly that by claiming the throne as his inheritance through his mother's line from Henry III which everyone knew was preposterous. He also backed it up with a touch of harsh reality by saying the throne 'was in point to be undone for default of governance and undoing of the good laws.' He raised his hand to show Richard's signet ring – a true sign that Richard had appointed him successor and as he sat down the Hall erupted into wild applause, chanting: 'Long live Henry of Lancaster, King of England!'

Of this moment in Westminster Hall which changed the course of English history forever, deposed a rightful king, and gave rise to a century of civil carnage, there is not one mention.

Instead I dutifully look at the place where Charles I stood when sentenced to death by Parliament in 1649. I see the plaques laid on the ground where various monarchs and Churchill have lain in state. In the guidebook they say that a Gunpowder Plotter was condemned here. These are all important notches in the bedpost of England. But they are looked over by a White Hart in the rafters and a Red Lion on the wall about which there is nothing.

I stand at the top of the stairs below the massive South window. Suited people, who all look about twelve, are bustling around on their way to running the country. This is the seat of Government and it is alive with smug people. I tried to stop one of them to ask him what he did and he looked at me in appalled horror and quickened his step away. I suspect he may have as much idea of under-privilege and social justice as Richard II. Even if it is untrue they all certainly give the impression this is so.

Riled, I head off to the Commons consoling myself with the thought that, like Richard II found to his cost, the ruler has to rule with the consent of the ruled. The debates that take place in both Houses are public ones and as such we can all be let in to hear our country being discussed. Ever since someone threw talc over Gordon Brown from high up in the public gallery, however, we are cut off from our elected representatives by glass. It is the first time I have been up there and sadly the point of the public gallery seems to have been utterly lost nowadays. The glass simply reinforces our alienation from the process by the fact that it feels like a zoo. It's horrible up there – we are unwelcome, mistrusted and unloved. Down below in the animal enclosure, the MPs say what they have to say in the most unedifying drawl. Both sides seem to know what a particular MP is going to say and seem not to be listening. They appear to be just going through the motions as if their lives don't depend on it. Sadly, other people's do.

The MP speaking as I sit and write in my notebook is boring not only others but obviously himself as he has an unfortunate habit of putting his hands in his pocket every now and then and rubbing his balls. How do these people get elected? What is the point of having a debate if no one can hear you? As an actor I don't stand on stage and in the middle of a speech start relieving an itchy testicle.

Dispirited, I get up and go to the Lords' red bit. At least they're not elected, so they have a right to be as unengaging as possible. The House of Lords is a lot plumper and rounder – richer – than the Commons. Somewhere in between the two is Britain.

At least in the Lords there isn't a big piece of glass between us. Whilst it is extraordinary to be able to witness the lungs of Government it is also depressing to know that it takes place elsewhere. Cameras eye my every move. I had to sign some piece of paper to say that I was going to be a good boy and not cause a disturbance. If you're allowed into the debate then I think you should be allowed to speak. The Lord speaking was inaudible and unintelligible: all I would have said was, 'Speak up.'

A few months ago the newly sort-of-elected Coalition Government opted to slash public funding to the Arts in a spurious bid to ease the country's unfolding bankruptcy and the House of Lords are now debating it. Were we allowed to speak at the Public Gallery the place would be packed with an awful lot more people with much louder voices than the mumblers down below. As someone who has made a living through being largely a stage actor, most of which is enabled through public funding, I stand to be out of work an awful lot more than I used to be. There are a lot of good, hard-working and talented people – not just actors but all the people that work behind the scenes – who may have one day risen to the top who will not be able to carry on working. This, in a business that for every pound it receives in Public investment brings back five to the Exchequer.

The idiocy and complacency of it is staggering. They say everyone has to feel the pain and that it's the most severe financial crisis since the Second World War. During the Blitz the theatres were full every night. A country cannot exist on bread alone.

All the shouting has been done, eloquently and rationally, months before and none of it seems to have made a difference. As there is no point at all in watching these debates, the people in the Public Gallery are a few foreign students pointing at the nice windows. The Bill will pass and even the Lords that are trying to be a force for good – I see Lord Puttnam sitting gloomily in his seat – will watch it glide idly by like a piece of shit on a river because there are bigger politics downstream.

Back in the Hall I get talking to a guide whose energy and enthusiasm for his place of work perks me up again. He tells me of a runnel built by Richard that ran from the kitchens to the river on the other side to siphon off the effluent. Just to stand in Westminster Hall is to travel through time. The smell, however, still lingers. But the fact remains that, with a little bit of frisking, whenever I want I can go and stand where Charles I was condemned, Churchill lay in state, Richard II gave up his crown to Henry Bolingbroke, and watch our Government at work. It is breathtaking.

I look at all the young suits who studied Politics, Philosophy and Economics at Oxbridge and got rushed into the policymaking departments of political parties. Of PPE they may know a little. Of the world they know perhaps a little less. They dash past me bustling through the Hall to somewhere else more important and I wonder if they ever stop and think. If they took the time to look maybe they would see – as Bolingbroke was about to find out – that a country does not live on bread alone.

Pontefract

Westminster Hall would of course not be here at all had the Gunpowder Plot of 1605 succeeded. The previous 40 years had seen a series of plots and counter-plots that would have the policemen who checked my bag as I came into the Hall twitching in their beds. Alongside the Throckmorton Plot of 1583 there were many, many others such as the Babington Plot and the Ridolfi Plot that tried and failed to get rid of Elizabeth and place either Mary, Queen of Scots on the throne or a succession of other potentially Catholic sympathisers such as the Earl of Derby or Lady Arbella Stuart. Each were thwarted by a combination of the all-seeing Cecil family and an almost wilful ineptitude on behalf of Catholics to keep their communications safe.

So the Elizabethan audience might have given a knowing nod in *Richard II* when the Duke of Aumerle is caught by his father, the hand-wringing Duke of York, with incriminating letters peeking from his coat of a plot against the new King Henry's life. York's protestations to the new King to execute Aumerle for treason whilst only minutes before lamenting the passing of the old King was perhaps also something that the Shakespearean audience knew something about. Loyalty to the right person kept you alive. It was choosing the right person that was the trick.

According to Shakespeare, Aumerle's life is spared by the pleading of his mother and his closeness in blood to the King, but in reality Henry only spared it on condition that he reveal all the names of his co-conspirators – whom he promptly put to death. The truth was that, like Elizabeth, Henry was facing many plots.

Richard was actually still in the Tower when Henry Bolingbroke was crowned as Henry IV at Westminster Abbey in 1399. The holy oil used to anoint the new King couldn't be administered because his head was crawling with lice. Still, as if to cement his relationship with his people, he was the first monarch to have English rather than French spoken at their coronation. Two days later his son, Henry of Monmouth, was proclaimed heir apparent and made Prince of Wales, Duke of Cornwall and Earl of Chester – titles still given to the heir today. In October of that year, in a secret session, Parliament decided that Richard should be kept in a safe, anonymous, secure place in order that he should not act as a focus for rebellion. Thus he was made to dress as a forester (not the first time he had gone in disguise), led down the Thames and eventually taken by boat to Yorkshire first to Pickering Castle thence to Pontefract, then known as Pomfret.

The division within the country was now all too clear. The Earls of Gloucester, Exeter, Salisbury and Surrey plotted to kill Henry and his sons. To focus support they used a priest as a look-alike for Richard and it was only because of Aumerle that the plot failed. Henry was merciless in his subjugation and the traitors' heads were displayed on London Bridge. Later, too, a caltrap was found in Henry's bed with poisoned spikes.

Henry's claim to the throne through his mother was proved to be nonsense by a committee yet it was convenient because he could then bypass the superior claim to the throne of the Mortimer family. They were descended from the third son of Edward III, Lionel, Duke of Clarence, and not the fourth son, John of Gaunt. The seven year-old Edmund Mortimer, Earl of March, had even been named as successor by Richard himself yet it was to the man who could actually rule, Henry Bolingbroke, that England flocked. Well, half of it. The rest lay in wait for a better chance – either to rally around the Mortimer flag or even hoping for a miraculous return of Richard himself.

But this was not to be. Richard was in the cold grip of Lancaster – the abortive Aumerle plot against Henry probably signed his death warrant. Put in the care of Thomas Swynford (one of Henry's step-mother's offspring), he was quietly starved to death.

The castle where he died is still there, just. Pontefract, nestled now in the junction of the M62 and the A1, is small and utterly unremarkable. There are no dramatic hills piling into the distance or vast Victorian statements of industry. They used to grow liquorice here in the deep sandy soil, hence Pontefract cakes, and there is still a sprig of it growing beneath the castle walls. How apt that something so sweet and sour should grow in such a place. It is a granite grey day as I arrive, the skies matching the vast pepper pot-cooling towers of the modern Ferrybridge Power Station looming over the town.

The castle is in the suburbs on a promontory surrounded by trees. Some of the walls survive and rise from neatly planted flowerbeds. It's nearly dusk when I approach the gates to read a notice saying the place shuts at sundown so I scamper up to the grass sweep of the inner courtyard. A woman in uniform talks to a bloke in what must be the caretaker's hut. Other than that I have the place to myself. I climb to the top of the battlements and the sky has miraculously cleared in the West – the sun sinking red into the town hall.

I can see the houses and public buildings are lined with the black soot of industry. There is memory in this castle but it is chiefly of another revolution, the Civil War, which saw the castle torn down. Now it merely sits, naked and unloved, in a sea of suburbia. New houses are built in its walls, the locals walk past and never look up. History overgrown with ivy and dogshit. I think of Richard speaking within these walls: '*I wasted Time and now doth Time waste me.*'

With the sun just a burning eyebrow on the horizon the woman in the uniform starts ringing a bell to call Time. Looking down on the grass courtyard, the chimneys of the power station, grey satanic mills, belch their steam behind it.

There is a small door in the grass under which lie the cellars and passages where Richard was imprisoned. As Shakespeare would have it he died here facing his enemy for the first time – taking down a few of his attackers as he faced the murder squad. However in the seventeenth century Richard's skull was examined and no marks were found to indicate a blow to the head which would at least have been a merciful release. He died broken, emaciated and bereft. It was said that he became so hungry he tore strips of flesh from his arms and legs to eat. The official line was that he had gone on hunger strike and recanted at the last, so there would be no suicidal offence to God, but he was too far gone and had just slipped away.

The woman still rings the bell and it tolls for me. Time. I am keeping her from going home. I walk from the castle past the liquorice and the dogshit and there's a notice by the gate that says the Queen still owns this castle. The Duchy of Lancaster became part of the Crown from this time onwards and they won't let this place go. They should tart it up a bit but then being drab and unloved is perhaps a fitting memorial to a dark deed by the man who now not only was the Duke of Lancaster but had stolen the throne of England in an almost bloodless coup unrivalled in English history.

To Shakespeare, the genius of Henry's actions are countered by the weight upon his soul: Henry is aghast that Richard is dead. He condemns Richard's killer to wander through '*shades of night like Cain*', but it is Henry himself that is condemned. Eden has been left and the apple crushed upon the ground.

Richard's body was in fact taken to London and lay in state at St. Paul's for two days where Henry held a Requiem mass and hired chantry priests to sing a thousand masses for Richard's soul. The body was then taken back to Eden: Richard was interred at the church of the Dominican Friars at King's Langley, now All Saints' Church. The beautifully decorated tomb that housed Richard's body is still there but stands empty. Henry's son later placed Richard in Westminster Abbey.

It had been important for the newly crowned Henry IV that Richard was seen to be dead. His usurpation was complete. His troubles, however, were only just beginning. Although many rebel leaders within the nobility were executed and their body parts disseminated around the country as a warning, it was the country as a whole that remained riven. As Shakespeare was to show in his next three History plays, change at the top does not mean that the bottom has changed at all.

✳

Two

I pull into a pub car park on the old road to Rochester from London. The road dives down to cross the Medway a mile or two to the East and as such it was an important place for highwaymen and thieves to prey upon the potential booty heading to Canterbury and France. It is also about a mile away from Cooling Castle built by Baron John de Cobham in the 1380s who had fallen from Richard II's favour but was restored to all his former lands by the new Henry IV. His daughter married Sir John Oldcastle who had been a friend of the youthful Prince Hal, Henry's son, but was later convicted of heresy because of his Lollard beliefs – a form of proto-Protestantism based on the writings of John Wycliffe in the fourteenth century.

His descendants, the Barons of Cobham, became very well connected and favoured by the new Queen Elizabeth as the flame of Protestantism kept old Sir John Oldcastle's name alive as a Protestant martyr. When the Lord Chamberlain, Lord Hunsdon, died in 1596, Baron Cobham took over and withdrew the official protection the troupe of actors that bore his badge of office could rely on. 'The Lord Chamberlain's Men', of whom Shakespeare was a part, could not perform. Fortunately, Cobham died a year later, and Lord Hunsdon's son took over enabling their star writer cheekily to name the anti-hero in his new play after the Cobham's revered ancestor, Oldcastle. This new character was a Knight of the Realm, grossly fat, indolent and a thief – far too Catholic to be comfortable to the likes of the Cobhams who took great exception to it all. By the time the *Henry IV* plays were published around 1599, Shakespeare had been forced to change his character's name to 'Sir John Falstaff'.

Baron Cobham had not always been so full of the strictures of the new religion. By 1571 Cobham had been tarnished by association with the Ridolfi Plot and spent many months languishing in the Tower despite previously having been in Elizabeth's favour. Like many closet Catholics he had been supportive of her tolerant stance on religion. Once freed from the Tower, however, this apostate proceeded to embrace Protestantism and Elizabeth's stricter enforcement with open arms. His embargo on the Lord Chamberlain's Men was done with the zeal of the convert. His daughter even married Robert Cecil, the son of Elizabeth's treasurer and chief enforcer, Lord Burghley. Like Sir Christopher Hatton, Cobham knew all about how to reform and conform. However, two of his sons later met traitor's deaths under James I when they plotted for the toleration of Catholicism and to place Lady Arbella Stuart on the throne. So perhaps Cobham's own zeal was all for nothing. Elizabethan England was full of such people who carried a flag that didn't match the bearer.

The fact remained that the longer Elizabeth ruled – the more successful she was in establishing new England as the underdog in the fight against Rome – the more indolent the general populace became to any sort of change. By the time Shakespeare was writing his plays, although England was in no way wholly Protestant in outlook it had also begun *not* to be Catholic but, as he shows us, there was still a way to go.

From the strict, courtly measures and beats of *Richard II*, in *Henry IV Parts 1* and 2, Shakespeare creates the round, glorious spread of England's orchard. The fat tree trunk upon which the apples grow is Falstaff who proceeds to lead the young Prince of Wales through the flesh of the old world. It is a world set not in the taverns of Mediaeval England but in the bustling *liberties* of Shakespeare's time. For Shakespeare, History is now.

Whilst the new King Henry is in London stamping out fires, his son is getting interesting in its bars. Hal's friendship with Falstaff, a fading Knight with a weakness for wine, women and song, is filling the space left by his absent, ambitious father. At Gad's Hill in Kent on the road to Rochester from London, Falstaff and his bedraggled band of drinkers and lowlifes try to carry out a robbery only to be frightened from their purpose and left running for their lives by the mischievous Hal and his friend, Poins. The life and spirit coming from these pages is matched only by the dullness and intrigue of the new Henry IV's Court.

But these heady days of plump colour and Catholic desires are finite and the Prince knows it. He turns to the audience:

> ### Prince Hal
> *I know you all, and will awhile uphold*
> *The unyoked humour of your idleness:*
> *Yet herein will I imitate the sun,*
> *Who doth permit the base contagious clouds*
> *To smother up his beauty from the world,*
> *That, when he please again to be himself,*
> *Being wanted, he may be more wonder'd at,*
> *By breaking through the foul and ugly mists*

Of vapours that did seem to strangle him.
If all the year were playing holidays,
To sport would be as tedious as to work;
But when they seldom come, they wish'd for come,
And nothing pleaseth but rare accidents.
So, when this loose behavior I throw off
And pay the debt I never promised,
By how much better than my word I am,
By so much shall I falsify men's hopes;
And like bright metal on a sullen ground,
My reformation, glittering o'er my fault,
Shall show more goodly and attract more eyes
Than that which hath no foil to set it off.
I'll so offend, to make offence a skill;
Redeeming time when men think least I will.

(Henry IV Part 1 Act 1 Sc. 2)

Reformation. I think the audience might have guessed where Shakespeare was going with this lad.

I park round the back of the 'Sir John Falstaff' pub and go for a walk. The pub itself is pretty drab, placed on the edge of suburbia, but it overlooks the fine, leafy spread of Kent away to the East. These days it is not too busy a road but I can hear the far away scream of the A2 a mile or so in the distance that follows Watling Street from Canterbury to London. Above, a crane swings listlessly in the wind, erecting a new department at 'Gad's Hill School', the main building of which is an old Victorian pile once owned by Charles Dickens. The modest pillars at the front of a red-brick façade conceal two benches that Dickens insisted came from Shakespeare's birthplace in Stratford-upon-Avon. Dickens himself described Falstaff as the 'greatest comic person that never was' and was perhaps the knave that inspired so many of his own creations. His study, he claimed, was the exact point where Prince Hal left his fat, sweating surrogate father, Sir John Falstaff, in the lurch.

Next to the school I walk down a lovely lane that suddenly becomes swathed in countryside as fields break out on either side. But for the hum of traffic it is as tranquil a spot as any in the garden of Kent. Down in the valley I can just make out the small crenellations of Cooling Castle, the Cobhams' ancestral home. I fancy I hear the silent reproach of the dispossessed, but it is now owned by Jools Holland so I suspect the colour has come back into its cheeks.

With my thoughts full of Shakespeare and Dickens, back at the main road a chorus of young children from some unseen classroom are singing, 'He's Got The Whole World In His Hands'. I stand and watch with glittering eyes the world around me.

Northumbria

For Henry IV, England was running like sand through his fingers. He had wanted to go on a crusade to divert attention from his feeble claim to the throne. President George W. Bush took a leaf out of Henry's book exactly 600 years later. Yet unlike the events in 2003 where a million people marched on London and made precisely no difference, this time a similar percentage of the population were beginning to make their presence felt. Not least the people of the North for whom the vagaries of Westminster have always been a passing ship in the night.

From the A2 to the A1. I'm 350 miles north of Gad's Hill driving from Newcastle to Berwick – a stretch of road that races through some of the most extraordinary country in England. I head north past long, beautifully carved beaches to my right, and billowy mountains to my left. It doesn't feel like England in truth. But then neither is it Scotland. To the west the Scottish border lies much further south, but here in the east England pushes northwards in this fist of land lined with castles and coasts, and the road reaches through Time. If the Berkeleys in Gloucestershire controlled the gateway from the south, and the Ardens patrolled the Midlands, so here in the north the Swintons still keep watch over History.

This place, however, is Percy and Neville country – the families of the Earls of Northumberland and Westmorland respectively. It is a tough, wind-etched, almost black and white place. As a consequence, so were the people. They fought hard over centuries to keep their lands in their own hands. In 1569 both families led a rebellion known as the Rising of the North which stirred up the predominantly Catholic North but was catastrophically organised and badly led. Nearly 600 men were killed and the downfall began of one of the great mediaeval families of England – Charles Neville, the Earl of Westmorland, ended up in Holland begging on the streets. The rebellion's chief aim was to achieve the marriage of Neville's brother-in-law, Thomas Howard, Duke of Norfolk, to Mary, Queen of Scots and place them on the throne in a union of Catholicism and untainted lineage so craved by those who hated Elizabeth and her mother's questionable Protestant marriage to Henry VIII.

To aid the rebellion the Pope issued the fatal Bull that exhorted all Catholics to aid in killing the Queen, which ultimately became so disastrous to Catholics everywhere in England. Shakespeare was five when all this was taking place and the name of the Percy family was being dragged through the mud by both sides. Over the next twenty years the consequences of the rebellion and other subsequent Plots squeezed the life almost completely from Catholic hopes of change. Thomas Howard finally lost his life over the Ridolfi Plot and the ensuing mutual suspicion eventually led to Mary, Queen of Scots being executed for treason in 1587 and the resultant Spanish Armada a year later, when Shakespeare was twenty-four.

So perhaps it is no surprise that the Percies appear largely in Shakespeare's plays. Their influence, for good or bad, was still close to the bone. Their courage, foolhardiness, side-switching and dithering was something to which his audience could relate. In the play *Henry IV Part 1*, having laboured to place Henry Bolingbroke on the throne, the Earl of Northumberland and his son, Harry Hotspur, are now recanting on their efforts and plotting to remove him. It is a *volte face* worthy of many a Tudor aristocrat.

Warkworth Castle, the home of Hotspur, is perched on the coast of wild Northumbria. The weather matches Hotspur completely. Shakespeare depicts him as an increasingly insane, hot-headed, cold-blooded young man who is the polar opposite of the partying Prince Hal. At his castle he waits for news of the impending revolt which involves a union of the Percies of the North with the Welsh, and the man who has a greater claim to the throne than Henry himself, Edmund Mortimer.

However, I too am accusing myself of hot-headedness. I just happen to be in one of the biggest blizzards to hit the country in forty years and I'm driving through it in a silly little MG with a soft top. I am the only person on the road and I keep thinking I'm about to die. The snow is horizontal. I thought motoring around England in a British racing green MG may have been somehow poetic. I do love it but it's a piece of crap. There's always something wrong with it and its ability to start or even turn corners is temperamental to say the least. When you're an actor earning next to nothing on tour and your car refuses to start when you have a show to perform, it's no joke. I have physically attacked it three times.

The night before, I had driven up to the North East with the pallour of a man approaching the block because the radio reports were filled with the area being covered in about two hundred feet of snow and people freezing to death just looking outside or some such guff which sells a paper. At Doncaster I had guffawed as light snow began to pattern the fields but by Durham it was a white-out and my cynicism had left the car along with any heat through the soft top. They were closing the motorway behind me. Creeping down the hill past the Angel of the North I had momentarily touched the brakes and turned sideways. I do not ever want to do that again.

Making an impromptu pit stop and staying the night with a friend in Newcastle, the next morning I was buoyed by the news that the A1 might be passable, so I dug out the car and set off to Percy country.

But the clouds which I can see now queuing up from the sea, like hungry horses, have brought havoc. Three-foot high piles of snow line the one lane of the main road. Nothing else is on it and all I am trying to do is get to safety. Suddenly, out of the white, I see a signpost saying Warkworth. I turn the wheel and carry straight on. This bloody MG is so light it's like driving a roasting tin. At the next turning, forewarned this time, I make the corner cheering victoriously and drive straight into a snow drift that could swallow a bus let alone the mid-life crisis that is this MG. It turns out I am in the one area where it is as bad as they say it is.

I dig myself out and reverse back on to the main road, all the time thinking life would be much better on a horse. There's no way I'm getting to Warkworth. It is one of a chain of castles all the way up this coast built to fortify against all manner of Scots, Vikings, Saxons, Celts and each other. The Swintons originally came from further up the coast at Bamburgh Castle and then moved north of the border to Berwickshire. But the mother of all these many castles is a little more inland where the Percies established their superiority since Norman times – Alnwick.

It takes a long time but by the time I arrive there it is bright sunshine so, for a laugh, I put the roof down. People in huge great 4x4s look at me askance as I drive past them in my silly little car with a buccaneer smile and a knowing wave. I stop outside a 'Gentleman's Outfitter' to stock up on underwear.

Alnwick is a very pretty town cobbled from the yellowy local stone burned black by time, and is utterly dominated by the largest inhabited castle in the country, excepting Windsor. The first thing you notice is walls, everywhere, lining the approach roads as you begin to realise you are nearing a fortress.

But even here – a place that spends most of the year in the teeth of ferocious weather – they have decided to batten down the hatches. Apart from the Gentleman's Outfitter and a card shop, Alnwick is shut. At the front of the castle I park next to a car that has two feet of snow on it. I walk down 'The Peth' to the river – the sun is out and what water hasn't frozen shines shockingly blue in the relentless black and white. From this bridge at the bottom of the hill the castle lies like a lion in its lair: it can't be seen all in one go, the power and ferocious beauty that awaits can only be guessed at.

There are wooden effigies of fighters and beasts on top of the walls apparently dating from 1300. They are striking in that they tell a story and frighten any invader but I can't help thinking they are a bit, well, crap. It's not their fault. They are strange in that they look like something put there for the tourists. They look a bit too Hollywood. My own lumpen vision of a fallen-down castle with bare walls and bulky battlements doesn't seem to fit. Yet here they stand atop the walls, frozen in action like a stopped film. But the castle lives and breathes and is most definitely not set in aspic – the current Duchess of Northumberland has, like a James Bond villain, planted a poisonous garden for people to ooh and ahh at. The estates still sigh with the seasons and its farms churn out life. Whilst the castle had its ups and downs during the Wars of the Roses, it was never successfully invaded. The Percies just couldn't be rolled over – they were far too canny, wealthy and heavily armed for that. In the 1500s the 6th Earl, another Henry Percy, fell in love with Anne Boleyn before Henry VIII did, for which he lost his head. His nephew, Thomas Percy, was the Earl executed by Elizabeth for leading the 'Rising of the North' and was later beatified by the Catholic Church. In the early 1600s another Thomas Percy, whilst not being of the direct male line, was made constable of Alnwick Castle when Shakespeare was writing *Macbeth*. Thomas was then hung, drawn and quartered as a Gunpowder Plotter – trying to kill a Scottish King called James I.

Through various incarnations (one inheritor had to change his name to Percy in the end) they still live here; they are still one of the richest families in England; and they still wander around British society today. At one point the main heir to the Dukedom, George Percy, was stepping out with the Duchess of Cambridge's sister, Pippa Middleton. So it goes on and on.

The town is of course defined by the castle but this time of year they don't want you to get in. The car park is terrible and you have to get out and walk past the recycling bins and the backs of the shops in order to get front of house, so to speak. Once you work out how to get there, all is well. It is a delightful, thriving – indeed, very rich town. On the High Street, shops full of cakes and goodwill glisten in the snow. In the crisp white and polished blue it seems the most perfect place to be. Yet soon the angry black clouds begin to form on the horizon and I head back to the MG.

In Shakespeare's world, too, the storm was always gathering. From the black and white of Northumberland to the bawdy red of a brothel in London, the darkness was always behind the door.

Eastcheap

The Boar's Head Tavern in Eastcheap is in the heart of the City of London and was also the heart of Falstaff's world. It's no longer there: it was burnt down in the Great Fire of 1666, rebuilt, then knocked down in the eighteenth century. Eastcheap is still prominent – lined with the banks and barricades of modern-day thievery. Splendid Georgian buildings rise in majesty from one of the oldest thoroughfares in Britain. At their skirts are the usual shops that have invaded every town and High Street in England but foreign banks with exotic-sounding names are there too and, looking up, the serried rows of office upon office disappear into nothingness. I try to imagine the pisspots and pints of Shakespeare's Eastcheap, but it is so far removed as to mean nothing.

Where the pub actually stood is now underneath the approach to London Bridge around the corner in Cannon Street. Over the river at the Globe Theatre there is a 'Boar's Head' sign in a glass case that once hung above the pub. It is certain that everyone watching these plays in London who was not an aristocrat or tourist would have known the pub – and probably known it for a brothel-house and den of inequity. But there was also a Boar's Head Tavern in Southwark, near the river by the south side of London Bridge, which in Henry V's time had been owned by one Sir John Fastolfe.

He was a Knight who had been slandered, wrongly, for cowardice in the French wars of the fifteenth century whom Shakespeare had already featured briefly in his earlier *Henry VI* plays. In *Henry IV Part 1* he states the Boar's Head is in Eastcheap so many times that we are under no illusions as to where Shakespeare wants his audience to picture the scene. Yet perhaps he was making sure that there were no repercussions from the authorities: Fastolfe's house, built by Edward II, was next door to the Boar's Head in Southwark and was called the 'Rosary', and was still called that in Shakespeare's day. So even picking 'Fastolfe' as a name was dangerous. Especially when that character came to represent a sweating, heaving version of Englishness loved by the audience: joyful, funny, quick-witted and guileful, strong of heart and ready to brawl – he is also drunk, lazy, quick to steal, weak of the flesh, doubtful of honour, fat and past it. The gentry, the peasants, the town and the country in one man. No Protestant work ethic here or rigorous self-discipline. This is do what you want, then confess your sins to God later.

The Rosary was knocked down in the eighteenth century, so I meet David Warner, who played Falstaff in The Histories, in a pub as close as I can get to it, but the house was almost exactly opposite the Tower of London – pretty much on the spot where the Mayor's office, known colloquially as the 'Testicle', now resides. The new buildings, built in the flush of the Millennium, are an awful lot better than the wasteland that lay here as the residue of the Industrial Revolution, but I physically cannot bring myself to go into the sleek and skin-deep patina of the wine bars that litter the place. So I take David to the 'Market Porter' in Borough Market a few hundred yards away. Within the cramped confines of dark wood and decent ale, I tell him of the Rosary, the divide of England, and why we have met here.

David is a *bona fide* film star as well as having famously played Hamlet, Henry VI and, latterly, King Lear in his long, glittering career. He's great company and I always think it wonderful to be having a drink with the baddie from *Time Bandits*. As a thin introvert he was obviously perfectly suited to play the role of the ultimate fat extrovert, Falstaff. But he pulled it off in style. We sit and talk about Falstaff as the belly of England – vice filling the void. It's an interesting discussion as David says that when he's performing he doesn't think in such a way.

'I was just worried about the fat suit,' says David, in conclusion.

After much warmth and laughter David leaves, and a young Irishman cradling a Guinness and a fine beard leans over and apologises for intruding.

'Did you know', he says 'that Joyce thought Falstaff Shakespeare's greatest creation? It's in Ulysses.'

Pitchers have ears.

I walk over the river, the water swirling like Charybdis and the skyscrapers of the bankers planted like Scilla in her lair, and meet some of my fellow Histories actors, who couldn't make it earlier, in a small pub called The Ship – round the corner from where 'The Boar's Head' in Eastcheap once festered. It's a tiny little tavern, all black windows and Victoriana, down a side alley that means the smokers can shiver outside with impunity. We gather with much hugging and rejoicing at being back together and proceed not to talk about the plays at all. Life gets in the way. Laughter and love are in great supply just as they are similarly for the unreformed Hal with his surrogate father, Falstaff, who banter and play long into the night. My own surrogate family leave me thus disheveled too.

In one of the outside world's intrusions a man from the Court turns up to tell Hal his presence is required in the morning because his father is now at war with the Percies, the Welsh and Edmund Mortimer. In order to prepare himself for a grilling from his father, Hal plays a game of roleplay with Falstaff where each takes the role of the King admonishing his son for the company he keeps. Like any perfect night in the pub, truth seeps through the seams.

> **Falstaff**
> ...but for sweet Jack Falstaff, kind Jack Falstaff, true Jack Falstaff, valiant Jack Falstaff, and therefore more valiant, being, as he is, old Jack Falstaff, banish not him thy Harry's company, banish not him thy Harry's company: banish plump Jack, and banish all the world.
>
> **Prince Hal**
> I do, I will.
>
> (Henry IV Part 1 Act 2 Sc. 4)

Hal's conversion is ever nearer.

In the scenes at Eastcheap the black presence of the political, policed and reformed world outside is a constant threat. With actors it's there too – in the form of low pay, unemployment, and the desperate search for the next job. But, like the Eastcheap regulars, as a consequence actors do know how to enjoy the moment: as Falstaff says, 'Watch tonight, pray tomorrow.' The world outside is why every one of us in that pub feels an empathy and a joy for each other and for living for today. We feel. We breathe as one.

My liver hurts. I need to go home.

The Marches

Deep in the heart of Mid Wales, in the bluffs of Ceredigion, the mountain of Plynlimon rises. It is said that a giant still sleeps there – he is so big the hairs from his beard were used to tether King Arthur's hound. From him seep two rivers, the Severn and the Wye, that flow to the sea far away and mark the boundary between Saxon England and Celtic Wales. The Severn flows North and East then glides southwards to Shrewsbury and on down through Worcester to Tewkesbury where it is met by the Avon coming in from the heart of England. After Gloucester the river spreads to the sea, where at its very mouth, the Wye is met again having made its own more direct journey through Hay, then Hereford, Ross and Chepstow. They are the twisting plaits of the giant's beard. It is in the land between the two rivers that the Marches lie, like Babylon.

The term 'March' applied to any area in the borderlands with England of both Wales and Scotland – it's from the Old French *marche*, meaning a boundary (from where we get to 'mark out' something, usually by pacing). There were many Lords and Earls allied to each area – hence the Earl of March in these plays. But nowadays the term seems only to refer to the Welsh border and more specifically the space in between 'the banks of Wye and sandy-bottomed Severn' stretching from Shropshire through Herefordshire and the Forest of Dean to the Bristol Channel.

It is a strange, magical area to this day – rural to the point of being the definition of it, remote, unlittered by tourists, backward, forward, timeless, independent and staggeringly beautiful. By an odd geological quirk, the soil is as red as blood and incredibly fertile, and while there may be people with three heads wandering around certain parts of it, it has quietly fed and watered the nation for all of its history.

It is also my home.

I was brought up here under the shade of an apple tree rooted in the very red earth that made the blossom white above me. Through the village the Wye stretched past on its journey to the sea, a lifetime and countless counties away. My father came from Shrewsbury on the Severn – his father from Salt on the Trent in Staffordshire just to the North. My grandmother came from red dragon Mid Wales and it feels like their blood met and trickled down the river and ended up in Hereford.

I know these lands. Every folded hill, hollowed oak, field and stream lined with memories of games, tumbles, digging and milking; hard work, hops, and straw in the hair; a stolen first kiss round the Maypole with its Queen. At least, that's how I sometimes remember it.

It was the Garden of England long before brash, close-to-London Kent made such claims to that title. Before London even became the capital. As the Anglo-Saxons swept across the land and forced the Celts into the mountains of the West (Wales), so the lands buffering those mountains that offered such fertile soil became more and more strategic. As the Celts became the Welsh (derived from the same Saxon word as Watling Street meaning 'foreigners') and Anglo-Saxons the Anglish, sorry English, so the area offered food, wealth, violence and mystery to both parties who sought to live by its bounty.

The Normans and Angevins came and went but still couldn't get to grips with Wales, even though Edward I built his massive ring of imposing castles such as Harlech and Flint all around its borders. As such, whilst still relying on the rich harvest the place produced, successive monarchs tended to leave the borders in the hands of the feudal lords who had been there for centuries. As long as the bounty came in they could do what they wanted – which they proceeded to with almost autonomous impunity. They acted like Kings of their own state. Indeed, there is still somebody who goes around proclaiming he is King of Hay-on-Wye to this day and that you need passports to get in or some such drivel. What is true is that they set up and ran fiefdoms of extraordinary wealth and terrible savagery, where the threat of invading Celts or a passing warring English monarch was only relieved by the cut-throat feuds of families acting as a law unto themselves. It is worth remembering that Henry Bolingbroke himself tapped into this rich seam by marrying the wealthy daughter of the Earl of Hereford, Mary de Bohun – and inheriting his father-in-law's title, which is why he is referred to as 'Hereford' in the beginning of *Richard II*. Yet still the land produced and from it came the harvest, fruit and magic.

The apple.

Red skin, white flesh.

When I was growing up in darkest Herefordshire we would go wassailing the cider trees on Twelfth Night. There would be lots of singing and standing in a circle around the tree with warm mulled cider, laughter and shouting. We'd bash the tree or the ground around it to wake it up and pin bits of cider-soaked bread to the branches, displaying the signs of collective insanity. Even at the age of nine I could see that we all saw the ridiculousness of what we were doing yet not only did it ensure a good harvest the next year, it made me recognise the people in my village. Stories were told, the breath came sharp on the winter's night, and my face lit up when I took my first sip of warm cider beginning a downward spiral I have enjoyed ever since. I loved every minute of it. (It is no surprise I became an actor. The sense of community – of shared experience – is all. To me, standing around that tree and singing a song is no more ridiculous in this modern world than a large group of strangers huddling together in a theatre and being told stories. In my view they are exactly the same.)

The orchards that still stand there today wash the world in cider and are a living testament to the womb of nature, history, violence and magic that bled into the fields and forests of the Marches.

In his wonderful 1927 book, *In Search of England*, H.V. Morton describes them thus:

> *Here lived those turbulent Lord Wardens of The Marches who sat for centuries with their hands on their sword-hilts and their eyes on Wales. When the whistle of an angry sword had become almost a novelty in other parts of England, it was one of the ordinary rural sounds in The Marches; when the sight of a man with a red throat shocked London they held no inquests in Shropshire; and while in less troublesome counties men were building cosy manor-houses the marcher barons were still reinforcing their keeps and deepening their moats – the first die-hards....*
>
> *It was with a feeling of reverence that I realised here in The Marches with Welshman always at hand, Englishmen were once too busy to kill foxes.*

Indeed.

Out of this mayhem came Roger Mortimer, Earl of March. Born at Wigmore Castle in Herefordshire in 1287, he swept from the rich and fecund Marches and made a bid to become King of more than all he surveyed when he shacked up with Isabella, Edward II's wife, and led a rebellion against the weak, ineffectual monarch. He it was that shut Edward up in Berkeley Castle and consigned him to an uncomfortable fate. For three years Roger ran England as *de facto* ruler until Edward's son, Edward III, outsmarted them at Nottingham Castle, banished his own mother and sent Roger to the Tower. Mortimer thence assumed the dubious distinction of being the first of many to have been hung, drawn and quartered at Tyburn – now the site of Marble Arch in London. Not the first clash of Town and Country in this sceptered isle.

But you could argue that Roger had the last laugh over Edward III. One of his daughters became a Berkeley. Another married the Earl of Warwick. His son died soon after him but his grandson was gradually restored to privilege at Court by Edward III, as he remained the head of a Marcher lordship so important to the wealth and stability of the country. His son, in turn, married Edward III's granddaughter, Philippa. It is their son who, according to Shakespeare, now relaxes with his new Welsh wife and, being descended from the third son of Edward III and not the fourth, has a greater claim to the throne than Henry IV himself.

The wound that Henry had lashed across England, one side red, the other white, was beginning to welt. His lords were saying one thing and plotting another; impersonators of Richard were popping up and proving focal points of resistance. Shakespeare conflates two Mortimers: the one with the actual claim to the throne – the Earl of March – and his uncle, another powerful Lord Mortimer from the Marches. In reality, the Earl of March was actually still a boy at this time and he and his brother were in custody, but their uncle Mortimer was indeed taken prisoner by the Welsh and, in the play, now enters their strange, heady, lotus-flowered world.

Somewhere in the *limen* of the Marches most of the rebels have gathered together in a summit. Shakespeare sets it nowhere other than in a magical place, where English and Welsh combine and the poetry of both create a rather astounding oasis in the middle of the high politics of the English Court and the low shenanigans of the Tavern.

Alongside Mortimer, Hotspur is there, with his long-suffering wife. So too is Owain Glendower who remains elusive and magical to this day. Although, in the scene, most of his magic seems to come because he says it is magic, not because it is.

Hotspur clearly suspects this too. He is very sceptical of Glendower's claims to powers of the heavens – that the earth shook when he was born, and such like.

Glendower
Why I can teach thee, cousin, to command the devil.

Hotspur
And I can teach thee, cousin, to shame the devil
By telling the truth: tell truth and shame the devil.
….

Mortimer
Come come, no more of this unprofitable chat.

Glendower
Three times hath Henry Bolingbroke made head
Against my power: thrice from the banks of Wye
And sandy-bottomed Severn have I sent him
Bootless home and weather-beaten back

Hotspur
Home without boots and in foul weather too.
How he scapes the agues, in the devil's name?

(Henry IV Part 1 Act 3 Sc. 1)

There is an inescapable line that exists between the rational, Protestant, martial Englishman and the rough Celtic warrior whose soul is based in the mists of mountains and magic, whose unity comes from dispossession, mutual loyalty and the land – much like the Tudor Catholics. It's still found in the rugby teams of both nations to this day. Indeed Hotspur later in this scene says of Glendower:

I cannot choose: indeed sometime he angers me
With telling me of the mouldwerp and the ant.
Of the dreamer Merlin and his prophecies,
And of a dragon and a finless fish,
A clip-winged griffin and a moulten raven,
A couching lion and a ramping cat,
And such a deal of skimble-skamble stuff
As puts me from my faith. I tell you what,

He held me last night at least nine hours
In reck'ning up the several devils names
That were his lackeys: I cried 'Hum' and 'Well, go to.'
                    (Henry IV Part 1 Act 3 Sc. 1)

In one speech Shakespeare captures the tension at the heart of Britain that still exists. There's many an Englishman that will have a good-natured, or ill-tempered, discussion with a Welshman that ends in 'Hum' and 'Well, go to.' Or the other way round. I grew up supporting Wales but living in England. Red and white. The truth is I grew up between the two.

Glendower's fighting and rebellious spirit, born from the cloudy crags of Snowdonia like the one Clive and I drove through, and hewed from the wrongdoings of feudal lords, has lit up history and Welsh resistance ever since. He grew up a descendant of the Princes of Powys, part of the Anglo-Welsh gentry that dwelled in the Welsh Marches who co-existed with the English Marcher lords. As comfortable with the English language as well as Welsh, he even studied law at the Inns of Court in London and then served in the army at Berwick-upon-Tweed – in the heartlands of the Swintons of the other Marcher country up North. He had fought under John of Gaunt in Scotland and even became a squire to Henry IV himself at the Battle of Radcot Bridge in the early days when Henry was quelling insurrection from his usurpation.

Yet it seems to have been a dispute with one of the other Marcher Lords, Baron de Grey, that kick-started a revolution. De Grey had some land in the Welsh Marches and Glendower argued with him over ownership. He appealed to Parliament in London, but de Grey was falsely able to claim that Glendower had failed to send some men to deal with the uprising Scots, proclaiming him a traitor in and around Court circles. This meant Glendower lost the case and it seems to have been this, along with the Welsh affinity for Richard II, that led Glendower openly to revolt and be proclaimed Prince of Wales himself.

In a few years, by the time of the fictitious scene Shakespeare describes, Wales and the Marches had almost become his own. He declared a Welsh Parliament and laid plans for a Welsh Church and two universities. The French allied themselves to him and, in an extraordinarily little-known foray, launched an invasion of England through Wales in 1404. They landed at Milford Haven and marched into England straight through the Marches into Worcestershire. About ten miles from Worcester they stopped and made ready for battle with the English ranged before the Severn. Each party eyed the other for *eight days* and then, for reasons utterly unknown, the French turned around and went back again. Within a few months they had completely dispersed.

For Wales and Glendower, however, the battle had almost been won as Henry was stretched fighting many rebellious fires in Scotland, France and the North. On paper then, the combined powers of the Percies of the North, Mortimer's semi-independent Marches alongside his claim to the throne, and Glendower's proven military worth, the Triumvirate looked a good horse to back.

So much so that they and their supporters drew up a 'Tripartate Indenture' where it was agreed that they would carve up England between the three of them. The Percies would get the North of England, Mortimer the South, and Glendower the Marches alongside his own kingdom of Wales.

It's an act of unspeakable hubris and one which Shakespeare latches onto with all the knowledge of an experienced Tragedian. After the bickering of Hotspur and Glendower, Shakespeare introduces the map of England into the room like Eris's Golden Apple.

Glendower
Come, here's the map: shall we divide our right
According to our threefold order taken?

Mortimer
The archbishop has divided it
Into three limits very equally:
England, from Trent and Severn hitherto,
By South and East is to my part assigned:
All westward, Wales beyond the Severn shore,
And all the fertile land within that bound,
To Owen Glendower: and, dear, coz, to you
The remnant northward, lying off from Trent.
And our indentures tripartate are drawn,
Which being sealed interchangeably –
A business that this night may execute –
Tomorrow, cousin Percy, you and I

And my good lord of Worcester will set forth
To meet your father and the Scottish power,
As is appointed us, at Shrewsbury.

(Henry IV Part 1 Act 3 Sc. 1)

There must have been a good deal of shifting in the seats when that little speech was played out, as the idea not only of Civil War but of 'Maps' was of prime national importance in Elizabethan England. The new art of Cartography was only just evolving as new technologies made it easier to map accurately the environs of the country. To have a map was to have information. To have information was to have power and control. William and Robert Cecil, the father-and-son team behind Elizabeth's continuing Protestant grip on power, could use maps to make sure troops and missives be detailed to one particular place or another with far more efficiency. They also used the potency of maps to enhance the idea of England – an England personified by Elizabeth. There is even one portrait of her standing on a map of England and Wales, the virgin in white with the red hair, protecting the soul of the land.

To see your country spread before you in all its glory was also artistically to bring it into being – all the clearings, villages and towns that had grown over time around the forests, rivers and valleys of our world could be seen, and heard, on a map. The songs and stories that told us who we are could be etched simply into the metal of the printers' block alongside a map of where they came from. The elision of History and Geography forming that new science of the Tudor age: Chorography.

Looking at the map now, the nearest point of the Trent river to the Severn at Shrewsbury is Salt. So the route that my grandfather took to adulthood by moving from one to the other neatly maps the partition of rebellion, as it would have been at Shrewsbury that all three areas – a United Kingdom, even – would have met: Glendower to the West, Percy to the North and Mortimer to the South. So it is a quirk of fate that in reality the Tripartate Indenture was drawn up a year after the battle of Shrewsbury in which Hotspur met his fate. It was signed by all the parties and Hotspur's father – but Shakespeare was never one to let the fickle hand of truth get in the way of a good story. He seizes on the overweening expression of rebellion and lets the audience hold their mouths in horror as the nemesis is played out.

Glendower never showed up at Shrewsbury – he was off fighting battles of his own in Carmarthenshire. It is perhaps very important that he was never seen to have been taken by the King. But his star was waning. Under the new directions of the grown-up Prince Hal, the battle for Wales shifted from less direct confrontation into political strategy: by the time he became Henry V, Hal had strangled them by embargoes, sanctions and conciliation. There is no doubt he took a softer line than the brutalities imposed by his father but when he did fight, his military genius slaughtered the Welsh into submission. He was also aided by willing Welsh henchmen like Daffydd Gam – who is particularly mentioned by Shakespeare as being one of the dead of Agincourt.

In reality it all ended with a siege at Harlech Castle where Mortimer died of starvation. It was this man's nephew, the real heir to the throne, who lived on in the custody and charge of the next two Henries. The little boy's sister, however, married the Duke of York's son – with huge dynastic consequences for the rest of the century.

After the siege at Harlech, when the English finally entered the castle Glendower wasn't there. He'd simply disappeared into the mountains. The magic lived on, somehow, by vanishing like a rabbit into a hat. Even as late as 1414 – a year after Henry V's accession to the throne – there were rumours that Glendower had been in talks with a certain Marches-based Lollard leader, our old friend Sir John Oldcastle. So much so that troops were even sent to castles on the border, but nothing materialised.

There are many myths and fables about what happened to Glendower, but the one that seems to lend most credence – about which the Owain Glyndwr Society themselves have written – ends with him living at his daughter's house disguised as a Franciscan Friar. Here he lived out his days as a tutor, his daughter's family on his knee. That house was in Kentchurch in Herefordshire a few miles from where I grew up. In England, yet not so. In Wales, yet not so.

His daughter, Alys, married Sir John Scudamore, Sheriff of Herefordshire and he had estates in Kentchurch and Monnington Straddle deep in the heart of the Golden Valley a couple of miles from the border with Wales. It is said that Glendower is buried there with the secret being kept by the Scudamores for 600 years. The Scudamores are still all over the Marches – I went to primary school with one. A grandson of Alys and Sir John was Sir John Donne – a high-level Yorkist courtier and progenitor of the De Vere family, Earls of Oxford, who wove their own particular web of magic around every monarch of the Tudors. Their bloodline flowed thence to the Cavendish family – still the Dukes of Devonshire to this day. But it is Glendower's legacy of survival, rebellion, magic and music that lives on in the hearts of every Welshman.

Glendower's blood, and that of old Roger Mortimer, both of the Marches, have spread from the giant, like the whiskers of the Wye and Severn, to the sea.

✳

Meanwhile, Falstaff is busy thinking Catholic thoughts. He speaks to Bardolph, the red-nosed regular of The Boar's Head:

Falstaff

Bardolph, am I not fallen away vilely since this last action? Do I not bate? Do I not dwindle? Why my skin hangs about me like an old lady's loose gown. I am withered like an apple-john. Well, I'll repent, and that suddenly, while I am in some liking. I shall be out of heart shortly, and then I shall have no strength to repent. An I have not forgotten what the inside of a church is made of. I am a peppercorn, a brewer's horse. The inside of a church! Company, villainous company, hath been the spoil of me.

(Henry IV Part 1 Act 3 Sc. 3)

The Protestants whitewashed the bewitching, colour-soaked paintings that sang from the walls and pillars of churches – no such succour for the soul should come from the hand of men and the outside influence of beauty. The harsh Germanic monochrome of religious vision precursing the harsh Germanic monochrome of Architectural Modernism some 350 years later with which we still labour today.

As part of his duties in serving the town of Stratford-upon-Avon, John Shakespeare, William's father, was required to whitewash the walls of the Guild Chapel. It is listed that he paid for it to be done in 1577. This was *four years* after it was supposed to be done and one can only imagine the feelings of John, a known recusant, liming the red paintings with white, and smashing the coloured windows which were replaced with clear glass. The 13-year-old William was at school next door.

William could certainly remember what the *'inside of a church'* was made of. If you go there now, you can see the images which were discovered in 1804. They shimmer ghostly through lime and the ages, colour-faded but still defiantly there. Having spawned characters like Falstaff and the colour of Eastcheap, or the green of Arden in *As You Like It*, or Bohemia in *The Winter's Tale* to pick but a few, perhaps the colours on those walls shine brighter today than ever.

Yet Falstaff is not about to waste away. Hal arrives at the Tavern with news – he has repaid the monies stolen from Gad's Hill and he is 'friends with his father'. What's more he has procured Falstaff and the boys a job. Sir Jack will be in charge of a group of infantry, ready to depart from Temple Hall the next day, where Hal will be with pay and weapons, to meet the rebels in battle at Shrewsbury.

Hal may be edging closer to Reformation, but like a secret smoker, he can't resist taking his little bit of life with him.

Shrewsbury

The 'Battlefield Enterprise Park' hoves into view under the pylons by the Shrewsbury ring road. Clive Wood and I are in the mighty Bongo trying to find the site of the Battle of Shrewsbury, and the name somewhat gives it away. We've driven along Watling Street taking the same route that the King, Hal, Falstaff and his cohorts used from London. The road leads straight to Shrewsbury over the top of the Forest of Arden. Falstaff even stops near Coventry to get booze and count the earnings he has made from taking bribes – Warwickshire providing a respite, about which Shakespeare knew a little.

But all we can find is an Industrial Estate just outside Shrewsbury. The fact that it's called an 'Enterprise Park' is perhaps a vain boast given its utter lack of enterprise in beauty and sympathy with its surroundings. There are signs to the 'Battlefield Visitor Centre and Car Park' but nothing to be seen. To the right is a car park and this, it turns out, is the Visitor Centre. Not even a shack to shelter by.

We get out and stretch our legs and I can feel the immediate snap, crackle and pop of static electricity as the cables from a massive pylon towering above us sing for their supper. This is the battlefield. We go up to the 'Viewing Area' where we get an even better view of the pylon. A little board tells us how, in 1403, Hotspur lined his troops up to the North on a ridge and waited for the King's forces to arrive from the South and East. They even had a parley – that great mediaeval technique to avoid any unnecessary bloodshed. The two sides trot out to each other and see if they can't make one last attempt to resolve things in more diplomatic ways.

Like Glendower, the Earl of Northumberland – Hotspur's father – never showed up. He was 'ill'. Perhaps because of the no-show of his father and Glendower, it has been suggested that Hotspur was actually willing to accept terms from the King. Not even Mortimer had turned up to fight. It turned out to be the Earl of Worcester who was the one trading insults. Certainly this is what Shakespeare shows us, with Hotspur not even being present at the parley and Worcester not relaying the King's peaceful and conciliatory message. Because of Worcester's actions, the two sides return to their respective forces with nothing resolved and a battle to start.

Falstaff is even present at the parley, and takes a very dim view of Hal's offer to fight Hotspur single-handedly. As the others prepare for battle he is left musing on honour in no uncertain terms.

> ### Falstaff
> *What is honour? A word. What is that word honour? Air. A trim reckoning. Who hath it? He that died o'Wednesday. Doth he feel it? No. Doth he hear it? No. Is it insensible, then? Yea, to the dead. But will it not live with the living? No. Why? Detraction will not suffer it. Therefore I'll none of it. Honour is a mere scutcheon: and so ends my catechism.*
>
> (Henry IV Part 1 Act 5 Sc. 1)

The old world is not impressed with the new.

No one is very sure what happened in the battle. What seems certain is that Henry IV's forces lost it, but Hotspur carelessly got killed and therefore the King won it. Simple as that. The entire right flank of the King's troops, it seems, gave way and ran. The centre began to crumble. Only the left flank under the command of the resurgent Prince Hal kept any order. But then he got an arrow in the face. It must have gone straight through the slits in his visor. Doubtless wincing as they went, Hal's followers got him off his horse and he managed to pull it out. He was later treated with 'honey and alcohol' and went under the Physician General's knife. He had a scar for the rest of his life.

Hotspur, perhaps buoyed by the general carnage, moved in for the kill. He and his men charged at the centre where the Royal Standard was hoisted aloft. It was cut down only to be discovered that it was Sir Walter Blunt and not the King who carried the flag. However, with the Standard having been deposed the word spread around the battle that the King was dead, but then Hotspur apparently lifted his own visor to celebrate and promptly got an arrow in the face as well. He wasn't as lucky as Hal and died where he lay.

As the King was apparently dead, the rebels started claiming victory and cried, 'Henry Percy is King!', but the very much alive Henry IV soon started proclaiming 'Henry Percy is dead.'

There was no answer.

It seems people then just stood around looking at each other rather shiftily, either side not knowing who had won. Considering that their leader was dead there wasn't much the rebels could do. It was all over. Henry IV had lost the battle and very nearly his own life, yet he still won.

Shakespeare's portrayal of the battle culminates with a big showdown between the young Prince Hal and Harry Hotspur. All of which is played out with Falstaff playing dead in the background.

Hal is victorious.

Hotspur

O, Harry, thou hast robbed me of my youth.
I better brook the loss of brittle life
Than those proud titles thou hast won of me.
They wound my thoughts worse than the sword my flesh:
But thought's the slave of life, and life, time's fool:
And time that takes survey of all the world
Must have a stop. O I could prophesy,
But that the earth and the cold hand of death
Lies on my tongue. No, Percy, thou art dust
And food for –

Prince Hal

For worms, brave Percy. Farewell, great heart.

(Henry IV Part 1 Act 5 Sc. 4)

In death, Hotspur talks of mapping the world with time. Chorography. The mediaeval, Catholic, conception of time was cyclical with the death of Christ at its centre like the bloodstream of the body coursing round and round the heart. It was now being replaced by History seen as a river, from source to sea, and therefore must have an end. Being at the centre of the hourglass of Mediaeval and Modern, the Renaissance Shakespeare could not help but be for all time.

Standing under the pylon, with slate grey skies and the rain coming in, it's a pretty dispiriting place. I can see Battlefield Church in the distance which may have been built atop the pile of bodies from the battle. There are two paths marked out on the map erected in the car park – the King's trail and the Hotspur trail which follow the lines of the armies as they faced each other. I can see a couple walking their poodle around them. The green fields don't seem to seep of the dead, and the wheat is giving nothing away. The battle itself was fought in a field of peas. As if bludgeoning people to death wasn't hard enough, doing it with pea plants cloying and tripping around your knees must be like running away in a nightmare.

I get a flask of tea from the Bongo and we sit and look over the fields. The Ring Road pelts by. The hum of the cables above us, like the silver whispers of the ghosts that died here, keep us company. Clive suddenly gets up and as Henry IV shouts with finality:

'Henry Percy is dead.' Like 600 years ago, there is no response. He shouts: 'Let's go down the pub.'

He's right. With the pylon and the Battlefield Enterprise Park in all its aching monotony, this place is not a fitting memorial to History. I take a look at the map and see a village a mile away called Allbright Hussey. If ever there was a place for me it's Allbright Hussey. We find that not only is there a pub, it's a hotel built in 1524 and has a manager called Malcolm.

The sun comes out and as we walk past the moat that fronts the hotel, there is a black swan picking at the grass by the reeds. Malcolm greets us as long-lost friends and we ask if we can sit outside. Other staff walk by with the flat faces of people who cannot get a word in edgeways and have long since died inside listening to the ever chirpy Malcolm. But he's good value. He gives us the rather posh menu and he says we can forget that and just have something like a steak sandwich if we prefer. As we sit outside looking over the battlefield from the other side, we are both hit by the most powerful sense of place and history. Having played Henry IV, Clive is very affected and can feel the presence of all this History and the character he played. The 'Enterprise Park' seeps away and I can feel the weight of this land all of a sudden. It is in our boots.

'They want to build an incinerator over there,' Malcolm says as he points towards Shrewsbury and the Parks and the pylons which you can't see from this beautiful spot, 'But we've got their number. We found out who they've bribed.'

The black swan still forages in the water, unaware of big business working its dark magic over the broken bodies of our ancestors. 'The moat is there to keep the Welsh out,' he says, 'They'd come and nick your animals, and crops, and your wives, if you didn't build a moat. The border was only just over there, you see, not like it is now, and they'd take everything.'

'And that black swan, she's absolutely psychotic. It's a lesbian. Lived here for a year with no problems with its partner who, when it died, we realised was a female too. We got in a male mate and within a week she'd clubbed it on the head and it was dead in the water. We got another one and put it the other side of the bridge so she could look at it and she just hissed. Absolutely psychotic. Horrible piece of work that swan.'

'The vet says that it's a warm-blooded creature, and any warm-blooded creature can go mad, he says, and I believe it with that one.'

I look out over the battlefield.

'Still, a little bit of insanity works in this industry,' he says, and then he recognizes Clive.

Which is, of course, what Hotspur didn't do in our staging of the battle. We had sixteen men all processing on stage in formation with swords, crowns, and the same long battle coat that Clive wore, all creating a slow-motion sword fight that was 'danced' as one by sixteen men. Hotspur, standing downstage, could not recognize who was the King and thus fights each one and each time thinks he has killed the King but discovers he has not. Eventually the kings clear to reveal Prince Hal, about to win his spurs – literally.

'Oooh, you're off the telly, aren't you. Thought I recognised you. Yes, they all come in here,' says Malcolm. 'Richard and Judy, I put them in the corner, they don't like to make a fuss. Michael Heseltine. What a nice man, although his wife made a fuss about the linguine, and he told her to eat it. Mind you, the royals. They're nice too. She's had a hard time of it, our Lizzie, what with all her kids and everything.'

I think of her ancestor, Henry IV, and looking over the bloody fields, think she may just have had it a little bit easier. Henry may have had an errant son – but, in his defence, Hal did get an arrow in the face fighting for his father's cause.

'Old Charlie with his hands in his pockets,' says Malcolm, 'I always wonder what he's doing with his hands.'

Well, Malcolm, perhaps he's feeling that arrow through the ages.

After the best steak sandwich I've ever had, we leave Malcolm. I take a picture of the lesbian black swan. I'm sure there's money in it somewhere.

The battle won, Henry dispatches his newly battle-blooded second son, John of Lancaster, with the Earl of Westmorland to Yorkshire to mop up the rebelling Archbishop of York and Hotspur's father, the Earl of Northumberland. The King and Hal are to go together to Wales and take on Glendower and Mortimer. A story that ends, untold by Shakespeare, in the wilds of Harlech Castle and the magical disappearance of the great Glendower. Falstaff survived the battle by playing dead. The fat belly of England is not quite ready to give up the ghost.

Shakespeare ends his first play, *Henry IV*, here on the field of Shrewsbury – the meeting point of a Union that never was. To this day Shrewsbury is split in two: No one can agree on how to pronounce the name. Of those that live there, some call it *Shroosebury*, and others call it *Shrohsbury*. Middle class or working class, Catholic or Protestant, Welsh or English.

Who knows?

Three

Henry IV was fighting to stay on the bucking horse he had fought so long to master. His kingdom was not convinced first by his usurpation and then his leadership. Shrewsbury did much to quiet the rebel voices but they lay in wait.

Glendower was proving his main focus. In 1404 Henry received money from Parliament to launch a massive expedition finally to defeat the ageing magician of the West. Which is what Richard Scrope, Archbishop of York, and his cronies in the form of the Earl of Northumberland, Hastings, and their armies were waiting for in their northern capital of York. When Henry's forces were engaged elsewhere their smaller power could become effective, so as soon as Henry set foot in Wales, 'the North' would rise up from nowhere and put things right.

Except Henry didn't go to Wales at all. Thanks to his son, John of Lancaster, and the Earl of Westmorland, Henry got wind of the conspirators' little meeting in York and stayed right where he was – back in the Marches. He wasn't going anywhere.

Like the subsequent Rising of the North in 1569, misinformation and hearsay got in the way of the conspirators. In 1569, indecision and vacillation – infected by grief – was a hallmark of the Catholic dithering under the yoke of a ruthless political system. Shakespeare starts *Henry IV Part 2* with Rumour, a spirit that sows lies and ill-feeling, known to us all. It informs the Earl of Northumberland, waiting nervously in Alnwick, that his son has actually been victorious instead of what really happened: he was carved up and posted to all parts of the kingdom as a warning to others. There is no greater barrier to effective rebellion than not knowing what is happening.

By the time Shakespeare shows the Archbishop of York and his fellow plotters at the Bishop's Palace in York, they are vacillating and wringing their hands like the finest Catholics of Shakespeare's day.

> **Lord Bardolph**
> *...in a theme so bloody-faced as this,*
> *Conjecture, expectation and surmise*
> *Of aids incertain should not be admitted.*
> **Archbishop of York**
> *'Tis very true, Lord Bardolph, for indeed*

It was young Hotspur's case at Shrewsbury.

Lord Bardolph

It was, my lord, who lined himself with hope,
Eating the air on promise of supply,
Flattering himself with project of a power
Much smaller than the smallest of his thoughts.
And so, with great imagination
Proper to madmen, led his powers to death
And winking leaped into destruction.

Hastings

But, by your leave, it never yet did hurt
To lay down likelihoods and forms of hope.

(Henry IV Part 2 Act 1 Sc. 3)

'Conjecture, expectation and surmise'. One can almost feel the dusky, smudged, candlelit discussions of plotters in the corner of a darkened room or perhaps a crypt under St. Etheldreda's at Ely House.

The Archbishop's Palace is a little way out of York, in Bishopsthorpe, and only tiny parts remain of the old structure in which this scene takes place. It is now an impressive hodge-podge of Mediaeval, Tudor and Georgian, lying languidly on the banks of the River Ouse. There has been an Archbishop in it since 1241 and the great Catholic hero, Wolsey, who was once Archbishop of York, made his way to power through this important office, even though he never actually came here.

This, and the throne which sits in York Minster itself, is the seat of power for the Capital of the North: the Romans built a huge camp here, Eboracum, and the Vikings built Jørvik, or York. It was the central hub in this Northern, wilder, Viking land that was bounded by the Danelaw line on Watling Street a hundred miles to the south. 'K' is not in the Latin alphabet, it was Scandinavian. It was virtually autonomous for most of its history, plying wool for its trade and playing politics with its leaders. There was even a Bishop of York present at the councils of Arles and Nicaea.

It is still prosperous to this day, as the cobbled mediaeval streets lace their way to the Minster which pitches and yaws up before you like a page from a pop-up book. The cosy, timbered buildings which lead from its skirts draw you in to neddy among the snuggeries: 365 pubs dance within the city walls.

Deep in the shadow of the West Façade of the Minster, is the 'Guy Fawkes' pub. The great talisman of failed rebellion was born in this very house. Here the fires still burn, and you can get a pint in a wooden cubby-hole and talk of terror and bluster and all things November.

Gloucestershire

Whilst Henry's son, John of Lancaster, and the Earl of Westmorland are heading North to meet the rebels, Falstaff is taking a more leisurely and roundabout route. He is wandering through the Cotswolds in Gloucestershire picking up human cannon fodder for the King's army along the way – and making money whilst he's doing it.

For Shakespeare to depict the *liberties* of London was one thing: a large majority of his audience would have been from just the very streets he was depicting. But now to draw a picture of basement rural life was markedly another. He was a country boy, well-schooled yet denied a university education either by his father's fall from financial grace or the taint of Catholicism. It could be both – nobody knows. A country boy that had not been to University was treated with extreme scepticsm by his contempories whose noses were fixed firmly to their Oxbridge rafters. Precisely because of this, no other writer at the time could place a scene in the middle of Gloucestershire and make it dance through the ages. Elegiac, wistful and tender, it is Shakespeare at his most accessible. It was not the middle of nowhere – to Shakespeare it was everywhere.

Warwickshire and Gloucestershire meet about six miles away from Stratford-upon-Avon. Travel around there now and it is not a huge stretch of the imagination amongst the moneyed Range Rovers, yellow custard cottages and the thatched weekend dreams of a modern-day Cotswold village to think that Shakespeare's characters are still meeting to this day: two blustery old Justices of the Peace are still to be found hee-hawing in the restaurant of most Cotswold pubs.

I've brought Geoffrey Streatfeild along to Chipping Campden – a beautiful little market town nestled on the edge of the Cotswolds in Gloucestershire. Geoffrey played Hal in The Histories and we have known each other for a long time and remain the greatest of friends. We've always said that we'll probably end up playing Justice Shallow and Justice Silence at some stage, so perhaps we are in training for it as we sit in the Red Lion and mull over friendship and beer.

Shallow is an old lawyer who trained in London but has moved to Gloucestershire for many a year. He knows Falstaff from his London days and he and his cousin, Justice Silence, have rounded up some potential soldiers for the great man to recruit on his imminent arrival. The names Mouldy, Shadow, Wart, Feeble and Bullcalf give a pretty good idea of the sort of people the two Justices have gathered together: the five bits of deadwood that line up for Falstaff's inspection could not be described as a lean fighting unit.

However, Falstaff is not worried by such a display and once the men that can afford it have quietly paid *not* to be picked for the war, he sweeps up his terrible recruits and leaves Justices Shallow and Silence gobsmacked by his choices. These characters are hewn from the hollow of England. Their terrible inheritance is to be forced to fight if they cannot afford to buy themselves out of service, and get sent to oblivion in the mud and blood of somebody else's battle. It is the lowest form of conscription.

What would help in a battle was to be fit and able, and one man in Gloucestershire came up with just such a way of doing it. Above Chipping Campden on the land that rises to the Cotswold edge is Dover's Hill, a stunning vantage point that overlooks the breadth of middle England with Stratford-upon-Avon a few miles to the North, the Vale of Evesham and the Malvern Hills to the West, with the River Avon picking its way through it all. At the top of the hill the ground dips into a natural amphitheatre and here it was, in 1612, that the 'Olimpick Games' were created.

Robert Dover, a lawyer at Gray's Inn in London, moved to Chipping Campden and created a series of 'Games' on the common land above the village. There had possibly been a 'church ale' taking place at the sight for centuries (an 'ale' was a mediaeval festival of feasting and drinking). But whatever Dover's personal reasons, it was done with the express permission of King James – hence the Red Lion pub in the village – who liked the idea of keeping the people fit and streamlined in the defence of the realm. Dover's main theme of these Games that took place in the centre of the country was that they were open to all – gentry and commoner alike – and featured horse racing, running, jumping, hammer throwing, sword fighting and, especially, a local variant named 'backsword' fighting. Wrestling was very popular but usually took the form of another local peculiarity known as *shin-*

kicking where the combatants hold on to each other and, er, kick each others' shins.

Robert Shallow refers to Falstaff as a good 'backsword man', and it is not difficult to believe that, even though these plays were written fifteen years before the creation of the Games, the traditions and practices were familiar to Shakespeare. Robert Dover may even have known Shakespeare as he was in London in the early 1600s and even wrote a pageant performed at Gray's Inn. He moved to Chipping Campden soon after Shakespeare had decamped back to Stratford-upon-Avon. Dover had been brought up in a Catholic family and even though, unlike most Catholics, he was allowed to go to Cambridge, he left early to avoid taking the Oath of Supremacy.

The Olimpick Games have been recognised by the 2012 Committee as one of the founding bricks in the modern-day Olympic heritage. In 1636 the *Annalia Dubrensia* was published with contributions from the likes of Ben Johnson and Michael Drayton, praising Dover and his achievements with the Games and giving lustre to English social life. The Games had already acquired the moniker 'Olimpick' long before the publication of the book, but the name alone represents the Renaissance fascination with Classical Mythology. What's more, to the Catholic Dover, the name was a useful secularisation of an ancient tradition based on a 'church ale' that nicely kept him out of jail and, indeed, in favour with the King. So much so that James I sent his clothes to be worn by Dover on the occasion of the Games, giving it the royal seal of approval. The sports were not just a personification of the bawdy merriments of 'Ye Olde England', they performed a serious function in keeping people fit either for farming, industry or war and played an important part in the wider English community.

As a consequence, the Games were shut down during the Civil War by the Puritans for being far too much fun, complaining of 'drunken behaviour and sexual licence.' James I and Charles I rather liked these sorts of endeavour and thought they defined a certain type of Englishness. It was the headlong rush against this strain of unabashed, naked silliness and drinking that was another piece of kindling to the fire of the Civil War. It pitched the Puritanical desire to label such impulses as 'devilish' against the Old English form of what-the-hell celebration and joy. The explosion of fun, drama and 'Britain at its best' attitude of the 2012 Olympic Games in London which sprang from the mire of depression that immediately preceded them was the embodiment of just such a history.

Robert Dover died in Barton, just outside Stratford-upon-Avon, in 1652. Charles II restored the Games and they ran until 1852 when the common land was enclosed by local landowners, one of whom had complained, again, that licentiousness was rife. In 1965, having been revived for one time only at the Festival of Britain in 1951, they were restaged and continue to this day. Which is why Geoffrey and I find ourselves on Dover's Hill on a whippy night in June, with about three thousand other people, watching tug-of-war, a gymkhana and shin-kicking.

The scenery is stunning, the green, dappled hill dropping down to the sun-dried plain below. People sit around the banks of the natural theatre singing songs and cheering the local village Queen as she is processed. A man on a huge horse and Jacobean costume, pretending to be Robert Dover, officially opens the Games and soon, to the cheers of thousands, two men grab each other and proceed to kick the shin out of each other. It's all taken very seriously by some people and not seriously at all by others. Both combatants have to don white coats and stuff hay down the front of their trousers for the ritual. They must then take hold of each others' collars and begin to kick the other's shins. The one who hits the ground first is the loser. There's one chap with the finest bald pate I have ever seen giving it a good go but invariably the man in his twenties, with endurance and strength on his side, comes out on top. He will walk taller in his local forever. With painful shins.

Standing on a hill overlooking the Avon and the warm heart of England, I cannot think of a stranger yet somehow more obvious pastime. Everyone is enjoying this spectacular if silly action, and the world is a very calm and rosy place – although that may be due to the copious amount of ale from the Red Lion that we drank down in the village. But I feel that I can spot Mouldy, Feeble and Wart just over there by the shin kickers. Bullcalf is certainly smashing up a piano in the next field. Shadow is standing too close to the newly elected village Queen. And there is Justice Shallow, decked out in green Barbour and deer-stalker, just as much a figure of fun as he was 400 years ago. Justice Silence is soon to be shattered by the jingle-jangle jaunt of the Morris Men as they start their dance.

This is not corporate. There is the touch of the earth here. The smile of the Green Man. It is not Protestant, Catholic, Puritan or even Olympian. This is nature, community and peace with the land. I fancy I can feel for what Shakespeare yearned.

I stand on the hill and look out over Arden.

A huge beacon is lit, to affirm our place in the world, that on such a clear night four hundred years ago would have been seen from all over the Forest of Arden to the north. Then we walk en masse in a flame-lit procession from the hill to the village. The night, the flames and the almost breathless hush of community move me almost to tears.

Geoffrey and I hit the Red Lion and hear the chimes at midnight.

Jerusalem

From one lost forest to another. Gaultree Forest used to lie just north of York, starting at the Bootham Bar gate and curving North and West for twenty miles or so. Once a Saxon royal forest it was cleared during the reign of Charles II. Beyond the growing spread of York's suburbs it is now rather unremarkable farmland, punctuated by the odd power station.

Here it is that the Archbishop of York has chosen to meet young John of Lancaster and the Earl of Westmorland in the field. But the Archbishop falls prey to one of the biggest stings in history when, at the parley, John agrees that the King should indeed listen a little more to people's demands and says the Archbishop and his followers will be fairly treated. All drink as brothers and the Archbishop disbands his joyous army. At which point John and Westmorland arrest them for high treason. With the rebel army disbanded a victory is scored without a drop of blood being shed.

Contrary to Shakespeare, King Henry IV himself came to York once the rebels had been duped and captured, having put his Welsh campaign on hold and turned his steely gaze northwards. He stayed at the Archbishop's Palace and was visited in the night by his closest friend and ally, a breathless Thomas Arundel, Archbishop of Canterbury, who had hot-footed it from London in order to stop the King killing a fellow Archbishop – a direct emissary of God.

The King politely assured him all was fine and ushered him from his chamber. Whilst Arundel was asleep, he convened a council and speedily tried all the traitors held prisoner in the Palace, including the Archbishop of York. They were all dead by daybreak. In the Elizabethan era, an Archbishop of York killed by the King must have chimed an awful lot of bells with an audience whose grandparents were alive when Cardinal Wolsey was defeated by Henry VIII. As it is, the last line that Shakespeare's Archbishop of York says to Prince John is simply: *'Will you thus break your faith?'*

It was said that the horrific skin conditions and burning limbs from which Henry IV eventually died started that very morning. Whatever the cause, Henry was almost certainly syphilitic and ill. What's more, having killed an Archbishop he not only alienated most of his people but also the Church – both in England and Rome. Yet he fought on. Henry only knew struggle.

Throughout *Henry IV Part 2* from the Battle of Shrewsbury in 1403, the Archbishop's rebellion in 1405, then the death of Henry in 1413, it is the red, fat, Father Christmas Falstaff, lovable old Falstaff feasting and fornicating on the body of England, that is the pendulum in the clock. The play beats to his time as the audience warm to his misadventures. But the great hulking figure of Henry is always a brooding presence, on and off stage. Far removed from the battlesome youth we saw at the beginning of *Richard II* who quarrels and fights his way to the throne, Henry is now a sweating, pustulating mass that heaves his body through Westminster Abbey to pray in a room just off the Dean's House.

The Jerusalem Chamber is still there, to the right of the West façade of Westminster Abbey as you look at it. Inside, a huge fireplace the size of a small room burns bright. Up in the corner of the ceiling, a bust of Henry IV looks down past the wooden-pannelled fust of ages. This is the room where he died with his son Hal weeping by his side.

The fact that there was a small reception in it after we had done our little performance of scenes from The Histories seemed strange. Clive and Geoffrey had staged the death scene of Henry at the foot of the altar and we had processed down the nave, a staggering Clive being helped by myself and Geoffrey, as the audience followed. On a small balcony leading to the Chamber, a song was sung written by Henry himself, as the audience down below stood holding candles.

To play a scene written 400 years ago about events 600 years ago, in the very place they are set, with a soundtrack written by the person whose death the scene is depicting, seems almost painfully English. To stand in the Chamber supping a glass of red wine and fiddling with a mushroom vol-au-vent seems even more so. It is strangely life affirming and comforting, wrapping history around us like a blanket.

In *Henry IV Part 2* it is in this very room that both father and son are finally, fully, reconciled to each other and Henry can let go, knowing whatever guilt that has come with the crown can die with him.

King Henry IV

...Therefore, my Harry,
Be it thy course to busy giddy minds
With foreign quarrels, that action, hence borne out,
May waste the memory of the former days,
More would I, but my lungs are wasted so
That strength of speech is utterly denied me.
How I came by the crown, O Heaven forgive,
And grant it may with thee in true peace live.

Prince Hal

My gracious liege,
You won it, wore it, kept it, gave it me.
Then plain and right must my possession be.
Which I with more than with a common pain
Gainst all the world will rightfully maintain.

(Henry IV Part 2 Act 4 Sc. 5)

George Bush Sr. couldn't have put it better.

'By cock and pie, sir, you shall not away tonight...' are the first words spoken after the death of Henry IV. It always completely shocked the audience, drawn as they were into the death of someone they had spent the previous three plays with. It is old England calling. It's Justice Shallow in his orchard back in Gloucestershire: 'Cock' means God, and 'Pie' is a mispronunciation of a Roman Catholic Ordinal (as in 'Pie Jesu'). Even whilst the great leaders are dying, the country is calling from the past: all the pomp of Westminster followed by a field in Gloucestershire where nothing happens apart from an old lawyer sorting out the planting of some red wheat with one of his workers.

As Hal, like England, is busy turning to stone with every passing minute, Shakespeare contrasts that with an Orchard and apples being brought in by a farmhand. Another Eden.

Stand on Dover's Hill with all the shin kickers and see the Forest of Arden stretch North. In the near distance just a mile or so away is the Vale of Evesham: the most fertile soil in Europe protected from the winds by the surrounding hills. Looking West, orchards spread away as far as the eye can see – on this early June evening the blossoms are still there, just, and all I can see is the white and red of the apple trees, mixed with the green speckled brown of the asparagus crops.

When we staged the beginning of this Orchard scene, as the preceding scene of Hal's rousing speech to his brothers ended so blossom began to fall as Falstaff et al were seen heavy and sleepy in Shallow's orchard and Justice Silence broke the silence by singing. The world is turning at its rightful pace.

It cannot last. The stone-grey hand of Henry's new authority is beginning to clasp. In London, Doll Tearsheet and Nell Quickly, the women of the Boar's Head Tavern, are arrested. However, thinking they are on the gravy train by dint of friendship with Hal, excitement is near fever pitch by the time Falstaff, Shallow, and the lads of the Tavern have arrived in London and are lined up in the crowds awaiting the new King after his coronation. Shallow has lent Falstaff a thousand pounds in the hope of advancement. Pistol is exhorting Falstaff to free Doll from prison once he is in power.

> **Falstaff**
> *Save thy grace, King Hal, my royal Hal!*
> **Pistol**
> *The heavens thee guard and keep, most royal imp of fame!*
> **Falstaff**
> *Save thee, my sweet boy!*
> **King Henry V**
> *My Lord Chief Justice speak to that vain man.*
> **Lord Chief Justice**
> *Have you your wits? Know you what 'tis you speak?*
> **Falstaff**
> *My King, my Jove! I speak to thee, my heart!*
> **King Henry V**
> *I know thee not, old man. Fall to thy prayers.*
> *How ill white hairs become a fool and jester.*
> *I have long dreamed of such a kind of man,*
> *So surfeit-swelled, so old and so profane.*
> *But being awake, I do despise my dream.*
> *Make less thy body hence, and more thy grace,*
> *Leave gormandizing: know that the grave doth gape*
> *For thee thrice wider than for other men.*

Reply not to me with a fool-born jest.
Presume not that I am the thing I was,
For heaven doth know – so shall the world perceive –
That I have turned away my former self,
So will I those that kept me company.
… as we hear you do reform yourselves,
We will, according to your strengths and qualities,
Give you advancement…

(Henry IV Part 2 Act 5 Sc. 5)

His Reformation is complete. The thousand stories painted in vibrant colour on the walls of his mind are whitewashed, limed and purified.

Falstaff is left with nothing.

Falstaff
Sir, I will be as good as my word. This that you heard was but a colour.
Shallow
A colour that I fear you will die in, Sir John.
Falstaff
Fear no colours.

(Henry IV Part 2 Act 5 Sc. 5)

Fear no colours. As Falstaff and the entire crew are arrested by the triumphant Lord Chief Justice, how many in the audience would not have seen their heritage, their country, and their parents' struggle go through the doors into oblivion?

Within the Guy Fawkes pub in York, or the Gloucestershire countryside, all I can see is colours. I hope I do not fear them.

*

Four

In the new world order the Church is also carving out its identity. Through all the posturing of the opening scenes in *Henry V*, it is the scheming Archbishop of Canterbury who seems to win the day: Henry wants to believe the Archbishop's ridiculous speech about the Salic Law giving him a divine right to the throne of France. The audience are left in no doubt: this is busying '*giddy minds with foreign quarrels*', as his father advised him. However, when Henry is provoked by the gift of some tennis balls by the King of France's heir, the Dauphin, the audience are with him: face must be saved, so give the French a good whipping.

Richard II had lost the throne through many things but one of them was making peace with France. War with the French was almost seen as the regal duty of most mediaeval Kings and it was only through civil unrest at home that Henry IV was unable to turn his full attention to them. Even Elizabeth's father, Henry VIII, had taken people's minds off the strife at home by leading an expedition to reclaim territory. His daughter, Queen Mary, finally lost Calais and with it went her heart and the last English foothold in France. Mindful of her broken country, Elizabeth resisted any attempts at warmongering by her male councillors. Her way was to tread carefully through the mire and in doing so propped the country up financially and sowed the seeds of an artistic, cultural and expeditionary flowering unsurpassed in English history. But forty years was a long time to keep the dogs at bay. Elizabeth eventually sent armies to Northern France and the Spanish Netherlands to help with the conflict both physical and spiritual against Catholicism – the embers of which threatened to blow across the Channel at any time. By the time Shakespeare came to write *Henry V* England had been engaged in a bloody and costly war in Ireland for five years and the lustre of Elizabeth's greatest victory, defeating the Spanish Armada, was fast fading. England was stretched like a taut wire between a draining and ineffectual Irish war on the one hand and the dismal mire of a field in Flanders on the other.

So to write a play about the English going to war with France and actually winning was good box office. The fantasy of England kept everyone happy. It still does. Shakespeare and the Lord Chamberlain's Men had just built The Globe Theatre in the *liberty* of the South Bank and needed a hit. What better than the continuation of the story about which Shakespeare had written, on and off, for nearly ten years.

Southampton

In the Great Hall in Southampton at the beginning of August 1415, Richard, Earl of Cambridge, was tried and convicted of treason. The panel that convicted him included his own brother – our old friend Aumerle, now Duke of York, and King Henry V himself. Also present was the very man Cambridge's plot had been trying to put on the throne, Edmund Mortimer, Earl of March. Cambridge, named after his godfather Richard II, was taken outside to the Bargate and beheaded – a lenient sentence for a traitor.

With him were two other men, Sir Thomas Grey and Lord Scrope of Masham (nephew of the ill-fated Archbishop of York). Grey was one of the clan that had annoyed Glendower and, alongside the Percies, still own most of the land north of Newcastle. Scrope was one of the most faithful of the King's servants, having been Lord Treasurer during Henry IV's reign and now looked after the financial affairs of the royal household. Most probably he had been paid a vast sum by the French to make sure that England did not invade.

The plot failed chiefly because of the man whom it was going to create King – Edmund Mortimer, Earl of March. He was the boy that Richard II had nominated as his successor and who had been kept in custody by Henry IV. He had been freed from housebound captivity when Henry V was crowned – Henry being much more secure in his accession to the throne than his father. Mortimer's unusual upbringing in what amounted to a golden cell left him a weak man and an inveterate gambler. He was given a generous stipend and lived at one of the biggest palaces in London, Baynard's Castle on the Thames, yet he still proved a focal point of resistance for those who had a grievance with the Crown or who still believed that the Dukes of Lancaster were usurpers.

The plot was massive in its intent. The Earl of Cambridge was married to Mortimer's sister, Anne, who had grown up back in the Mortimer homeland of Herefordshire in the Welsh Marches. Mortimer himself would raise an army from the New Forest and march to Wales to be proclaimed King. There he would wake the sleeping giant Glendower from his retirement, which would in theory make the Scots come on board. Grey (tacitly aided by the new Earl of Northumberland, son of Hotspur) would help the North to rise up. The King and his brothers would be killed in Southampton on 1st August by Cambridge and Scrope as the fleet was being prepared for France. Mortimer would then be proclaimed King.

Mortimer even enlisted the help of none other than the famous Lollard conspirator, Sir John Oldcastle, who was now in hiding back in Herefordshire. Two years before Oldcastle had escaped from the Tower (some say Henry turned a blind eye because of their earlier friendship) and spurred on 20,000 Lollards to march on London in the first great uprising of Henry V's reign. It had failed but, like Glendower, Oldcastle was still a potent mystical force, if not a physical one.

It was a huge plan which may just have worked had not Scrope, the man closest to Henry, taken exception to the inclusion of Oldcastle. He didn't want the taint of heresy, the unclean mark of a different attitude to God, to be upon the body of the new King. Whilst the conspirators were in Southampton with Henry preparing for his expedition to France, Scrope told Mortimer in no uncertain terms that Oldcastle was not to be used.

Smarting from his telling off, Mortimer ran home to tell his Dad, or rather the only proper authority figure he'd ever known – Henry. Within hours the conspirators were rounded up and the many-headed beast of rebellion was cut down once more.

One of the biggest plots of the Mediaeval Age was brought down by a disagreement over the man whom Shakespeare said died a martyr – Oldcastle, a man who refused to change his faith and way of belief in the face of death. A recusant. What a man to pick as your belly of England. It is classic Shakespeare to pick a Protestant icon under which to hoist the banner of a different world – time and again it had kept him from prison. But the success of the character, and all it represented, meant it was becoming defamatory. No wonder Shakespeare changed the name. He was in hot water and paddling hard.

A few of the ports used by Henry V have long since been flap-dragonned by the sea, or eaten up by land. Smallhythe and Winchelsea, for example, lie marooned on land, yearning out at the sea. But Southampton has survived, and how. Sheltered in the centre of the South coast of England it lies on the estuary of two rivers much further inland than its rival Portsmouth – a neighbour more concerned with military naval power. Southampton is the mercantile dock, trading oil and goods around the world, and it is huge. The ferries to France are dwarfed by the mountainous hulks which simmer on the dockside full of oil or containers carrying everything ever made from China.

The Great Hall where the Earl of Cambridge was tried for treason still exists within the confines of a pub rather unsurprisingly called the 'Red Lion' on the High Street. It is clothed in a Victorian façade and surrounded by warehouses, nevertheless the Hall remains, even if held in an architectural prison.

I can barely see the ceiling, high up past the dusty beams and the yellowing paint. The smell of chip oil and rancid carpets is intoxicating and I begin to regret the fact that there is no smoking in these places anymore to hide the grease. Perhaps rashly, I order some food and a pint of 'Hampshire Rose', then go for a look around. What would normally be one of the dingiest pubs imaginable is transformed by the Hall rising from the bar. There's the usual *faux* bits of mediaeval tat – a suit of armour here and some 'Ye Olde' signs there. But there is real age too, beneath the dust. A fireplace to match the one in the Jerusalem Chamber is a tell-tale sign that big things used to happen here – the chimney breast rises past the gallery that lines half of the hall. It is startlingly easy to feel a semblance of the trial where Henry, Mortimer and York passed sentence on their kinsman.

Apart from a man crunched over a pie in the front of the bar, I am alone in the place. There is, however, a parrot that starts whistling as soon as Stevie Wonder comes on the sound system, providing an interesting accompaniment to my mediaeval thoughts. I sit next to the fireplace that has seen so much – this place was granted its pub licence in 1511, ninety-six years after Henry V sat in judgement here. The barmaid reads the paper and behind her in a frame high up on a wall is an ancient flag with a barely discernible White Rose, so I ask her what it is. She looks up and says, 'Sorry, love, I have no idea. Something to do with Henry V, innit?'

Mistress Quickly is alive and well and living in Southampton. At that moment Bardolph walks in. He has lank hair and sits in the corner sniffing through the finest carbuncular nose I have seen in a long while. According to their website there are twenty ghosts here. Whatever the reason, he – in fact the whole place – makes me shiver.

I make myself sick from the biggest ham, egg and chips I have ever had. Apart from in America, I have never had such a plate of food. Sadly the coleslaw is going off and the chips are ever so slightly bitter, but the parrot cheers me up with his whistling. It even says something that ends in '…ick.' It could be sick. Or Nick. Maybe he has a hotline to the ghosts. Or Stevie Wonder.

I waddle out into the light and the Bargate is resplendent down the other end of the High Street where the traitors lost their heads. It stands alone in a hotch-potch grey of new buildings. This city was virtually eradicated from the map in the Second World War. It was as bad as Coventry but being an old port, and therefore on the front line of England and its relationship with the world, it doesn't seem to be mentioned as much. Four hundred and seventy-six tons of bombs were dropped by the Luftwaffe on Southampton during November 1940. Five hundred tons in one night in the same month at Coventry.

Like Coventry, it seems to have knocked the stuffing from the old place. I go to a tower on the mediaeval walls – quite a lot of them still exist – and from it I can see an area of wasteland that stretches down to the docks. This is the centre of the city. Behind me the 'West Quay' shopping centre floods its victims with bargains.

Yet there is still a spirit here – I suppose a port will always be replenished. As well as Henry departing for France, the *Mayflower* sailed from here, as did the *Titanic* and other ships carrying millions of émigrés to North America. Their produce has found its way back.

Beside the Bargate, in the exact spot where Cambridge and his fellow traitors met their gruesome end, a beautiful Carousel with golden horses spins musically amidst the shoppers. A man sits beneath the most exquisite metal lion that stands proudly from the Bargate and rolls a fag. He drinks a can of Special Brew as the fairground organ rises and falls.

The gleaming eyes of the horses shine manically in the sun.

France

At the end of *Henry IV Part 2*, there is an epilogue in which it is promised that the story would continue:

> *One word more, I beseech you: if you be not too much cloyed with fat meat, our humble author will continue the story, with Sir John in it, and make you merry with fair Katherine of France, where for anything I know, Falstaff shall die of a sweat, unless already he be killed with your hard opinions. For Oldcastle died a martyr, and this is not the man.*
>
> (*Henry IV Part 2 Epilogue*)

Apart from keeping him out of prison, this is Shakespeare acknowledging the great role Falstaff was playing in his version of History: the roguish, old English everyman was stealing the show. But in *Henry V* he does not make an appearance and dies offstage before Henry has even got to France. All the other flotsam from the Boar's Head are there, but Falstaff is gone.

Who knows whether it was because Shakespeare had had enough of writing fat comedic parts because one of his star turns, Will Kempe, was good at it? Maybe Kempe himself had had enough. Or maybe the Catholic sympathising aristocrats like Lord Strange and the Earl of Southampton, who quietly protected their genius writer and his players, called time on the salty character who rubbed so much into the fresh wounds of new England. No one knows.

Either way, with the Reformation of Hal, old England is dying. Gone is the Orchard and the colour is fading fast. Far from England being ablaze with the fire of youth wanting to go into battle, Shakespeare gives us the tired dregs of a once vibrant world being dragged to war by its heels. Pistol, a war-wrecked Ensign who appears briefly and alarmingly in *Henry IV Part 2*, is doing his best to fill the large hole left by the sweating Knight and has married the Tavern's landlady, Mistress Quickly. But Pistol is no Sir John – having neither the wit nor standing to thrive. He has charisma, but it's spent. Doll Tearsheet is in the hospital, the diseases of her trade having finally caught up with her. Nym, another casualty of war, is aggrieved that Pistol and Quickly are married. Bardolph is the peacemaker and henchman still. The Boy continues to serve.

Without making an appearance, Falstaff, the barrel of England, is dead – broken on the shore of the New World. In the aching description of Falstaff's death given by Mistress Quickly, we see a man reduced to a single point of suffering crying out for God. And drink. And women. The apple tree has withered and gone.

So too are the boys, off to France, to fester in a foreign field.

Standing on a ferry from Dover to Calais, Geoffrey Streatfeild and I look out over Old England's white cliffs. The massive harbour walls loom large and bland, wrapping the port in the arms of Albion. We're both feeling excitement – firstly at going on a trip with a friend and secondly because crossing the Channel is always special, whichever way you are going.

The mighty Bongo is safely tucked below decks. On the dashboard lies a moth-eaten copy of *Henry V* that Geoff used in rehearsals and it feels a little valedictory to have it on display when eventually we rumble off the ferry through the badlands of Calais. We sheepishly remove it but have it to hand as we speed southwards over the Somme.

From the battlefields of Crecy and Agincourt in the mediaeval era to the Somme and the Bulge in the twentieth century, it is a historically blighted place. The beautiful pastureland that hides the blood of millions now plays host to hundreds of massive wind turbines counting with each turn the cost of pride and folly. They are a rather beautiful and fitting memorial.

A small proportion of those lost souls died further south at Harfleur, near the modern port of Le Havre, in 1415. Lying on the Seine estuary, the small town is now a little way from the coast, but was laid siege to by Henry when his ships arrived from Southampton in the first week of August. In the suburbs of a nondescript French town lie the tumbledown ancient walls around which, in the imagination of a man 400 years ago, a notion of England was built.

> **King Henry V**
> *Once more unto the breach dear friends once more*
> *Or close the wall up with our English dead.*
> *In peace there's nothing so becomes a man*
> *As modest stillness and humility*
> *But when the blast of war blows in our ears*
> *Then imitate the action of the tiger*
> *Stiffen the sinews summon up the blood*
> *Disguise fair nature with hard favoured rage*
> *Then lend the eye a terrible aspect*
> *Let it pry through the portage of the head*
> *Like the brass cannon let the brow o'erwhelm it*
> *As fearfully as doth a galled rock*
> *O'erhang and jutty its confounded base*
> *Swilled with the wild and wasteful ocean.*
> *Now set the teeth and stretch the nostril wide*
> *Hold hard the breath and bend up every spirit*
> *To his full height. On on you noblest English*
> *Whose blood is fet from fathers war proof*

Fathers that like so many Alexanders
Have in these parts from morn till even fought
And sheathed their swords for lack of argument.
Dishonour not your mothers now attest
That those whom you called fathers did beget you.
Be copy now to men of grosser blood
And teach them how to war. And you good yeomen
Whose limbs were made in England show us here
The mettle of your pasture let us swear
That you are worth your breeding which I doubt not
For there is none of you so mean and base
That hath not noble lustre in your eyes.
I see you stand like greyhounds in the slips
Straining upon the start. The game's afoot
Follow your spirit and upon this charge
Cry 'God for Harry England and Saint George!'

(Henry V Act 3 Sc. 1)

Not surprisingly the French aren't that fussed about the walls of Harfleur. They are still there, sort of. They are just a small clump of stones to the south of the town overlooking the river. They once defended against the sea but the estuary silted up many years ago. There's even a small archaeological dig taking place – either that or they are just nicking the stones for local buildings. But the walls, in truth, are pretty drab and someone has built a modern house slap in the middle of the main section.

The town itself, unlike its history, is nicely unremarkable. Its high watermark was left by the sea 500 years ago. There are signs for an 'Office de Tourisme' and in an effort to learn more we head there, but is nowhere to be found. Following yet another sign that leads to nowhere Geoffrey mutters, 'The beauty of this Office de Tourisme is that it leads you through the whole town in trying to find it, thereby taking away the need for it.'

We eventually find it across a park and pick up a map of where we had just been. The man behind the counter starts laughing at our French.

'Oui. Henry ze fifth was just here in ze park,' he says in answer to our question, 'It was very 'orrible, yes.'

It was indeed. In all Henry lost about 3,500 men in a disastrous two-month summer siege that ended in disease and starvation. Henry eventually took the town but at a searingly high cost and with no seeming point to it at all.

Tired from our unforeseen hike around the town, we settle down to a coffee in a beautiful small square, dappled with sun, to watch the locals buying bread. There are precisely no tourists (perhaps they were all lost), but a more French scene one could not hope to find. Beside us a small bridge teeters over the river that fed the town during the siege in 1415. Then, courtesy of our new-found map, we realise we are on 'Rue des 104' named in commemoration of the 104 men that lost their lives in kicking out the English from Harfleur in 1435. So the 3,500 English that died in their own excrement amid the dysentery and disaster outside the walls of Harfleur did so for twenty years of English rule.

The walls which the English so celebrate every time we have to force ourselves back to a task ('Once more unto the breach...'), the walls that stopped a King in his tracks, aren't on the map from the Office de Tourisme at all.

Like the 'sceptered isle' speech of John of Gaunt in *Richard II*, the point Shakespeare makes with 'Once more unto the breach' is often forgotten: Henry's speech was of no use at all to the quivering English anti-heroes of Pistol, Bardolph and Nym. Despite Henry's finest exhortations to stiffen the sinews, they are not going anywhere. A cheer must have gone up in the theatre when the Boy, in response to their situation, says, '*Would I were in an ale-house in London; I would give all my fame for a pot of ale and safety.*' I have never known an English audience not to laugh. They are finally forced up to the breach by a Welshman, Fluellen. Only the Boy – the servant hired by Falstaff – is left behind to shine a light on the real workings of these cowards. In a speech as undermining as Henry's is tub-thumping, the Boy elucidates the other England:

> *As young as I am, I have observed these three swashers.... Three such antics do not amount to a man.... They will steal anything and call it purchase.... They would have me as familiar with men's pockets as their gloves or their handkerchiefs, which makes much against my manhood, if I should take from another's pocket to put into mine; for it is a plain pocketing up of wrongs. I must leave them and seek*

some better service: their villainy goes against my weak stomach, and
therefore I must cast it up.

(Henry V Act 3 Sc. 2)

Shakespeare holds a very clear and harsh mirror up to the true England. Heroes? Here they are, in all their shame. From bankers to football matches, we're still doing it today. Who knows whether the audience – aristos and groundlings alike – cheered or fell silent?

Yet, in the same scene, here are the beginnings of a modern United Kingdom: the Welshman, Fluellen, is joined by an Englishman, Gower; an Irishman, Macmorris; and a Scotsman, Jamy. All are of equal rank, Captains, and their voices are as eloquently mixed as they still are today. Macmorris is an underminer – literally digging under the walls to blow them up and is enraged at the different orders coming from on high, whereas the pedantic yet courageous Fluellen considers that things have to be done in the right order. Still, Macmorris questions the Welshman's right to know anything about the Irish nation because all the Brits think of his people is that they are a *'villain and a bastard and a knave and a rascal.'*

> **Fluellen** *Look you, if you take the matter otherwise than is meant, Captain Macmorris, peradventure I shall think you do not use me with that affability as in discretion you ought to use me, look you, being as good a man as yourself, both in the disciplines of war, and in the derivation of my birth, and in other particularities.*
>
> **Macmorris** *I do not know you so good a man as myself. So Chrish save me, I will cut off your head.*
>
> **Gower** *Gentlemen, you mistake each other.*
>
> **Jamy** *Ah, that's a foul fault.*

(Henry V Act 3 Sc. 2)

The tone is set for the next 400 years.

However, whatever the growing mix of these isles, the new world can never rid itself of the old: Bardolph – the willing dogsbody of Falstaff's England – is hanged by Henry for stealing a *pax* – a small Catholic relic from a church. Pistol exhorts Fluellen to appeal to the Duke of Exeter to stop it, but the Welshman will have none of it.

Fluellen *Ancien' Pistol, I do partly understand your meaning.*

Pistol *Why then rejoice therefore*

Fluellen *Certainly, Ancient, it is not a thing to rejoice at, for, if, look you, he were my brother, I would desire the duke to use his good pleasure and put him to execution; for discipline ought to be used.*

Pistol *Die and be damned. And figo for thy friendship*

Fluellen *'Tis well.*

Pistol *The fig of Spain!*

Fluellen *Very good.*

(Henry V Act 3 Sc. 6)

'Figo' is a Spanish, Catholic, phrase for contempt.

The little village of Azincourt lies just north of the River Somme, 50 miles inland, and surrounded by farmland and woods that stretch and billow prettily. From the disaster of finally taking Harfleur, Henry had been hoping to press on to Calais and safety for the winter, but the French succeeded in blocking his path over the doomed River Somme, thus he was forced to turn inland and march the fifty miles to a bridge that could finally be taken.

By this time the vacillating French had begun to get their house in order. Their King, Charles VI – ever so delicately monikered Charles the Mad – was, as his nickname suggests, of little or no use and the French were riven by internal factions. But the ailing Henry was a sitting duck so the French put aside their differences and began to congregate near the Somme.

Having crossed, Henry marched north again but knew that he was surrounded, so he turned to fight. He took his weary troops, all 5,000 of them, to a field just outside the village of Azincourt – a field which lay between two woods, thus making his smaller numbers less exposed in the trees. Seeing his position, the French troops – 20-30,000 of them – lined up to the south, and the two armies sat down to wait until morning.

There is no fanfare when you drive into Azincourt. Like Harfleur, it's understandably not something the French celebrate. It's just a small country lane with crap mediaeval figures every few hundred yards. But there is a museum, so Geoffrey and I pull in to visit.

There's a chap at the counter who looks rather surprised to see us. He immediately starts speaking in English to us (like Henry, the French can see us coming) and shows us the way in. We are the only people there. I want to like it but it's not really a very good museum – a modern piece of armour, quite a lot of old bits and pieces from the battlefield, and a video room that isn't showing any videos. But there is a wonderful, huge model of the battlefield with all the figures, trees and relief built into it in great detail. It's a thrilling representation of how the battle commenced, and of how the English could so startlingly win, when faced with impossible odds. There is also a long list on either side of the museum walls of some of the dead. On both sides, it is a numbing and depressingly familiar roll call of ordinary names. In his research for playing Henry V, Geoffrey found out there was a Streatfeild listed as an archer at Agincourt but there is no record of how he fared. We scour the long wall of English names – Brown, Smith, Ward, alongside more prosaic mediaeval names such as 'Bramshulf' and 'Lychebarow', but of Streatfeild there is no trace. He must have survived, I suppose: his progenitor returning some 600 years later.

The battlefield is a mile or two away across unhedged, freshly tilled fields that give little sign of the carnage. We drive round what would have been the back of the English front line – where the boys and the luggage were placed for safety, and park up in the spot where an ancient obelisk stands to the memory of battle, gnarled and phallic in the late afternoon sun.

The forests that lined the battlefield are long gone, making it seem wider than it would have been. But the small rise that lay between the French and the English is very apparent: the gentle lilt in the ground hiding from the French the slaughter that was going on ahead as they charged towards the foe. We clamber our way in the heat and the light – so different from the late October day in 1415 when it had rained for weeks on end and the ground was a mushy quagmire into which all the French horses sank into oblivion. At no distinct point, we stop and fall silent. There's no sound but a warm, gentle wind, playing across the land.

I remember the day when Geoffrey got asked to play Henry V in The Histories. I knew I was playing Pistol, and our excitement at the thought of spending two and half years with these characters was only matched by the trepidation we felt at such an undertaking. Now here we were, having long since done our play, but still drawn back to discover why these characters played so much on our consciousness and that of the audience. Two friends playing at soldiers again.

Having done Henry for so long, Geoffrey begins to find a power in the place – standing literally in his footsteps. He is back in character and loving it.

'It is a place where I would go for a glorious charge.'

Yet there is more here. More in the ground. The French have no story here, but for the English, it is part of us.

Shakespeare portrays Henry, padding about his camp on the night before the battle, as a hero consoling his men before their meeting with destiny. But he also accosts Henry with the spirit of the English yeoman – the ordinary man in the street. Whilst Henry is disguised, Shakespeare challenges him with Pistol, who takes him back to the roaring days in the Boar's Head, and with three common soldiers – Bates, Williams and Court – who are waiting for their reckoning. Shakespeare challenges the King in every aspect of who and what he is. His past, present and future.

> **Henry V** *Methinks I could not die anywhere so contented as in the King's company; his cause being just and his quarrel honorable.*
>
> **Williams** *That's more than we know.*
>
> **Bates** *Ay, or more than we should seek after; for we know enough, if we know we are the King's subjects. If his cause be wrong, our obedience to the king wipes the crime of it out of us.*
>
> **Williams** *But if the cause be not good, the king himself hath a heavy reckoning to make, when all those legs and arms and heads, chopped off in a battle, shall join together at the latter day and cry all, 'We died at such a place' – some swearing, some crying for a surgeon, some upon their wives left poor behind them, some upon the debts they owe, some upon the children rawly left. I am afeared there a few die well that die in a battle, for how can they charitably dispose of anything when blood is their argument? Now, if these men do not die well, it will be a black matter for the king that led them to it – who to disobey were against all proportion of subjection.*
>
> (Henry V Act 4 Sc. 1)

A subject challenges the monarch's word and is allowed to live. Here, on a field in France 600 years ago the King was saved by his men, and in the imagination of an Elizabethan playwright 200 years later,

England had a revolution: the King is but a person. In Henry's only soliloquy he says:

> And what have kings that privates have not too
> Save ceremony, save general ceremony?
>
> (Henry V Act 4 Sc. 1)

The groundlings in the front of the theatre and the aristocracy sitting at the back must have been rendered speechless by such a thought: England, the red-haired Queen Britannia, is built on nothing but ceremony and the yeomanry prepared to uphold it.

There is no doubting the majesty of Elizabeth, but the reality for the struggling yeomen of England was that Britannia was built on cast iron security and a brute will to survive about which they had no say whatsoever.

The story of the battle is achingly simple. Henry chopped down trees and turned them into stakes which he drove with ease into the soft ground. He had trained his fighters hard and well. Though ravaged by illness, they had discipline, battle hardness and organisation; better technology with their longbows; and a will to live and get home. The French were a loose collection of ill-disciplined nobles, mercenaries and *pésants* with nothing on their side but numbers. The English yeoman, the archer, the fighter, stood up and faced the enemy.

Henry charged, halted and retreated, and let the French charge toward them into a sharpened death as they broached the hill and rode straight into the stakes on the other side. Combined with the mud, and the hail of arrows that descended upon them, with each wave of charging French so the wall of dead climbed even higher. It was carnage. The plucky underdog won it and we still love that dog to this day.

Far from the glittering death that Shakespeare gives him, Aumerle – the Duke of York – was actually by now grossly fat and useless on his poor horse. He died either of heart failure or simply fell off and then died. Nobody knows. Certainly there seem to be no accounts of anyone attacking him. Indeed, after the battle no one could be bothered to ferry such a huge deadweight back to England, so they boiled him down in a vat overnight and sent his considerably lighter bones back to Fotheringhay where they still lie to this day.

Shakespeare depicts Pistol grabbing a French prisoner from among the melee in order to squeeze a healthy ransom from him. This was to be denied, however, as Henry gave the order to kill all the French prisoners. It is an act that has rung through the ages as a callous war crime, answered only by the French stealing around the back of the English lines and killing all the boys who looked after the luggage. Geoffrey, firmly behind his character, is full of support for Henry. If he'd been there and seen the French rallying – which some say Henry did indeed see – what with too many prisoners being guarded by fighting men the primary objective would be to win the battle and get rid of the prisoners. But nobody knows the absolute truth, or Henry's motives. What seems to be the case is that with victory almost assured many of his men refused to obey such an order – even under the threat of hanging. In the end he had to fall back on 200 of his most trusted archers who did the deed. Upon such thorns is the myth of England built. And Pistol, of course, has nothing to show for his scavenging.

Probably in the region of 7,500 French were killed that Crispin's Day, October 25th, 1415. Some say the English lost about 1,500, most believe it was considerably lower – if a few hundred. What is true is that it was a comprehensively lop-sided victory for Henry who in one afternoon wiped out most of the French nobility. All but a few of the aristocratic families in France lost someone at Agincourt. Shakespeare gets the numbers horribly disproportionate, saying 10,000 French died and only 29 English killed. Even so, as a mark of respect, Shakespeare has Henry read out the names of the French dead. I have appeared in this play three times now, and it is always staggeringly moving when these names are read out. Not only is it all too familiar in our modern world but it is moving because the people upon whom the myth was built – the slaughtered French – are recognised even amidst a sea of heroic rhetoric and derring-do.

Just four names on Henry's side are read out: The Duke of York; the Earl of Suffolk; Sir Richard Keighley and Davy Gam, Esquire. Dafydd Gam – the old Welsh turncoat who had helped Henry fight Glendower, and who saw his King to the greatest victory of all and seal his questionable throne for good – died at the last hurdle.

Indeed, Welshness plays a considerable part at the end of Shakespeare's play. Many feel that Fluellen is in part based on popular depictions of Gam himself – well-schooled and particular in the courses of the wars, brave and loyal. Also Gam was a man who turned his back on the old magic of Glendower's uprising and fought him with all the zeal of the converted. Henry's Welshness – he was Prince of Wales and born at Monmouth after all, is so big an issue in the immediate aftermath of the battle that it throws into sharp relief the swaying flags of St. George. It is this proto-Puritanical Welshman, Fluellen, that affirms how Henry has turned away his past.

> **Fluellen** *..as Alexander killed his friend Cleitus, being in his ales and his cups, so also Harry Monmouth, being in his right wits and his good judgements, turned away the fat knight with the great belly-doublet. He was full of jests and gipes and knaveries and mocks – I have forgot his name.*
>
> **Gower** *Sir John Falstaff*
>
> **Fluellen** *That is he. I'll tell you there is good men born at Monmouth.*
>
> (Henry V Act 4 Sc. 7)

Here, too, Shakespeare presents Henry with Williams, the yeoman who accosted him with his own conscience the night before, and Williams is unashamed:

> **Henry** *It was ourself thou didst abuse.*
>
> **Williams** *Your majesty came not like yourself, you appeared to me but as a common man; witness the night, your garments, your lowliness. And what your highness suffered under that shape, I beseech you take it for your own fault and not mine, for had you been as I took you for, I made no offence: therefore I beseech your highness, pardon me.*
>
> **Henry** *Here, uncle Exeter, fill this glove with crowns,*
>
> *And give it to this fellow. Keep it fellow,*
>
> *And wear it for an honour in thy cap,*
>
> *Till I do challenge it – Give him the crowns –*
>
> *And captain, you must needs be friends with him*
>
> **Fluellen** *By this day and this light, the fellow has mettle enough in his belly. Hold, there is twelve pence for you...*
>
> (Henry V Act 4 Sc. 8)

It is a fantasy and a dream, of course: This England that is allowed to stand up for its truth in front of the monarch and the State. It's interesting to note that alongside John Shakespeare in the list of recusants fined for not going to church in Stratford-upon-Avon were the names of Bates, Court, Fluellen, Gower and Bardolph. They stood up for what they saw as their truth and paid for it.

Pistol is finally sunk by a leek. Fluellen has had enough of the derision of an Englishman abroad and quietly beats Pistol up and forces him to eat a leek.

Pistol, the last remnant of Falstaffian England, is spent. Everyone else from the tavern world is dead – the Boy slaughtered by the French in the battle; Nym has been hanged as well as Bardolph. Pistol even reveals in his final speech to the audience that his wife, Nell Quickly, is dead from 'the malady of France' (venereal disease). He is the last.

Yet he hauls himself up:

> **Pistol**
> *To England will I steal, and there I'll steal*
> *And patches will I get unto these cudgeled scars,*
> *And swear I got them in the Gallia wars.*

(Henry V Act 5 Sc. 1)

He may have had a Welsh 'correction' – but the old 'skimble-skamble' magic might well just claw on in the netherworld of Eastcheap.

For Shakespeare, the bleeding heart of old England was alive but made to wander in the dark corners, force-fed a diet of the new world.

One thing strikes Geoffrey and I as we walk back towards the obelisk at Azincourt: the French description of the battle, written in a little glass case, is very different from our English version. They simply say that the 'arrows caused confusion and panic' in the ranks, whereas the English shout of the slaughter and brilliance. Yet in his play, Shakespeare has Henry issue a strict order to his men: *'And be it death proclaimed through our host/ To boast of this'.* Geoffrey points out that all we have ever done is boast of this and listened to the bits we want to listen to.

The ridiculous tub-thumping that is sometimes allied to Agincourt and Henry's Shakespearean speeches, is part of the English condition just as much as the hollow ceremony of ages gradually turned to substance by Time.

What with all this Englishness around we sit in the still, late afternoon sun in the middle of the battlefield at Azincourt and have a flask of tea.

Driving from Azincourt to Rouen, I begin to feel a sense of dejá vu as the road snakes through many of the names read out on the list of the dead so respectfully detailed by Shakespeare. Rambures, Fauconbergue, Marle all fly by on signposts that for us lead not to a place, but a person who died in a battle 600 years ago. Yet they also read like the pages in a book of battles through the ages – Crecy, Azincourt, Abbeville, Somme, Amiens, Ypres. A fellowship of death. The vastness of these deaths silence the drive, as one by one we pass fields of war graves, billowing white from the past.

> *This story shall the good man teach his son,*
> *And Crispin Crispian shall ne'er go by,*
> *From this day to the ending of the world,*
> *But we in it shall be remembered.*
> *We few, we happy few, we band of brothers.*
>
> (Henry V Act 4 Sc. 3)

The people that died at Agincourt will forever have a play in memorial to their lives. The millions that died in these foreign fields 500 years later have a stone and ceremony. As we drive, the combination seems almost unbearable.

After Agincourt Henry returned to England a national hero and all question marks about his right to be King were gone. The great battle was not necessarily the high watermark of Henry's reign – being declared the heir to France in 1420 was arguably his finest hour. He also married Katherine, the King of France's daughter. Yet in 1422 he died, pure and simple. Just like that. What the Catholics of the late Tudor era would have given for that to happen to Elizabeth – as had happened to her sister. For Henry, it was probably of typhoid whilst campaigning again in France. Three months later, mad Charles VI himself died. Who knows what may have happened had Henry lived?

His accession to the French throne was not a *fait accompli* by any means and there were many French nobles who completely ignored the treaty that recognised Henry as the heir to the King of France – hence he was still campaigning. But he did leave behind him an infant son. There was a prophecy doing the rounds at the time which stated that 'Henry born at Monmouth should win all, Henry born at Windsor should lose all.' Henry implored the pregnant Katherine not to give birth at Windsor but as he was off fighting in France she saw fit to go straight there and promptly gave birth to one of the most ill-starred monarchs this country has ever had.

So it all made no difference – within thirty years the English were kicked out of France for good, and the old divisions of Red and White would govern England for a generation, this time in a new form. Roses.

Thus far with rough and all unable pen
Our bending author hath pursued the story
Mangling by starts the full course of their glory.
Small time but in that small most greatly lived
This star of England. Fortune made his sword
By which the world's best garden he achieved
And of it left his son imperial Lord.
Henry VI in infant bands crowned King
Of France and England did this king succeed
Whose state so many had the managing
That they lost France and made his England bleed,
Which oft our stage has shown and for their sake
In your fair minds let this acceptance take.

(Henry V Epilogue)

Five

Henry's body was brought back from France to be buried in his tomb at Westminster Abbey just yards from Richard II in the shrine of Edward the Confessor. He lies beneath a Chantry Chapel he had commissioned before his death, the building of which was overseen by his mourning wife, Katherine. His armour, or 'achievements', that he wore at Agincourt used to be on the beam that rises above the chapel until the 1970s but were taken to the Abbey museum to be preserved. All that's there now is the small stub of the beam which served as the hanger.

As his kinsmen and generals placed him in his tomb, they effectively sealed up their hopes with it. Henry's two brothers – John of Lancaster, Duke of Bedford, and Humphrey, Duke of Gloucester – had to fill the gap brought about by a tiny infant King. Henry V had done so much to cement his weak claim to the throne – his leadership so strong and successful, his deeds considered so miraculous – that when he suddenly departed the stage no one quite knew what to do.

An awkward reality was that Henry's incessant campaigning bled his England dry and the country was nearly bankrupt. Devoid of such a charismatic and resourceful leader they could not hope to subjugate the rest of France. Indeed, all the English activities had succeeded in doing there, apart from gaining land, was to foster a sense of nationhood previously unseen in most parts of France. Thus, with a child at its centre, the new English Court split into two main factions – those favouring the continued war across the Channel and the potential revenue it may bring in the acquisition of new lands, and those wanting peace, stability and the coffers that grew from a stable country.

For now, the thorny problem of the Mortimer succession seemed to have died with the Earl of March who left no issue. But his sister, Anne, had a son by Richard, Earl of Cambridge – the man killed for treason at Southampton. This junior Richard was still only fourteen years old when he should have inherited the March estates from his maternal uncle, but the Regency Council established after Henry's death resolved to give Baynard's Castle to Queen Katherine, and the March estates to possibly the richest man in England – Henry Beaufort, Bishop of Winchester.

Beaufort was immensely powerful. Whereas Henry IV, Henry V and the young Henry VI were the progeny of John of Gaunt's first marriage, the Beauforts were the offspring of Gaunt's third marriage to Katherine Swynford. Thomas Beaufort, Duke of Exeter, was the son of John of Gaunt and a loyal and effective servant to Henry V, figuring largely in Shakespeare's play. His brother, Henry Beaufort, Bishop of Winchester, proved himself to be one of the cleverest and most ruthless operators of the mediaeval era. Using the inherited lands from his father, and those of the Church, he had become wildly rich through the wool trade and began using that money to secure influence in England and Europe. He had loaned Henry thousands of pounds for his campaigns in France thus the Crown owed him a debt he was careful to maintain – hence the bequest of the March lands to him after Henry's death. Almost limitlessly ambitious, he couldn't quite inherit the Crown beause he was a Churchman and by dint of birth, so he set his sights on becoming Pope instead. He never got there, although he did become a Cardinal in 1426. He became one of the chief power-brokers in England and may well have ruled the roost entirely but for the tireless efforts of his nemesis and chief sparring partner, Humphrey, Duke of Gloucester.

Henry V's youngest brother was born in 1390 and had attended Oxford, thereby gaining the most classical education of the sons of Henry Bolingbroke. Created Duke of Gloucester in 1414, Humphrey was wounded at Agincourt and had served Henry, whom he idolised, with distinction and loyalty. Perhaps because of his education and military service he was even-handed, fair and consistent – and consequently loved by the people. Yet with his own class he was self-serving, ambitious and frequently pig-headed. The perfect mediaeval gent, in every respect.

When Henry V died, given his status as heir to the French throne he willed that his brother John, Duke of Bedford, be Regent of France and that Humphrey be Protector of England and guardian of the infant King. But by the time the Regency Council set up after Henry's death had their way, Gloucester was relieved of any sovereign authority. He was named 'Protector and Defender of the Realm and the Church in England' until the King came of age, but he was to show deference to Bedford, his elder brother, when Bedford was in England and he effectively couldn't do anything without the Council ratifying it.

Not for the first time, and certainly not for the last, Gloucester blamed Henry Beaufort, Bishop of Winchester. He suspected

Winchester wanted to be Protector himself, and given the Bishop's mighty wealth and influence, the two major players at home were in an inevitable collision course with the young King caught in between. Indeed, whilst Gloucester had been appointed Protector of the Realm, it was to the Beauforts – Exeter and Winchester – that little Henry was given for safe-keeping and nurture.

Thus the system for the next twenty or so years was created with two massive planets revolving around the tiny sun of Henry VI, whilst other lesser satellites were to make their presence felt and make occasional bids for supremacy. It's no wonder that the world of division between two opposing and intractable views so appealed to Shakespeare.

The unprecedented explosion of literary and intellectual talent by the time Elizabeth's reign was in full swing is in no small part down to the seismic shift in culture brought about by her father, Henry VIII. His father, Henry VII, had started the social ball rolling by promoting people of the mercantile class into positions of authority because half the aristocracy were either dead or untrustworthy after the chaos of the Wars of the Roses and the Plague. By the time Henry VIII was in power, for the first time such eminent minds as Sir Thomas More and Cardinal Wolsey could rise to the top of the tree having been born in comparative poverty. Many of them, especially Wolsey, were put in their place by Henry VIII and the Reformation – yet the money and land released from the Dissolution of the Monasteries gradually trickled down through the hierarchy giving rise not only to previously impoverished people gaining an education, and thus perhaps becoming playwrights, but other people having the money to see the fruits of their labour.

As a consequence, at no time in English history have we seen such a flowering of artistic thought. London was the head of it – almost a separate country from the old Catholic body upon which it stood. Its eyes and ears, Oxford and Cambridge, were close by and these fed the growing mass of thought and wonder that were the playhouses of London. As long as you were Protestant.

Although Oxford in particular still had lingering sympathies for the old world, Catholics were excluded from the great universities which led many great minds and sons of aristocracy to go abroad and be educated. Some even suggest that this is why Shakespeare never finished his education and seems to disappear off the historical compass for seven years: he was off being educated in Paris, or Douai, or Rome or wherever. Of course, once again, nobody knows.

Nobody knows anything about Shakespeare's *Henry VI* plays either, which established him as a potential leading light amongst the sparkling glory of the Northern Renaissance. They remain a bone of contention amongst scholars and the theatrical community, as they present many contradictions, curiosities and authorship debates that have wittered on and on for centuries. What seems to be the consensus is that eight or nine years before he was at the height of his powers when completing *Henry V*, *Hamlet*, *As You Like It* and the like, Shakespeare the young actor and novice writer was putting the finishing touches to these plays that seized on the division of England and made it his own. The Oxbridge educated minds churning out their efforts amidst the frenzy of the English Renaissance looked down their noses with considerable alarm at the 'upstart crow' that came from nowhere and so eloquently stole their thunder.

They are palpably the work of a passionate young man honing his craft – as evidenced by the fact that many parts of the plays are utterly useless. As an actor, I am quite prepared to acknowledge that Shakespeare had an off day occasionally and wrote some garbage. And not just in his early plays: try making sense of some of the Bohemia scene in *The Winter's Tale* to a thousand perplexed people every night, for example. Or try listening to Touchstone in *As You Like It* for more than you have to and it's impenetrable. It may well be brilliant poetry but most of it quite rightly gets cut because it doesn't work dramatically and is ever so dull. There is so much hagiography of his work that I fear we lose the fact that it can be alienating and boring if treated with anything other than healthy respect – then we can turn it into some of the most powerful shared experiences we can offer to each other. Treat it too respectfully and it becomes po-faced nonsense.

There is a lot of dross in these three plays, some of it written by Shakespeare and some of it written by other people. The writing style of high rhetoric and rather stiff formality which mirrors some of his predecessors such as Robert Greene, Peele and Marlowe begins to soften and mature during the plays. There are staggering glimpses into the man's genius peppered throughout – the Temple Garden scene and the death of Talbot in *Henry VI Part 1*; most of *Part 2*; the first act and the ensuing Battle of Towton in *Part 3*; the birth of young Richard, the hunchback, into the towering figure of evil that would become his first great creation to ring through the ages in *Richard III*. In *Henry VI Part 1*, as an actor you can tell when you walk on stage when it's a bit written by Shakespeare – the audience sit up and the play becomes accessible and interesting.

What seems to be the most common view is that Shakespeare wrote what is now *Part 2* first then progressed with his characterisation and dramatic licence in *Part 3* – and subsequently took some plays written by a few of his contempories that dealt with the events leading up to his first big hit, and re-wrote and fashioned them into a 'prequel' to capitalize on the Box Office. Collaboration amongst playwrights was very common at the time, and Thomas Nashe who had previously written with Marlowe is considered to be the chief culprit in writing a lot of *Henry VI Part 1* along with two or three other unidentified authors. After the success of what we now call *Part 2* and *Part 3*, it seems the Shakespeare name was now a big enough draw to pull in the punters.

Whatever its provenance, Shakespeare's name was put to *Henry VI Part 1* by actors that were in his company, Hemmings and Clondell, who published the *First Folio* in 1623, seven years after his death. As such, we must consider that however bad some of it is, and however much revision was done by the man himself, it was readily considered to be part of the Shakespeare canon and representative of the man and his work.

The play starts breezily with the funeral of Henry V at Westminster Abbey where Shakespeare bluntly chooses to represent the state of things by having this tangled web of Dukes, Earls and Bishops argue over the grave. When we staged this explosive first scene of *Henry VI Part 1* in The Histories, Geoffrey Streatfeild, as the ghost of Henry V, walked down through the bickering lords processing around his grave and lay atop his own coffin, buried in the stage, until the new world order slammed the doors of the stage down upon him. It is an extraordinary first scene of a play, not least because it crams into five minutes what in effect took about fifteen years, but the important points and people are there: the lords are arguing (with Gloucester and Winchester, especially, at each other's throats); they receive news that their newly conquered land in France is crumbling due to inaction; the brave and noble Lord Talbot has been injured and taken prisoner in the first ever English loss against the French. So Bedford, Regent of France, will leave to sort it out, Gloucester will check the Tower for ammunition and money, and Exeter will look after the young King. Phew. The last word goes to Winchester:

Each has his place and function to attend:
I am left out; for me nothing remains
But long will I not be Jack-out-of-office.
The King from Eltham I intend to steal
And sit at chiefest stern of public weal.

(Henry VI Part 1 Act 1 Sc. 1)

So far, so dastardly. It is the first scene of a play written, or revised, by a young man fresh out of the morass of an England torn asunder by the Reformation. The division he knew so well feeds the enmity between the two characters that tear each other apart for the next two plays – Gloucester's reply to Winchester's proclamations that the Church's prayers made Henry so prosperous is succinct and dangerous:

Gloucester
The Church? Where is it?

No wonder the plays were a hit.

Rouen

Geoffrey and I are swept like pooh sticks into Rouen. The road keeps tumbling down and the one time we want traffic lights to stop us, to catch our breath and to establish where we are, is of course the one time we are carried along on a river of green. We swoop into the central town square over cobbles that surely can't be for everyday access, and on a hunch we turn right, only then realising that our hotel is in front of us and we have arrived. It's the most remarkable entrance to a town I have ever made. We haven't stopped once for navigation, traffic lights or junctions and yet here we are.

It's a cheap hotel I booked on the internet and has the benefit of being slap in the centre of town, yet my room looks as though it has been decorated by Satan. Black bedspreads hover amid dark brown walls, but other than that the place is warm and cleanish. Half an hour later, in the balmy evening sun, we go out to take in the town.

Captured by Henry V in 1419, Rouen became the capital of English rule in Normandy and the focus of English advances across France. For thirty years or so it was a corner of England. It was here that Joan of Arc was burnt at the stake for heresy and witchcraft: a subject close to Elizabethan hearts now that the perils of believing in the wrong thing could land you with the same fate. From Homer to Star Wars, the struggle of a martyr against the imperial dark forces has always been good box office and never more so than in Tudor England, where the stories mirrored the mystification and struggle that greeted their fathers as their country changed from one power to another. So Joan of Arc appears in all her glory for most of *Henry VI Part 1* where we see a beautiful freedom fighter giving the promise of redemption and sex in equal measure accompanied by lots of violence. The prescription for a blockbuster has not changed in 400 years.

With her great adversary, Lord Talbot, we get James Bond in armour. I played the Earl of Salisbury in The Histories whilst suspended from a ladder about 30ft above the stage. After a brief chat with Talbot, I got blown off the thing by a guy swinging on a rope from the other side of the theatre, and hung there dripping blood whilst Talbot dropped to the stage and fought the renewed French and the newly minted Joan. It was a suitable *coup de théâtre* to kick-start the action of Lord Talbot's adventures – he is the flower of English chivalry and the one person to continue the legacy of Henry's desire for France.

In reality, Talbot was impulsive, brilliant, brave to the point of disbelief, and in our modern world we would probably brand him psychotic. It comes as no surprise, then, that he was a mad Marcher Lord – one of the same breed that gave rise to the Mortimers and the Glendowers. His father was Richard, Baron Talbot of Goodrich whose broken castle still stands on the border with Wales near Ross-on-Wye. Having married his own step-sister, who brought with her the inheritance of Hallamshire, his elder brother died (besieging Rouen) and his niece shortly after, so he ended up inheriting the whole family estate.

All this made him a significant landowner – the amount of 'Talbot' Inns around the country are testament to the spread of wealth and influence enjoyed by his progeny. However, he got into hot water with Henry who banged him up in the Tower over a little disagreement, some say, about religious belief. Nobody knows the truth as his imprisonment may have been simply over an argument with the Earl of Arundel – but it could also have been through Talbot's association with Sir John Oldcastle whose Lollard rebellion swept from the Marches to London in 1414. Either way, he was inside for a few months and, let off the leash, proceeded first to bludgeon Ireland and then France – fighting so much like a banshee for Henry V that he was branded the English Achilles. Even once the tide started to turn after the arrival of Joan of Arc within the French Court, Talbot spent his time hammering away with honour and barbaric insistence, Canute-like in his fortitude. French mothers to this day quiet their babes with his name. Talbot, not Henry, is the bogeyman.

His battle plan was simple and effective – fall at the enemy with speed, precision and utter disregard for your own or other people's life. In the days when to go into battle with a lumbering army was a slow and drawn-out affair, Talbot was like a nifty tank division. He regularly got into trouble with his own side as his spur-of-the-moment decisions placed many others in peril, but invariably he won out. On one occasion he famously attacked a convoy of French soldiers when heavily outnumbered, but the speed, surprise and ferocity of the assault won the day and thus negated the need for a long siege.

In the play Talbot faces his nemesis in Joan of Arc – the force of heavenly nature who turns an inept and despairing French Court into a defiant, cohesive, fighting force. She is called 'Pucelle' which in French can mean virgin *and* whore. White and red. She springs from the earth. To Shakespeare she is nature, a Green Woman, that harnesses the spirit of Mary, Mother of Christ, to save her country from the foe. The Dauphin calls her 'Astraea's daughter' who in Greek mythology was the personification of 'Justice'. It also just happened to be a moniker applied to Elizabeth I who in the early part of her reign, through tolerance, peace and understanding, was seen to be presiding over a Golden Age of the Renaissance. So Joan is a Goddess in many forms – a Catholic martyr on one hand and a female representation of power and justice allied to Elizabeth on the other.

In the play, Joan achieves one of her greatest victories by persuading the Duke of Burgundy from the English side. She is at her magical best when simply using words to beguile the Duke to the French side. Burgundy is no match for her and with him on side, the scene is set for a final showdown between Joan and Talbot in which the chivalric flower of Henry V's honour will finally be brought down.

The actual History is somewhat different: Talbot may well have fought against an army inspired by Joan but he was certainly never killed by her actions as the play shows. Neither was the Duke of Bedford, who died soon after Joan's star briefly shone and not as a consequence of her storming the gates of Rouen.

Her story is brief and legendary: a country girl from near Orleans she gained access to the waning, dissolute French Court and turned them into a fighting force. Engendering a renewal of French pride, she achieved a notable victory against the English at Orleans and within a few short months, turned the tide of the war in France's favour.

In reality, it was only later that Burgundy turned back to the French side – thus depriving the English of the vital bridgehead they needed to secure their goal. It was, in fact, Burgundy that got the better of Joan when she was caught by him and sold to the English at Rouen after only a few months of country-changing deeds. Put on trial as a witch in which the outcome was inevitable, she was brought through the streets of Rouen by Bedford and burnt at the stake in the town square.

Geoffrey and I almost immediately find the magnificent cathedral which looms into the night just around the corner from our hotel, and we both stare in wonder – our necks arching backwards to appreciate its full grandeur. It is a hugely impressive building until we realise that it isn't the cathedral at all and Rouen is filled with hugely impressive buildings. Through the pottering mediaeval streets lined with busy shops, garlicky restaurants and delicate cobbles, we sheepishly find the actual cathedral soaring into the stars. The closeness of the streets make it bigger somehow. It is almost impossible to know where to start looking – there is so much to take in. The South door has masonry so delicate it feels woven, and the West facade is as glorious a piece of art as I have seen. Lace-like towers point to the great metal spire that disappears upwards like a taut umbilical cord.

We retreat to the safety of a restaurant in the shadow of another glittering church, Saint-Maclou, and eat Steak Frites on a table outside whilst the youth of Rouen parade beautifully in the warmth of an Indian Summer evening. Games of pétanque quietly clank and chink among the close walls. Caught up in the heady whiff of it all, we drink a wonderful amount of wine. It seems to go down all too easily when you're sat amongst the French, the smell of lobster in the air. We talk of how our lives and friendship have been inextricably woven into Shakespeare's History Plays – our own history governed by History. In a gloriously French place that was so potently English for a small time, we clink our glasses together and toast friendship, history in all its forms, and the inconsistent glory that is being an actor. In a town far away from England, I am very, very happy.

In the town square the next morning, I feel almost guilty to be so content. You can see the actual spot where Joan was burnt. They have kept the same mounds and hillocks that were features of the time, and by placing a simple plaque in a beautiful flowerbed the chorography is perfect. In this little gap in the concrete, this bloom of nature that so lit up her world could be seen amongst the backdrop of the city waking up. There is a surprisingly beautiful modern church that looks like a crocodile's tail as it weaves around the square where she died. It reminded me of Coventry, although here there was no toothless cathedral to look blankly over the new, but a simple flowerbed. It is no less eloquent. It is a place to breathe.

Joan was a woman fighting for her country and the freedom of her people, burnt as a witch and a heretic. Yet her work had been done. In breaking the siege at Orleans, Joan had provided the glimmer of light that the French needed to turn the tide. She is shown to be as resourceful and committed as any of the dispossessed fighting for their right to freedom and belief. With Henry V gone, the aura of invincibility that the English purveyed was punctured irrevocably. For the English, France became sand through their fingers in the space of twenty years.

The young Henry VI, boy king of England, stopped to watch Joan's trial on his way to be crowned in Paris. All his coronation achieved was to knit the French closer. They had a new figurehead in the re-invigorated Dauphin, himself crowned King of France at Rheims a few months earlier. A few years later, Bedford was dying and wished only to negotiate an honourable peace before the inevitable loss that England was to suffer. The Duke of Burgundy did finally switch to the French side and took with him the vast resources and lands that could feed such an English campaign.

The Regents of France that were subsequently sent out by the English Council to spearhead the War became more and more interested in what was going on back home. Through all the scenes of *Henry VI Part 1* in which Talbot appears he embodies the spirit of the Old World and is the chivalric, martial bastion of mythic England that we so cling onto even to this day, yet he sticks out like a sore thumb from the seething mass of Lords, Earls and Dukes that are vying to take control back in England.

Talbot, and thus England, only lose because he is let down by the bitter factions and deadly games of his fellow power brokers – events all too familiar to the play's Elizabethan audience: in 1591, when this play is roughly thought to have been written, the Earl of Essex led an expedition to help the Protestant Henry of Navarre in the siege of Rouen. The whole project went off more with a whimper than a resounding bang – let down by bitter factionalism at home. England, the tolerant bearer of religion that was the flower of the Northern Renaissance, was fast becoming a useless fist clothed in an old glove. It was fighting a war abroad, the cause of which it was not party to, and the execution of which was undermined by in-fighting at home. *Plus ça change*.

Geoffrey and I sit in a café in the beautiful square in which Joan was burnt and take in the morning sun, nursing our hangovers and sipping our coffee thoughtfully, wondering how far we have come in the ensuing 400 years. Not far away, the old cathedral that is still very much alive begins ringing out Time in deep sonorous bells.

It is time to go home. Back to England, somehow clearer from afar.

The Temple Garden

Also in attendance at the burning of Joan was Cardinal Henry Beaufort whose Palace of Winchester still stands, albeit a little forlornly, on the South Bank next to the old Clink prison to this day – a few yards from the newly constructed Globe Theatre. It has a towering rose window that now sees nothing but bricks and mortar but it gives a broken semblance of the majesty with which the Bishop would have ruled his own little fiefdom, his *liberty*.

It was to these 'Liberties' that Shakespeare arrived to strut and fret his hour upon the stage and emerge as a writer in the 'powd'ring tub of infamy' that so fed the country boy's imagination. The prostitutes that adorned the top tier of the theatres were always powdered white to detract from the worst effects of aging and the pox, and wore white headscarves, all of which earned them the nickname Winchester Geese. So when, in *Henry IV Part 1*, the factional Duke of Gloucester calls Winchester just such a name, the groundlings down the front may have raised a comical eyebrow at a peer of the Realm splashing about in the vernacular of the Liberty.

With the Reformation came the death of the Mystery Plays and Pageants that so permeated old Catholic England, so the concept of watching a 'Play', certainly in a specifically designed theatre, was relatively new – and to the people who couldn't read, it was also the first time they could experience their nation's History, so the language use was inevitably contemporary. The themes of division and the swaying of the masses to the winds of the aristocracy were bitingly satirical and the battles of Gloucester and Winchester are peopled throughout with common folk affected by their strife. Long before writing of the Boar's Head, Shakespeare was keen to show who was paying for the squabbles of the nobles.

According to Shakespeare, one of those aristocratic squabbles took place directly opposite the fleshpots and denizens of the South Bank, on the other side of the river in the Temple Garden. Stand outside what is now the National Theatre and a small patch of green can be still seen across the river behind the Embankment. The Garden provides a moment of stillness in the middle of London that can rarely be bettered.

The Temple Garden is still a 'liberty' governed by no one. It falls between the jurisdiction of the City of London a street to the East, and the City of Westminster a street to the West. On the *limen* between the two. The two Inns of Court that surround the Gardens, the Inner Temple and the Middle Temple, get their names from the Knights Templar who built the Halls back in the twelfth century as well as the infamous Temple Church that lies close by. The whole complex has changed much over the years due either to ruination by revolt or the Luftwaffe. The Middle Temple Hall has the first recorded performance of *Twelfth Night* in 1602 and remains host to theatrical performances all year round, and the Gardens sweep down to the Embankment in a wonderful anomaly of space in a crowded area. This place, this bubble, in between two Cities, built by the Templars and rebuilt after the Second World War, is set firmly amongst two ages – Mediaeval and Modern. In between law and lawlessness, the liberty, it is a breath, a little scene. The perfect garden, in other words. An Eden.

It is also, of course, a garden of Law as the Inner Temple and Middle Temple Inns of Court surround them. As the lights of our modern culture began to shine from the foundry of the Elizabethan age, so the issues of what is right and wrong in modern Law were being forged here under the gaze of Elizabeth, Astraea's daughter.

For Shakespeare, the Temple Garden was a place rich in recent Elizabethan history – not only was it the garden of one of the main Inns of Court, it was part of Essex House, owned first by Robert Dudley, Earl of Leicester and then by his step-son, Robert Devereux, Earl of Essex. Hence Essex Street and Devereux Court still being there today. At the time Shakespeare was writing in the early 1590s, Essex was the up-and-coming power broker amongst the aristocracy and the new favourite of Elizabeth after the death of his step-father, Dudley. This particular Garden, having been destroyed at one stage by the Peasant's Revolt and patronised by Dudley, needed no introduction to the combined groundlings and aristocracy piled into the theatre over the river who all trod a fine path between the State, the Law and the gallows.

It is into this Garden that Shakespeare throws a group of mediaeval young men shaping England's destiny and watches them fall – it is the garden between two worlds, red and white. All the main protagonists of the causes of the Wars of the Roses are here: The Earl of Suffolk; the Duke of Somerset; the Earl of Warwick; Richard Plantagenet – heir to the Duchy of York AND the Mortimers; a Vernon and a lawyer. A potent mixture.

In 1415, William de la Pole, Earl of Suffolk, inherited his title when both his father and elder brother were killed at Harfleur and Agincourt respectively. He had himself been seriously injured at Harfleur so missed the glory that would follow on Crispin's Day. His great-grandfather had been a wool merchant from Hull who rose in the new world created by the Black Death and whose son eventually became Chancellor to Richard II, being created Earl of Suffolk in 1385. Although the 1st Earl fell from favour with Richard's fall, his son and grandson were staunch Lancastrians who gave their lives for Henry V, and William eventually became co-commander of English forces in France. So within four generations they had risen from nothing to be powers behind the throne. New money, in other words. The phrase 'jackanapes' derives from this Earl who reached high beyond his station: their coat of arms bore a leash and collar which looked unfortunately like the tethers that held monkeys, colloquially called 'Jack Napis', or John of Naples, the port that shipped them in from Africa.

Suffolk needed money and lands, having comparatively little of either without ancient lineage to back him up. By being charmingly brilliant to the young Henry VI he managed to secure a lot of both. In Court, Suffolk allied himself to old moneybags Winchester who had his hands on the purse strings of an increasingly insolvent England. Both wanted peace in France to stop the financial haemorrhage the war created, or in Suffolk's case to bring an honourable end to a hopeless cause as well as to feather his own nest at home. The question remained: how do you withdraw from a long, drawn-out conflict without making the previous years of fighting utterly moribund? We are still looking for an answer.

Suffolk was a serious political figure having done so much for Henry V, and also done so much to lose a lot of France – it was under his, not Talbot's, guard that Orleans had been lost to Joan of Arc. But he was not the only culprit – the entire Court was tainted in one way or another with the stench of growing defeat. However, the young men coming through, inheritors of a world in which their fathers had either been slain or absent for many years abroad, were not so discoloured. They were eager to make their way in the literally do-or-die world of an English Court with no sovereign at its centre.

The Earl of Warwick, Richard Neville, was just such a man. His father was the Earl of Salisbury, but Warwick inherited most of his titles through a particularly sharp marriage: his father-in-law was Richard Beauchamp, Earl of Warwick, whom Shakespeare conflates with Neville. Whichever Warwick it was, the fact remains that Neville inherited vast tracts of land not only in the Midlands but a lot of the fertile southern Marcher lands in Wales and Herefordshire.

This would put him into direct conflict with Edmund, Duke of Somerset, who also thought he owned the lands through marriage. He was a Beaufort – the grandson of John of Gaunt and nephew of the Bishop of Winchester. His brother, John, had been the first Duke of Somerset, but spent most of his life in France fighting what turned out to be a losing battle not only against the French but sanity. Imprisoned in France for seventeen years, John had returned to England only to be given generous amounts of money from an impoverished Crown to command various armies back in France – which he proceeded to lead with a staggering ineptitude. Returning to England a broken man he most probably took his own life, which left the young Edmund inheritor of the Somerset estates. Sadly, those estates yielded little in the way of solid funds – a fact which his uncle Winchester and the young Henry VI tried to redress through offering Somerset various appointments which could yield important amounts of money.

These appointments, alongside his brother's ineptitude, brought him into open dissention with the man who stood to receive more than all these Lords combined – Richard Plantagenet. Four years old when his father, Richard, Earl of Cambridge was executed by Henry V for the Southampton Plot, he was thirteen when married off to Cecily Neville, daughter of the Earl of Westmorland – and thus became the uncle of Warwick. But the moment the corpulent Aumerle,

Duke of York, fell childless and sweating off his long-suffering horse at Agincourt everything changed. Even as the fat old boy was being boiled down, people were wondering if the rightful inheritor, Richard Plantagenet, would ever be made Duke of York. His father had been attainted – so Richard could not inherit the Cambridge lands – but it had been the loyal, childless, Duke of York that had died thereby opening the blood line for the boy to inherit the great York estates. Richard's mother, Anne, had died giving birth to him but she was sister to the rather useless, and childless, Edmund Mortimer, Earl of March. Once Mortimer died in 1425, Richard became the sole meeting point between the third son of Edward III – Lionel, Duke of Clarence – and the fifth son, Edmund Langley, Duke of York.

Put simply, this little orphan boy stood to inherit not only a good proportion of all the lands and money in England, but a potentially superior claim to the throne than the boy King himself. He was hot property. Too hot.

It is this radioactive young man who storms into Shakespeare's play in the Temple Garden. The scene is simple. In order to resolve an argument, Richard Plantagenet, yet to be created Duke of York and therefore a lowly commoner, picks a white rose and challenges the others to pick one with him, if they think he is right. Somerset, in response, picks a red rose and likewise challenges the others to side with him.

Suffolk, a staunch Lancastrian, cannot choose anybody but Somerset. Warwick, having equivocated like the tightrope walker he would show himself to be in the future, picks a white rose – Plantagenet is, after all, virtually family. That leaves a dead heat. So the aristocrats turn to the others. Standing in the spotlight is a Vernon.

Lady Elizabeth Vernon was married to the Earl of Southampton, Shakespeare's principal benefactor at this time. Elizabeth Vernon herself was descended from Talbot, and Southampton's mother was a Montagu – one of the few major aristocratic families allowed to keep its Catholic practices and patronage during the Elizabethan era. Hardly surprising then that a Vernon picks a white rose – the symbol of the Virgin Mary, the Mystical Rose of Heaven.

However, as ever, it all comes down to a lawyer in the end. By law, it seems, Plantagenet is right and the lawyer picks white.

Richard Plantagenet

Now, Somerset, where is your argument?

Somerset

Here in my scabbard, meditating that
Shall dye your white rose in a bloody red.

(Henry VI Part 1 Act 2 Sc.4)

And so begin the Wars of the Roses.

It was only in the nineteenth century, thanks to this very scene, that the term Wars of the Roses came to represent the feud between the Houses of York and Lancaster. I go to the Garden now on a warm summer's afternoon. There is a small gate that at certain times is open to the public, and a restaurant within puts its tables on the terrace by the Temple Hall to enjoy the view and the white and red roses put here to commemorate the union of make-believe and history. All the car horns, sirens and blare that is the soundtrack of London seem muffled and distant in the folds of the grass. The roses smell as sweet and joyous as the wars that are named after them were terrible. Before she died, Margaret Thatcher would come here every week and water the roses. It seems she just couldn't stop harvesting the crop of division.

I walk around the gardens, down to the Embankment, where a beautiful avenue of London plane trees tumble in the sun. This is still a resting place for lawyers and, it seems, their prey – a very worried-looking man with a red face passes me, puffing his cheeks with a preoccupied stare. Elsewhere, a barrister clothed in the curious neckwear of his profession sits upright on a bench fast asleep. His hands are clutching his balls in a protective clinch rivalled only by footballers. I wonder if the red-faced man and the ball-clutching lawyer are connected?

I can only imagine that the lawyer in Shakespeare's scene would be adopting a similar position once he knew what resentment he had unleashed.

In dramatising the lives of the ancestors of the aristocracy who ruled England with such a tight rein, Shakespeare was playing a high risk game. Like a lawyer, he had to tread a fine line between representation and slander – in portraying one Duke of Somerset, for example, the present Duke may well be shifting angrily and lethally in his expensive seat. Suffolk, Somerset, Warwick and Richard Plantagenet burst into the Temple Garden, and the play, mid-argument. Many an actor has spent long hours considering what it is they are in arms about, but Shakespeare's audience would have taken the cause for the argument in their own way. In 1564 a certain John Hales had been imprisoned for writing a pamphlet on the thorny and increasingly relevant issue of Elizabeth's succession, whereby he had proposed that the line of the Dukes of Suffolk should be considered. By 1572 Parliament was forbidden to debate the issue and by the mid-1570s Elizabeth had banned all talk of her succession – you were likely to end up in the Tower for any overt speculation. So when a lot of aristocrats come pelting onto the stage, most of whom have names that conjure images of more recent claims and rebellions to the throne, having an argument in the Temple Garden of all places, and palpably not declaring the subject of that dispute – it is a fair bet the audience knew exactly what they were arguing about. For this scene, Shakespeare couldn't even say he was simply relying on Tudor chroniclers – none of whom mention anything about an argument in a garden – so he was subtly commenting on his own world through the portrayal of another. However mediaeval these characters seem, they have Elizabethan sensibilities running through them like a stick of rock.

Shakespeare was also schooled in Rhetoric and found it simple to say something merely by pointing out that he was not saying it (Brutus is an honourable man, say). Never was this more apparent than when we performed The Histories with HRH Prince Charles in the audience. They are plays about his ancestors after all and you start to find some pretty sharp lines about the nature of kingship when you know the heir to the throne is sitting in the same room. I could almost feel the seething young author boiling up and slapping the aristocracy in the face. Nevertheless it is all clothed in the adulation of History and you feel in a strange sort of way that Prince Charles must come away satisfied that whilst his ancestors are almost completely insane they remain glorified.

Perhaps that is the English: they maintain a healthy two fingers to a monarchy they clearly adore.

Holy Trinity Church

In portraying one story and telling another, it is the characters that bubble away under the surface with whom Shakespeare can perhaps more easily pack his punches: the Bishop of Carlisle or the gardeners of Eden in *Richard II*; Falstaff/Oldcastle in *Henry IV* or Bates, Court and Williams in *Henry V*.

In *Henry VI Part 1* he chooses a Warwickshire man through and through. Any actor working in Stratford-upon-Avon either lives or goes to parties in Avonside – a group of apartments sheltering by the river as it swoops down the weir. From there you have to walk past Holy Trinity Church to get to the theatres, thereby passing not fifty yards from Shakespeare's grave. After certain performances I'm sure I could hear the old boy turning as I walked past. But as you walk the avenue of lime trees on the Church path, the one name that stands out more than any other is 'LUCY'. It lies carved into many stones, under which lie the graves of one of the most distinguished of Warwickshire families. Lucy is everywhere in Stratford-upon-Avon. Lucy's Mill, Hampton Lucy – they were a huge family and had their seat a few miles from Stratford at Charlecote Park – where Elizabeth I visited Sir Thomas Lucy, an ardent Protestant, in 1572. It was here that the boy Shakespeare had his apocryphal brush with the aristocracy by poaching deer.

Who knows what run-ins the younger Shakespeare had with the man who passionately rounded up so many Jesuits, Ardens and other recusants and stole their lands and culture? Sir Thomas's great-great-great grandfather, Sir William Lucy, gets namechecked no less than three times in the space of a few lines. Whoever was writing this stuff wanted the audience to know who this man was. There is no mention by chroniclers of a Sir William Lucy fighting in France and yet here he is in the play as the go-between for the despairing Talbot and the Regents of France. Sir William was actually a Yorkist who died in 1466, yet here in the play he gets all the best lines and even talks directly to the audience:

> **Lucy**
> *Thus, while the vulture of sedition*
> *Feeds in the bosom of such great commanders,*
> *Sleeping neglection doth betray to loss*
> *The conquest of our scarce-cold conqueror*
> *That ever-living man of memory*
> *Henry the Fifth. Whiles they each other cross,*
> *Lives, honours, lands and all, hurry to loss.*
>
> (Henry VI Part 1 Act 4 Sc.3)

Nobody knows what Shakespeare's relationship with the Lucy family was. The fact remains that Sir Thomas was extreme in his efforts to quash Catholicism and recusancy in a County that remained resolutely attached to the old ways – extremism followed on both sides. Shakespeare may have been trying to please them or he may have been simply using the name. In typical Shakespearean fashion, by using someone who was so against his mother's family he may have been keeping himself out of trouble in flattering them, whilst using the mouthpiece to reveal his own thoughts. Whatever reason, the funnel between the stage and the audience in this particular play – the most eloquent commentator on the division of the English nobility – is a Warwickshire man from Stratford-upon-Avon.

As Lucy points out – the great hope of a lost past, Talbot, is swept into the deep divide opening up in England. *Khaos*, in Greek, means 'gaping void'. Thomas Nashe, who may have written some of the play, related that the audience in Elizabethan times were reduced to tears at the death of Talbot and it was no different when we performed it. It remains one of the most powerful deaths in all of Shakespeare – a precursor to Lear and Cordelia, even Horatio and Hamlet – when Talbot wraps his arms around his dead son and speaks his last breath:

> **Talbot**
> *Come, come and lay him in his father's arms:*
> *My spirit can no longer bear these harms.*
> *Soldiers adieu: I have what I would have,*
> *Now my old arms are young Talbot's grave.*
>
> (Henry VI Part 1 Act 4 Sc.7)

The Talbots, however, were still very much alive in Shakespearean England. In the 1580s, Talbot's descendant was his great-great-grandson, Francis Talbot, the 5th Earl of Shrewsbury. He was one of the most equivocating men in the Tudor era – enthusiastically backing Henry VIII's marriage to Anne Boleyn yet retaining his Catholic faith. He had prospered, however, under Protestant Edward VI and backed the accession of Lady Jane Grey, but was pardoned immediately by the Catholic Queen Mary I and rose to be one of the most powerful people in the country during her reign. He and his son, George, both received Philip II of Spain when he arrived in the country to marry Queen Mary, and their approval eased the passage for such a Catholic consort. Dying two years into Elizabeth's reign, he was on her Privy Council and a regular attendee at Court yet was allowed to keep his Catholic faith to the end. In order to preserve himself and his line, he had bolstered the very thing that was to diminish his faith.

His son, George, it seems, was no different. His wife was the infamous Bess of Hardwick and together they were given the custody of Mary, Queen of Scots. By the time Shakespeare was writing his first *Henriad*, Mary was dead and so was George, but not before both of them had been accused of an affair by Bess that, whether true or not, brought scandal to the entire Court. One can only imagine the delicate juggling act of equivocation George had been required to do – keeping his hands clean for Elizabeth whilst holding the hopes of Catholics within them. It must have required some doing, especially when his wife started flinging accusations around the Court that he and Mary were lovers.

The Queen of Scots, of course, was a tricky person to hold prisoner. Mary's first husband was King Francis II of France, who had been known as 'le Prince Dauphin d'Auvergne' before his coronation. Mary was therefore 'la Princesse Dauphin d'Auvergne' as well as Queen of Scots. In one episode of *Henry VI Part 1* – nowhere to be found in History or any of Shakespeare's sources – our hero Talbot is nearly taken prisoner by the Countess d'Auvergne but outsmarts her. Backed by soldiers and his wit he becomes her captor treating her fairly with chivalry and martial courtesy.

Later in the play Joan of Arc carps over the corpse of Talbot – which is also wildly historically inaccurate. Talbot died twenty years after Joan, in the final battle of the English wars in France, in Castillon, at the age of sixty-six. So it is a complete fabrication of Shakespeare to put the two together. It is merely a representation: a woman – zealous, witty and able, defeats the noble, big-hearted, yet ineffectual Talbot, who represents something from another age. Put together, these three characters – the Countess d'Auvergne, Joan and Talbot – become a greater allegory for the Elizabethan era: they are Mary, Queen of Scots, Elizabeth I and George Talbot, 6th Earl of Shrewsbury. In the heap of dead limbs on stage that are the Mediaeval Talbot and his son, lie yet more broken and equivocated dreams of old, tolerant England. Talbot's scream of pain may well be Shakespeare's too.

Six

Meon Hill

Stand atop the, er, interesting new tower of the otherwise beautifully reconstructed Royal Shakespeare Theatre in Stratford-upon-Avon, and the hill which dominates the skyline is a square lump of land that sweeps up the sides of the Cotswold Hills from the Avon. Meon Hill is a dramatic flat-topped, Iron-age fort, gilded by a single ash tree like a candle on a cake. It is visible from miles around and has a history as dramatic and singular as its geography. When I first came to Stratford and asked about the hill that stands so clearly in the distance, people looked askance when saying the name and told me I didn't want to go there. It's creepy, they said. Witchcraft and murder.

Folklore has it that Shakespeare got his three witches of Macbeth from the stories swirling with the wind around this place. According to that same folklore – and by that I mean perfectly sane people who sit in the pub and talk of the weather and normal things – witches still dance around 'that tree' on Midsummer's Eve. Tales of Black Dogs patrolling the hill through the ages have always abounded and things were made even worse when there was a particularly gruesome murder on its slopes in 1945 and 'witchery' was cited.

Sir William Clopton, who fought at Agincourt, is buried in the church, St Swithin's, at the base of the hill in Lower Quinton, and his estates, most notably Clopton House just outside Stratford-upon-Avon, form the basis of many ghost stories upon which local folklore says that Shakespeare created some of his characters. Charlotte Clopton, who was mistakenly buried alive in the Clopton family crypt in Holy Trinity Church just yards from where Shakespeare was to have his final resting place, is said to have given rise to Juliet; Margaret Clopton, who drowned herself in a well which is now round the back of Clopton House may have spawned Ophelia. Both, it is said, still potter about the house and gardens.

I live in Clopton House and haven't seen a thing. Mind you, I live in the old servant's quarters so the ghosts might not deign to visit. I regularly stand on top of Meon Hill, in my opinion the most unsung Saxon hilltop in Britain, and am yet to see a witch, or even an eye of toad.

On a good day you can see eight counties from up there. To the West, the Malverns and thence the Marches hover in the distance. Dover's Hill is a few miles away around the edge. Here you can see as far East, North and West as the earth will let you. It's like flying. The beauty, vigour and sweep of the landscape are life-affirming. No black dogs.

But there are more things in heaven and earth, Horatio.

James VI of Scotland, married to the Princess of Denmark, wrote a highly influential thesis on witches in 1597 called 'Demonology', which proved to be the apogee of a movement he himself started in 1590 about Scottish witchcraft. He felt that in his stormy travels to Denmark in 1589 he had been the victim of attempts by witches to kill him. Indeed during his early Scottish reign as many as 300 'witches' were accused – a hundred of which were put on trial. It is not known how many actually died as a result. Among other things he accused some of melting a wax effigy of him, and others of 'perverted rites' in Berwick – though what that had to do with killing James, we'll never know.

A lot of it, it seems, was to blacken the name of the husband of his mother, Mary, Queen of Scots. Earl Bothwell may have been partly responsible for the death of James's own father, and understandably James was a little aggrieved. But James was anyway only following in a tradition established by Henry VIII after the Reformation, whose Witchcraft Act of 1542 was the first to define such a practice as a felony. All the skimble-skamble magic of old was now out of place.

Mirroring their Catholic ancestors' missionary zeal, the Protestant will to demonise the reverence of wells, springs, rivers and hills into 'popish' or pagan idolatry knew no bounds. What mattered was a personal, white-walled relationship with God. The paranoid and the paranormal became one.

James became a great positor of the new Christian Theory that one 'witch' could not act alone and that there would always be help, or a coven of witches, nearby. In one fell swoop this was the insecure, new religion seeing ghosts at every turn and suspecting 'witchery' with its tail wrapped around every branch. The Serpent was tempting Eve with the rich, juicy Red apple of living, life and earth so afeared by the new Wittenberg philosophy.

Though less of an issue in England, the stories of Scottish witch trials that were so rooted in the religious division of the day left a huge mark on the chattering classes in London struggling under the rule of a woman who was becoming less a paragon of virtue and fountain of life, but more of a threatened, toothless old crone. The female that had given birth to the nation was now becoming the default image of male fear of female power, a witch. For Shakespeare, writing in the early 1590s, to throw in the burning of Joan and show her finally to be a witch relying on the 'lordly monarchs of the North' is both good box office and a little close to the bone.

Perhaps it is the loss of her virginity that precipitates her downfall – a course of action so publicly avoided by Elizabeth I and so disastrously embraced by Mary, Queen of Scots – but whatever the reason, it is the new world order that burns Joan. Richard Plantagenet had finally been given his inheritance and became Duke of York and consequently one of the richest, most powerful people in the land. He was also made Regent of France but this was long after Joan had been burnt by the English in Rouen. For Shakespeare, however, it is the newly-minted, rose-tinted Duke of York and the Earl of Warwick, the new inheritors of a world heading for Chaos, that fan the flames underneath her.

As Joan begins to burn, watched by the sneering York and Warwick, her 'spirits' leave her so her desperation becomes startlingly Protestant. She talks of her captors as devoid of 'Grace' – the Lutheran doctrine of salvation:

> **Joan**
> *Because you want the Grace that others have,*
> *You judge it straight a thing impossible*
> *To encompass wonders but by help of devils.*
>
> *(Henry VI Part 1 Act 5 Sc. 4)*

This is a direct slamming of the old 'skimble-skamble' ways that preceded the Reformation, which she of course had been guilty of using herself. Her father, a shepherd of the land, is there to remonstrate with her but she forsakes him and pleads that she is actually from 'the progeny of kings'. She tells them she is a virgin, but that is laughed at, so she tries another tack: if women were with child, they were bound by law not to be burnt as it was considered the unborn child was innocent. So she says she's pregnant, and names Alençon, and then, in desperation, Reignier, as the father.

> **Richard Duke of York**
> *Why here's a girl. I think she knows not well,*
> *There were so many whom she may accuse.*

Warwick
It is a sign she hath been liberal and free
York
And yet forsooth she is a virgin pure
Strumpet, thy words condemn thy brat and thee.
Use no entreaty for it is in vain.

(Henry VI Part 1 Act 5 Sc. 4)

It is interesting to note that the two nobles Joan arbitrarily names as fathers of her child, Alençon and Anjou (Reignier), are the names of the two Catholic, French nobles picked as husbands for Queen Elizabeth I during her reign who, in the end, she refused to marry.

Astraea's daughter, Justice, was dead.

Back at Westminster, the Chaos around Henry VI was growing wider. The Regency Council was split down the middle about how to extricate themselves from the war in France or continue fighting. Gloucester, now the heir to the throne and free from having to kowtow to the late Bedford's authority, was still a keen promulgator of war, but the tide was turning. By the time the young King Henry finally assumed control of his throne, the country had been at war for nearly twenty-five years since his father had set sail for Harfleur from Southampton. The English were fighting increasingly desperate and ineffective campaigns and the Council knew that the money had run out. It could be argued York himself was made Regent of France not only to get him out of the way, but because he was the only one who could afford to pay his troops. A fact about which he was not pleased and eventually came home complaining bitterly that he couldn't be expected to shoulder the burden.

Into this vacuum stepped the red rose of the Earl of Suffolk. What's more, he brought with him a Queen. He managed to negotiate with Reignier, the duc of Anjou, and titular 'King of Naples and Jerusalem' that his daughter, Margaret, should marry King Henry VI. It was an audacious coup which sidelined the plans of the English Court and many throughout Europe. It was only later discovered that in order to cement such a deal he had agreed to hand over the regions of Anjou and Maine so hard-won by the English over the preceding twenty years.

So thrilled was the young Henry by the thought of such a woman, that he made Suffolk first a Marquess and, later, a Duke pretty much on the spot – thereby placing him at the centre of English aristocracy and power, and putting the noses out of joint of most of the rest of the Council who didn't agree with a such a course of action, like Gloucester, York and Warwick.

Born in 1430, Margaret was fifteen when she was brought to England, without a dower, by the shining new Duke of Suffolk – the hard-fought lands of Maine and Anjou flowing off into the air like her wedding train. Henry was twenty-three and like any young man of that age was keen to marry as soon as possible. Once he had seen a picture of the delectable Margaret he was smitten, and the priapic young King sent many envoys across the water to secure both her and the peace that Suffolk and the Cardinal Winchester so urged.

When we first meet her, born from the maelstrom of Joan's death and the disintegrating French wars at the end of *Henry VI Part 1*, in Shakespeare's imagination Margaret is fairly near her actual historical self in that she is instantly assured, extremely clever and knows her own power. She has inherited the spirit of Joan, and the Duke of Suffolk is infatuated from the word go. There is no clear evidence, either in Shakespeare's sources or in other historical records, that Suffolk ever had an affair with Margaret – although he was accused, as were others, throughout Henry's reign. For Shakespeare, however, Suffolk's motivation for getting her to marry the King appears to be so he can have her for himself, thus winning power through influence. In a scene bristling with innuendo and word play, Margaret is the one that comes out on top, as it were, stamping her trademark wit and aloofness all over Suffolk's urbane charm.

To an Elizabethan audience, a Suffolk having a secret affair, and one that could prove the downfall of the throne, was all too familiar. In 1553 the then Duke of Suffolk, Henry Grey, conspired to place his own daughter, Lady Jane Grey, on the throne. For his pains both he and Jane lost their heads when Queen Mary I was swept to power after Jane's nine-day reign. However Suffolk's second daughter, Catherine Grey, still had as strong a claim to the throne as her sister – a fact which made her a particularly glowing ember in Elizabeth's fiery new Court five years later. Philip II of Spain planned to marry his son off to her and the Privy Council even planned to wed her to the Earl of Arran, the heir to the throne of Scotland.

But she chose love. Edward Seymour, Earl of Hertford, secretly married her and when she fell pregnant – thus letting the cat out of the bag – the Queen was enraged. She slapped them both into the Tower and had the marriage annulled instantly. Whilst there the couple had another son, but the eldest was not only the potential heir to the dukedom of Suffolk but also might just happen to be the king of England. This was when Elizabeth decided to ban all talk of succession, both public and private, and in so doing making the succession the only thing that people wanted to talk about. So when John Hales published his pamphlet supporting the 'Suffolk' line, he condemned both himself and Catherine Grey. She died in the Tower.

By the time Shakespeare came to write his History plays in the early 1590s, Seymour was twenty years older and so was Elizabeth. The matter of succession was now an urgent matter and Seymour reignited the Suffolk debate by petitioning the Queen to have his marriage legalised, therefore declaring his sons legitimate and the rightful heirs of the Duke of Suffolk. Unsurprisingly, given the fact that they could also be kings of England, it didn't happen and in 1594 he was sent back to the Tower. He never asked again. The boys were only legitimised seventy years later by Charles II in 1660, distant enough for time to have thinned the blood. To the Elizabethan audience, however, a Suffolk controlling the strings of power and being a star-crossed lover at the same time was simply the way things always were.

The mediaeval Suffolk's schemes were equally divisive. For one high-powered woman at Court, the arrival of Margaret was a disaster. The Duke of Gloucester's wife, Dame Eleanor Cobham, was comparatively low-born for a Duke's wife – she had been his mistress whilst he sensationally divorced his first – but may have had designs on reaching the very top when her husband, the heir to the throne, might become king. According to her detractors she decided to enlist a little spiritual help in achieving her aim by engaging the services of a witch.

Who knows whether this was true or cooked up by the enemies of Gloucester to finish his political career once and for all, but the fact remains she too was tried for witchcraft, and once again – in *Henry VI Part 2* – Shakespeare shows the whole rigmarole to a quivering audience.

It's still very contentious to this day. Of the hundreds of times I have performed this scene at the RSC, I have seen people in the audience crossing themselves every time. The story is clear: Dame Eleanor wants her husband to be king and is told by him in no uncertain terms to stop having such thoughts. She doesn't listen and engages the help of a shadowy priest, Sir John Hume, to gather a witch, Margery Jourdayne, and two other 'helpers', Roger Bullingbrook and Thomas Southwell, to investigate by sorcery if Gloucester will ever become king. To an

Elizabethan audience this may have been shocking enough to gather a few excited whispers but when Shakespeare actually shows them practising their dark arts they must have gone crazy. If it still perturbs people enough to cross themselves to this day then what did it do to the audience then?

> ### Roger Bullingbrook
> *Patience good lady, wizards know their times...*
>
> *[Stage direction] Here they do the ceremonies belonging, and make the circle; Bullingbrook or Southwell reads 'Conjuro te' etc. It thunders and lightens terribly then the Spirit [Asnath] rises.*
>
> (Henry VI Part 2 Act 1 Sc. 4)

'Conjuro te' is taken from a Jesuit exorcism ceremony where a circle is created and eventually the spirit exorcised from within it. Indeed, the presence of a Southwell on the stage, explicitly named, was contentious to say the least. Robert Southwell was a leading poet and Jesuit – the sect formed in the Counter-Reformation in Europe which denounced the double standards of the old church but still remained resolutely Catholic. He was in hiding in London at the time this play was written but a few years later was eventually captured by the notorious Richard Topcliffe, William Cecil's chief enforcer. He was tortured mercilessly but would not talk and so was tried and found guilty of treason in 1595. To the Catholic community he instantly became a martyr to their increasingly desperate cause.

To have witchcraft portrayed on stage was bad enough, but to have a Southwell doing it was even worse. As ever, Shakespeare can claim deniability by claiming his historical sources as fact, but typically he chooses to focus the lens directly on it.

His facts were right, however: Eleanor was indeed condemned with three 'witches', Jourdayne, Bullingbrook and Southwell, who were convicted and put to death. Eleanor was given life banishment, by dint of her status. She was sent to Leeds Castle and then imprisoned in the crypt under Peel Church in the Isle of Man where she died twelve years later. According to the local folklore of both Leeds Castle and Peel Church, both places are haunted by a Black Dog.

The scene takes place at the Gloucesters' royal residence at Greenwich. Humphrey built his own palace there, Bella Court, on the grounds of which he built a fortress which is now long gone, but the Observatory stands there today. At Bella Court 160 years later, King James's wife, Anne, Princess of Denmark, commissioned the beautiful

Queen's House that still stands wonderfully proportioned and flanked by its newer minders of the Naval College buildings. I have often stood amongst the hummocks and hollows of Greenwich Park – evidence of the Danish occupation here 1,300 years ago – and marvelled at the grand sweep of landscape, history and art.

It is also nice to think that on the spot where all the horses in the Olympics trotted and danced their way to victory in front of the Queen's House, there may have been some dabbling in the dark arts 600 years before. It is now the place where Time comes full circle every day.

For Shakespeare's Eleanor, time has run out. Asnath, the 'spirit', is busy predicting the future when the Lords of England storm in and arrest them. The all-seeing State has stamped the ungodly insurrection in its tracks but not before Shakespeare has shown the creepy crawlies scurrying from the light when the rock is lifted from the soil.

However, the first to fall into the Stygian river bordered by White and Red Roses was the mighty Duke of Gloucester, and with him the memory of Henry V. Gloucester had been fighting a losing battle ever since his elder brother, Bedford, died in Rouen in 1435. The wind in the English sails in France was seeping away, and all those on Cardinal Winchester's side that promoted peace and a secure economy at home were winning hands down. Agincourt was a distant memory. Indeed, in Gloucester's final scene, the hapless Duke of Somerset arrives at the scheming, internecine Court to declare of France to the King:

Somerset
… all your interest in those territories
Is utterly bereft you: all is lost.

King Henry VI
Cold news, Lord Somerset: but God's will be done.
(Henry VI Part 2 Act 3 Sc. 1)

WHAT?!

I think back to Harfleur, when Geoffrey and I stood on the white walls, pootling about amongst the bleached debris: Henry V's dreams, broken and empty. Thirty years and they were gone.

The stage was now set for England to turn from its neighbour and tear itself apart.

Seven

Bury St. Edmunds

I am reminded of the walls at Harfleur when I sit within the ruins of the Abbey at Bury St. Edmunds, in East Anglia, that housed the Court Assembly hosted by the Duke of Suffolk in 1447. Slap in the middle of the small city, all that is really left of the place are two fine gatehouses that appear like remaining teeth in an old, old mouth. But this is no Pontefract, forgotten and lost. The gardens that range around the broken walls and mounds are beautifully laid out and colour a deep sense of cherished History. Though ruined, the Abbey seems an integral and loved part of the city.

It was founded in honour of St. Edmund, a regional King who fought and died for his beloved Anglia against the marauding Danes, and whose cause was taken up by the Kingdom of Wessex against the Danes in the 900s, and thus became the patron saint of new Angleland, England, long into the Middle Ages. The Abbey was at one time spectacularly rich, even running the Royal Mint in the 1300s, and as a consequence was stormed and rebuilt every so often by the penniless workers who lived in the growing town around it. But it was all pulled down in the Dissolution of the Monasteries by Henry VIII whose sister, Mary Tudor (progenitor of the Suffolk line that had a claim to Elizabeth's throne), was buried here and whose body, in a fit of guilt, he had reinterred at a church around the corner.

But the Abbey legacy lives on. It had its own brewery, as the monks were on a strict diet of eight pints a day. It's a wonder how they built anything at all, but the Greene King Brewery is still a major presence in the small town – its huge vats clearly visible, steaming and glinting in the evening sun. There's also a large sugar factory here, so at times the town smells like it has just had the biggest party you could ever imagine. In a wonderfully symbiotic quirk of fate, the Brewery still owns the Theatre which toils away beside the ale. I have performed there a number of times and its fine Georgian architecture gives an intimacy, and genteelness, that belies the nature of the building next door.

Perhaps all this is why the ruins of the Abbey are still so looked after. It is a warm, summer evening when I sit in the Abbey confines and I decide to walk into town. Cobblestones clothe the inevitable car park that bounds the Abbey walls and spread up through interesting, prosperous old streets into market squares filled with traders packing up at the end of the day. The money that the mediaeval rioters so lacked is very much in evidence now – a more prosperous place you could barely wish for. It's on the commuter belt to London and is still making money from its beer and sugar. The red brick and white flintstone buildings that so colour the East of England are mellow and pastel in the evening sun, glowing like embers on the rich fire of old Albion.

It is incredibly easy to imagine the scene here in 1447 when the Duke of Gloucester, his wife recently exiled, arrived at a Court convened in the heartlands of the Duke of Suffolk to be arrested for plotting illegally against the Crown. Even Richard Plantagenet, Duke of York pitched in to damn him. The downfall of the last surviving son of Henry Bolingbroke was complete.

No historian can say whether Gloucester died of a heart attack or whether he was poisoned, but he died in his bed in Bury St. Edmunds a broken man. He may have been bullish, pompous and self-serving but then most of the English Lords of that time were. Some might say they still are. But the overall impression is of a man in tune with his people desperately fighting for his brother's dream, holding his arms aloft and shouting to the very end, borne down by the sharks that circled him. Perhaps that is why Shakespeare's sources such as Holinshed, Hall and Fabyan portrayed him as 'good' Duke Humphrey. By the time they were writing, in the early Tudor era it was handy to write some good things about a Lancastrian as their King had claimed the Crown representing them. For Shakespeare, a tolerant Duke Humphrey lacked cunning in the new Machiavellian world. Bulls have no power against the musket.

For Winchester especially, Gloucester's death was a valedictory moment. His old foe from the death of Henry V onwards was finally put to rest, yet both he and Gloucester were dinosaurs from another era. More importantly, they were Lancastrian dinosaurs. Winchester, one of the bastard Beaufort sons of John of Gaunt, was only powerful so long as a Lancastrian remained King. He, too, did not bargain on the clever ruthlessness of the new generation coming through or on the pull of the White Rose.

One of those White Roses, the Earl of Warwick, was in no mood to hang about. In the play, word gets out amongst the people of Bury St Edmunds that the 'good' Duke is dead and they are after Suffolk and the Cardinal Winchester's blood – pinning the crime directly on the Red Rose side. Warwick skips onto the stage having pacified the mob and proceeds to impersonate the finest Columbo in the mediaeval era. He even goes so far as to bring the bulging-eyed corpse of Gloucester onstage – an act of bravado of which Peter Falk would have been proud and that proves Gloucester didn't die peacefully in his sleep. Henry is convinced and knows full well who is responsible. He turns to Suffolk, promptly banishes him, and walks off congratulating Warwick. Just like that.

For Suffolk, a man at the height of his powers, it is a long way to fall. There is nothing he can do and bidding goodbye to his Queen and lover, his rage is impotent and absolute. Such was the price of ambition.

For the Bishop of Winchester – the most ambitious churchman of his time – life just wasn't the same without his old sparring partner. For Shakespeare, Winchester cannot survive without Gloucester. Back in his Palace, the Bishop takes to his bed and never leaves it. Here, writhing in agony and having horrific visions of Gloucester, he is visited by the King. In his death pangs he confesses to complicity in Gloucester's death.

> **King Henry VI**
> *Ah, what a sign it is of evil life*
> *Where death's approach is seen so terrible...*
> *Lord Cardinal, if thou think'st on heaven's bliss,*
> *Hold up thy hand, make signal of thy hope.*
> *He dies and makes no sign: O God forgive him.*

Here we have a Cardinal – a high priest of Catholicism – paying the price for a scheming, bloated life of high living and immorality. Just what the Protestants enjoyed.

> **Warwick**
> *So bad a death argues a monstrous life.*

And yet:

> **King Henry VI**
> *Forbear to judge for we are sinners all.*
>
> *(Henry VI Part 2 Act 3 Sc. 3)*

Those in the audience who fought for tolerance of religious worship could begin to like this boy King.

In reality, once Gloucester and Winchester had died, Suffolk became astonishingly powerful, virtually running the country single-handedly for three years. He almost completely ignored the Regency Council, and young Henry VI was powerless or too weak-willed, probably both, to do anything about it. The country was broke, merchants heavily taxed, and the Lords that followed Suffolk profited inexorably from the public's decline. Inevitably the tide of public opinion rose against Suffolk until he was solely labelled with losing France, murdering Gloucester and having an affair with the Queen. His subsequent banishment by a King with no more cards to play laid him completely without protection, and his murder on a boat crossing the Channel was simple and almost inevitable.

In four generations, the de la Pole family had risen from merchants to the power behind the throne. In one over-reaching instant Jackanapes was gone.

And yet. His extraordinary deeds were enough to graft his genes to the English Rose forever. The night before he surrendered to Joan of Arc in 1429 he had managed to de-frock a nun, Malyne de Cay, and through the ensuing daughter, Jane de la Pole, various offspring eventually married back into the great Talbot line and the Earls of Shrewsbury. Also, his legitimate sons (by Alice Chaucer, granddaughter of the poet) switched sides and ended up fighting for the White Rose – Suffolk's grandson was even declared heir to the throne by his uncle Richard III, and became a figurehead for those who opposed Henry Tudor after Bosworth.

I walk back to the grounds of the Abbey in Bury St. Edmunds with the high evening sun colouring the tumbledown walls that heard the Assembly in 1447. The walls are a stark example of what took place during the Reformation. The Abbey itself, its surrounding lands, and the town it owned, had been a Liberty which therefore ruled itself, and the pre-Reformation Crown had no choice but to sit back and watch the inevitable and dangerous mêlée: England's soul, bloated by years of rule by Abbeys such as this one, was in desperate need of Reform.

However corrupt and avaricious the Church had become, it is nice to think that even though the Abbey was taken away, the town still has the best bits left over – the brewery, the theatre and sugar are woven into its modern-day prosperity. Like a lot of towns in England, Bury

St. Edmunds was founded upon the fruits of the land – drinking and playing. I love it.

The Duke of Suffolk is buried in Wingfield – twenty miles away on the Suffolk/Norfolk border, as if permanently standing guard. The sun finally sets on the Abbey in Bury St. Edmunds as I walk to the Rose & Crown. I toast the sly old fox's memory, and the Abbey that originally brewed the ale I am drinking now, and the fact that corrupt, avaricious, seemingly intractable corporations can be brought down.

Eight

Stratford-upon-Avon sits in the bowl created by the Cotswolds and Meon Hill in the distance, and the rising fields of the Welcombe Hills, round the back of Clopton House nearby, where the tell-tale marks of Saxon and mediaeval farming still stripe the ground like lines on an ancient face. Ridges and furrows, put there by oxen year after year, are carved out of the earth and have yet to be wiped clean by History.

It is a public place, bequeathed to the people of Stratford-upon-Avon when the final owner of all this land and Clopton House itself, Lady Beecham, shuffled off in the 1970s. The ridges and furrows have primarily remained because by and large through History this place has been under the stewardship of one family or another residing at Clopton since mediaeval times.

Lady Beecham once claimed that Shakespeare got married in the secret Catholic chapel that existed here for many years – a bricked-up rose window tucked away behind a wardrobe in the top floor is the only evidence of the chapel now – and whether or not this is true we shall probably never know. But it is not too fanciful to think that the reason why the land outside has remained the same is in some small part down to Shakespeare. By the mid-1500s all land was owned by the aristocracy, or the Church, or the increasingly wealthy merchant class rising up the ranks. A fact some of the aristocracy are still bemoaning 500 years on. One of the few facts we know about Shakespeare is that by the time he had made his fortune in London in the early 1600s, he had a share, or tithe, in some of the land at Welcombe co-owned by the Clopton family. The combined landowners wished to enclose the land. This meant turfing off the resident farmers who eked out a living from these ancient strips, then planting hedges, and filling the resultant fields with more profitable sheep and livestock. It turns out it may have been Shakespeare who flatly refused. There is a quotation attributed to him that he could not 'beare the encloseing of Welcombe.' It is hotly debated – as is everything else about Shakespeare – but the fact that the land is still there, pretty much as it was, is testament to the fact it was never enclosed.

The economy of progress versus the needs of people on the ground is not a new phenomenon – the avaricious snatching of the ruling and mercantile classes is clearly laid out in the tapestry of England. As I look from the Welcombe Hills the patchwork canopy that enclosure created is spread beautifully across the hills into the distance. To the north, the Forest of Arden is long gone. Looking down the hill I can see the vast ugly bulk of three or four supermarkets, or 'out of town' shopping centres, spreading from the town like fat white leeches. The desperate farmers who supply the milk at a loss are picketing them. The faceless corporate rape of the land, and those who work it, goes on.

So I have some degree of sympathy for the poor man in Shakespeare's play who, like the modern-day dairy farmers, has come to petition fruitlessly against the enclosure of his lands. It is just one of the many examples in this particular play where the common people form the Breughelesque, even Bosch-like, background with which he paints his picture. It was a dubious *carnivale* in London that greeted the young playwright from the provinces.

Ale. Obviously it's a drink and most violence in England still emanates from the vast quantities downed on a weekend. Back in mediaeval times it was about the only thing you could drink as the water was rank and likely to send you to the privvy quicker than ten pints of ale may do the next morning. The word *ale*, however, was used as a suffix – the Parish-Ale, for example, was a get-together where ale was brewed for the celebration of the Parish, and a Church-Ale did the same. Whitsun-ale, lamb-ale (at lamb-shearing time), clerk-ale and leet-ale all were regular and important parts of the mediaeval world, and used chiefly as a mode for the community to come together, spread a little money around and party. The Bride-Ale, at a wedding, performed the same function – from which the word *bridal* comes.

The words *festival* and *carnival* have similar etymology, but their much-argued roots stem from deeper meanings combined with the ancient European traditions of ritual, community and magic. The *ale* or *-al* suffix may well even come from the *Lupercal* – the cave in which Romulus and Remus were suckled. The *Lupercallia* was a great Roman festival that lasted two days from February 13th to 15th in which the goat of fertility was ritually sacrificed, which is why Valentine's Day is where it is. (The *Lupercallia* replaced an even older fertility rite called the *Februa* from which we get the name of the month.) *Carnivale* traditionally takes place before Lent in February and is rooted in either celebrating the last of the meat before fasting, or eating each other carnally as Winter ends and the Spring approaches.

Either way, the great festivals of flesh and madness that still sweep through our hearts whether it be Glastonbury, the Olympics, May Day or Dover's Hill, danced and sang their way around Europe for centuries, delighting the people and terrifying the authorities. Based on the old shamanistic traditions of the Green Man in the forest and dancing in the face of him, the chief aim of *ale* was to confirm and celebrate our identity, our community. To thank the Land, not the Lord, for keeping us alive. To give us light, to strengthen ourselves together, to say 'It's all right.' To banish our collective fear of the rustling leaves in the forest, the heart of darkness, the black hole in our minds: Khaos, the gaping void. The Green Man. The red eyes of the Devil. The Lord of Misrule. By becoming *him*, acting him out, we could make him real, laugh at *it*, conquer it.

The inherent problem with that, of course, is that it is indeed about misrule. During Carnival all rules of society would be stripped apart. The Green Man is about fertility as well as Chaos, so at all the Ales which the community shared, fornication and drunkenness, even violence, were openly permitted or at least a blind eye turned. The game of football sprang from just such a root. Performances of stories, religious or otherwise, were joyously heralded and the towns, villages and fields filled the air with life. The peasants would dress as Lords, men as women, and vice versa. It was life-affirming in all its sweaty, community-filled, orgiastic glory, like the pantomimes that are their bawdy inheritors.

Carnival was fine if the strict template of society was in place. The feudal system – where the Lords and commoners knew their social strata and stuck to it – was perfect. But with the gradual dismantling of society and the new wealthy middle class enclosing land, community was bunk as well as history.

As a consequence, people filed to the towns in search of money and survival. During Carnival, those people that had once overdone it or acted destructively could no longer be held in check by their peers who knew their mothers, brothers or friends. Anonymity became a cloak behind which many a dark heart could retreat. The rustling leaves in the forest became the people themselves, creeping between the buildings. Ale, Festival and Carnival, instead of being a celebration and usefully tolerated by those Lords in power, now became a threat. The Lord of Misrule was not only feared by the Authorities, it was feared by itself.

Theatres were a way of bottling the now terrifying anonymity of the new Carnival and keeping it safe, just about. It became the setting for its own carnival every day. It's not called a 'play' for nothing. Within the theatre walls anything could happen. The groundlings festering in the front, and the monied ranks sat behind them rattling their jewellery, were all in the same place experiencing the same play. *Misrule* was standing on stage arms outstretched, tongue lapping, firmly inviting everybody to the party. There is no distinction between an audience and a crowd apart from the walls of a theatre.

Theatre, in its history of *ale*, *festival* and *carnival*, the rejoicing of the land, community and misrule, is a perfect distillation of time and England. It is not a luxury. It is vital.

Which is why Queen Elizabeth I so loved and hated it at the same time. It was constantly being closed down and yet performed privately at Court. Plague was very often the excuse, but the overriding sense of fear of the madding crowd packed into these new theatres is palpable. It was justified: Riots, much more than infection, did indeed emanate from these new-found places where people were crammed so close together. The civic authorities hated it and yet actors performed with a Royal Licence that exempted them from the Vagabonds Act of 1572, which declared that *'all fencers, bearwards, common players of interludes, and minstrels (not belonging to any baron of this realm, or to any other honourable person of greater degree), wandering abroad without the license of two justices at the least, were subject to be grievously whipped and burned through the gristle of the right ear with a hot iron of the compass of an inch about.'* Harsh for telling a story or singing a song, but that's what fear of rustling leaves in the dark of the forest does for you.

So as a country boy, perhaps it's no surprise that in Shakespeare's first great play we see him place *misrule* centre stage in the form of the great ringmaster himself, Jack Cade. Having set the play from the viewpoint of the privileged Kings, Dukes and Lords that so often are the sedan chairs of History, Shakespeare tips them out and gives us the bloody, sweaty, filthy trail upon which they travelled. He gives us the heart of darkness.

Jack Cade, a man of Kent, is about to riot his way to the White Hart.

Southwark and the City

I'm heading into London late on a Saturday night after a show and it is like being in a forest at night with leaves rustling in the dark. However, this is no imaginary threat as I know something real and dangerous is actually there. As I drive through town the beast of the urban forest appears: faceless, masked men run ducking through orange. The stark smell of smoke, cordite and fear in the air is terrifying. A strange yellow, simmering emptiness. Thankfully I see not a single act of violence but its aftermath lies scattered and etched into the streets. Barracked into my friend's flat, the blighted, burning wasteland that is the High Street at the end of his road feels like a cork keeping us in a hellish bottle.

There seems to be no one specific reason why people riot, whether it be through fear, malevolence or ignorance. The times dictate. But it is usually impotence. Impotence in the face of poverty, government (religious or otherwise) or corporation. Shakespeare was no stranger to rioting as the Elizabethans, especially Londoners, were fond of exploding into violence at a moment's notice. The mediaeval era was not only fond of a riot, they very often escalated into full-scale rebellion.

In 1450, England was broke. The old Suffolk/Winchester/Somerset/Margaret faction that favoured cessation of the war, and lorded it over a weak and ineffectual King, had feathered their own nest with such impunity for so long, they were as corrupt as the bankers or corporations are perceived to be today. To sue to France for peace was just about understandable if you had no money, but when the money that was left was used for the Lords' own purposes, it was tantamount to treason. For that the country finally rose up.

It was easy for Richard Plantagenet, Duke of York. He simply painted himself as someone who cared for the country and could run it. With Gloucester gone, only York stood up for firm governance, law and order, and a strong England that could happily give France a good slap. The people, especially Londoners, loved him as a consequence.

Having been kept out of trouble by being packed off to Ireland by the ruling faction, York was now much stronger with Suffolk and Winchester gone. As Suffolk's body washed up on the shores of Kent, it seemed somehow to ignite the penniless and defeated soldiers that landed from a resurgent France. Every step that took them to London increased their fury and played perfectly into the hands of York.

In May, a group of sheriffs and aldermen fuelled by the rage of national disgrace, met in Ashford in Kent and very quickly elected as their leader a man called Jack Cade – a prosperous gentleman of intelligence and experience, who may well have fought in France, such was his military expertise. Perceived as a man of integrity, his standing in the community landed him the part and he proceeded to operate with strict discipline on his motley bunch of rebels. Nothing was to be taken, no rioting or looting was to take place, and he hanged those that stepped out of line.

By the time they marched to London and stopped at Blackheath, the band of 5,000 men included MPs, knights, sheriffs, squires and even a man who had fought at Agincourt. Their demands were simply the removal of all the King's Suffolk-led advisors; restrictions on government spending which would reduce penal taxes; and an entire review of the judicial system to avoid corruption and bribery. So far, so decent. It has a ring of today about it.

But then Cade changed his name to John *Mortimer*.

No one knows whether the Duke of York was actually involved with this rebellion or not, but the fact that Cade felt able to call himself such a provocative name – recalling the family with the superior claim to the throne – meant that the finger was duly pointed in York's direction.

The King had no doubts that York was behind it all and resolved that these rebels wanted to supplant him. Luckily, he was in Council at the time in Leicester and managed to secure the help of all his favoured Lords in gathering a swift and effective army. Showing uncharacteristic decisiveness, he marched to London and placed 20,000 men on the north bank of the Thames by London Bridge, with even the people of London arranging a bristling flotilla pointing south towards Kent.

Cade knew when to retreat gracefully, and he pulled back to Sevenoaks, there to assess Henry's next move. In response, Henry led his army over London Bridge and prepared to descend upon the rebels in the true spirit of his father. But Queen Margaret could not bear to see her diddums husband go into battle, so in what could have been a final bid for effective leadership he failed spectacularly. He split his army into two, deciding to stay with his half in London and sent Sir Humphrey Stafford with the rest of the army to issue terms to Cade at Sevenoaks.

Seizing his opportunity, the battle-hardened Cade tore them apart. Henry's disaffected men promptly switched sides and with his army swollen by more popular opinion from Sussex and Surrey, Cade swiftly headed back to London. He swept through Blackheath and, with no little disregard for its meaning, made his headquarters at The White Hart in Southwark. Henry, Margaret and the Court fled to Kenilworth.

The White Hart is not there anymore – it was pulled down in the 1800s but not before it appeared in the Pickwick Papers by Dickens, another man of Kent. The George Inn, next door, on what is now Borough High Street, gives a good example of the kind of place it was

– although rebuilt in 1676, it is a huge coaching inn that would have been the main stop on the journey to London from the South East, the equivalent of a train terminus now. The Tabard, where Chaucer left for Canterbury, used to be a few doors down.

Four days after the riots in London that so inflamed the nation, The George is where I go now to sit and have a pint. It's a beautiful place with layered wooden galleries and satisfyingly creaky floors. It is crowded on all sides by the monotony of office blocks pushing in at it, but it does at least have a little courtyard in which to breathe. Inside, cloistered rooms smell of beer, woodsmoke and polished varnish. In winter, the mulled wine and the many-paned windows steam up the outside world into a cosy, fuzzy focus. The trouble is it's full of bankers.

Get to The George just after work and you haven't a prayer of getting a pint. Its proximity to London Bridge railway station means it is still fulfilling its function, after all these years, by lubricating the travellers that head South-East from London. I'm there at four o'clock, but they all seem to knock off early these days. Perhaps there's not much to do in banking apart from replace the windows. The swaggering talk of the Futures market is excruciating, so I leave – past all the commuters and three boarded-up shops – to walk over London Bridge to The Guildhall.

This was not such an easy option for Jack Cade, still calling himself Lord Mortimer, who camped out at The White Hart waiting to see how he could negotiate the drawbridge at the southern end of London Bridge which was hoisted firmly closed against him. It was the only bridge at the time, and the houses and shops that lay along its breadth must have smelt the hordes massing meters away with their mix of swords, meathooks and pitchforks. But the force was with Cade by now, and the next day even rebels from Essex turned up at the Aldgate. So the Mayor of London, urged on by Cade's supporters within the City, finally relented and ordered the drawbridge to be lowered. In came Cade, unchallenged and cheered by the people of London. Wearing the knight's spurs of Sir Humphrey Stafford, he went to the London Stone near Cannon Street and exclaimed, 'Now is Mortimer lord of this city!'

Cade's vengeance on the money men and advisors that had brought the country to its knees sliced through the City. Lord Say, one of Suffolk's greatest advocates, who as Treasurer of England was utterly ruthless and self-serving, was released from the Tower where he had taken refuge and dragged by Cade along with twenty others to The

Guildhall to be tried. When Say refused to honour the validity of the Court, he was summarily beheaded. So too was William Crowmer, the Sheriff of Kent, and both their heads were placed on spears and made to kiss.

Standing at The Guildhall now, I watch the serried ranks of suits filing past me. Unlike Southwark back over the river, the streets have been cleaned up and the windows seem intact. Deep in the heart of the City – no longer the beating, living centre of London, but just the money-making part – the present building of The Guildhall was only ten years old when Cade held his session here in 1450. The Guildhall stands as a bastion of 'The London Corporation' which proudly boasts its heritage of hosting nearly 600 years of corporate events. How lovely. Although to some this may be the definition of Purgatory, it is as important a cog in the machinery of England as Royalty or the peasants. None could have happened without the other.

They still don't let me in, though. I look around and idly picture for a moment the sight of two modern bankers' heads kissing on spikes as the evermore crazed hordes, drunk on success, shout and leer in an expurgation of hate, jealousy and impotent rage made real. In my imagination, at least, it's surprisingly easy to picture. The Guildhall is an extraordinary-looking place – reminiscent of a small Gothic cathedral. It has a metal spire only reaching a few meters rather than the hundreds of feet of somewhere like Rouen Cathedral, as if acknowledging that they weren't too bothered. In a time when the country has once more been brought to its knees by greed and corruption, this place at the centre of the Square Mile has come in for much abuse. The bland materialism that emanates from here, that so patronises both the haves and have-nots, and lies like a blanket over the towns and cities, stifling any individual expression into impotent, riot-making rage, is palpable.

Though the image of two severed bankers' heads satisfies me for a second, it also sends shivers down my spine. Whatever combination of political and financial meltdown, private pain, and materialism that led to the riots of 2011, I think back to the fear I felt at the end of the road where I was staying. When we staged The Histories all the people that fuelled the rebellion were a strange mish-mash of ghosts from previous plays and elements united in their rage against the collapse and abuse of their society. We even had a modern-day banker in a suit that we dragged from the audience and hung on stage. I think back to the burning images of hooded thieves stealing televisions from smoking shops, and shudder. The streets of England are lined with enough scars.

The problem was, Cade was human. All the thousand natural shocks that flesh is heir to cannot be smothered by the mob or materialism. Cade went wild. Empowered by his own prowess, the looting crowd that was sitting just under the surface of his disciplined leadership now began to spill like molten lava. The streets began to run not with red wine, as he had suggested, but blood. Caught up in the moment, he looted jewels that ultimately belonged to the Duke of York and once his followers saw this they either started tearing up the city or, as the Londoners did, stopped dead in their tracks and beheld the animal they had unleashed on their city.

Having gone back over the river to The White Hart to rest and presumably lick the slaver from his foaming mouth, the Londoners dashed over the bridge and tried to raise the drawbridge. There then followed a huge fight that lasted all night in the cramped confines of the shops and houses lining the bridge. At times it was only about eight feet wide and the carnage must have been awful, with reports of mothers and children leaping from their homes into the water.

Cade eventually blew up the drawbridge, thereby separating the two forces and calling a halt to the fight. Two hundred Kentish men were dead and forty-two Londoners. The damage had been done, and the air began to seep from his tyres very quickly. Sensing this, the Queen and several bishops finally arranged for a Cardinal to parley with Cade, and pardons were drawn up for him and all his men.

He withdrew to Rochester to regroup, but retribution was swift. He was hounded out of town, this time by his own people and his pardon was withdrawn as it was in the name of John Mortimer not Jack Cade. Hunted down to a garden by a Sheriff of Kent named Iden, he was set upon and killed like the bankers before him.

The rather extraordinary thing about Shakespeare's representation of Cade's rebellion is that it sticks fairly closely to the truth. He didn't have to layer, codify or embellish anything. In Cade he could see a perfect parable for mob rule. True, he makes Cade more of a 'common' man, more rising from the gutter, but in Cade's actions Shakespeare follows the script perfectly. He gives us the speeches and wildfire that everyone wants to hear ('Let's kill all the lawyers'), and at times it feels like a manifesto that Marx might write 300 years later.

Shakespeare unsurprisingly makes the garden in which Cade dies Iden's own garden. Into this man's mouth who has the surname very close to that of Adam's garden, he puts the manifesto of middle England:

Sir Alexander Iden

Lord, who would live turmoiled in the court,
And may enjoy such quiet walks as these?
This small inheritance my father left me
Contenteth me, and worth a monarchy.
I seek not to wax great by others' waning,
Or gather wealth I care not with what envy:
Sufficeth that I have maintains my state
And sends the poor well pleased from my gate.

Jack Cade, like a wasted Johnny Rotten, is flinging words at middle England as much as his sword:

Cade

...I'll make thee eat iron like an ostrich, and swallow my sword like a great pin ere thou and I part...

Iden promptly beats the famished and spent common man of England upon whose bones new Jerusalem is built.

Cade

O, I am slain!... Wither garden, and be henceforth a burying place to all that do dwell in this house, because the unconquered soul of Cade is fled.

(Henry VI Part 2 Act 4 Sc. 10)

That soul of Cade is still there, unconquered.

I leave the monied, over-reaching spires of the Guildhall where on this very spot the Treasurer of England was beheaded for misgovernment. With a final shiver of fear, I head for the train.

Nine

St. Albans

St. Albans is defined by the road around which it was built and its proximity to London – a day's horse ride away. It formed the first or last stop on the great Roman Road through England, Watling Street, that Falstaff and his ailing crew staggered up on their way to Shrewsbury from Eastcheap. The architecture of pebble, flint and brick is similar to the east of England, yet it sits firmly on the dividing line between east and west that is the Roman Road. It is about ten miles east of Eden, or King's Langley as it's known, and it was here in St. Albans' streets that the first blood in the battle between York and Lancaster was drawn.

Nobody knows whether York wanted to be King all along and was merely playing an exceptionally long and clever game, an almost real-life chess. The bottom line is that he marched on the King – ostensibly to rid him of his corrupt and inefficient advisers that were bringing the country to its knees, chief among them the Duke of Somerset. But he still marched on his own King.

Whichever way, Shakespeare's York can finally speak his mind.

> **York**
> *False King, why hast thou broken faith with me*
> *Knowing how hardly I can brook abuse?*
> *King did I call thee? No, thou art not King:*
> *Not fit to govern and rule multitudes*
> *Which dar'st not, no, nor canst not rule a traitor.*
> *That head of thine doth not become a crown...*
> *That gold must round engirt these brows of mine...*
> *Give place. By heaven that shalt rule no more*
> *O'er him whom heaven created for thy ruler.*
>
> *(Henry VI Part 2 Act 5 Sc. 1)*

And relax.

Standing on stage as Somerset, I could always feel the audience exhale. All the built-up tension of York's path to power, which had started a play and a half ago, was released. For an audience in Elizabethan London who were not even allowed to talk of the succession – with all the tension of what the future may hold, it must have seemed a heady fantasy.

York's rebellion may actually have been put down by Henry and Margaret, had it not been for the Earl of Warwick whose pockets overflowed with the bounty of inheritance. His hand, though, was forced by the corruption and greed of Henry's councillors to act on York's behalf. Once he and his father, the Earl of Salisbury, turned to York, the Lancasters had a fight on their hands. So for the Elizabethan audience quivering in the stalls, the stage was literally set for an almighty showdown between the peers – some of whose descendants were sitting behind them in the expensive seats. They, too, would have sat forward with interest as the open wound of England was now to be exposed.

But Shakespeare seems concerned with another kind of Elizabethan allegiance:

> **Salisbury**
> *My Lord, I have considered with myself*
> *The title of this most renowned Duke*
> *And in my conscience do repute his grace*
> *The rightful heir to England's royal seat.*
>
> **King Henry VI**
> *Has thou not sworn allegiance unto me?*
>
> **Salisbury**
> *I have*
>
> **King Henry VI**
> *Canst thou dispense with heaven for such an oath?*
>
> **Salisbury**
> *It is great sin to swear unto a sin:*
> *But greater sin to swear unto a sinful oath:*
> *Who can be bound by any solemn vow*
> *To do a murd'rous deed, to rob a man...*
> *And have no other reason for this wrong*
> *But that he was bound by a solemn oath?*
>
> *(Henry VI Part 2 Act 5 Sc. 1)*

In one speech, the Oath of Supremacy that subjects took to Elizabeth as head of the Church of England, was side-stepped. The safety of the theatre, the *carnival*, gave the man who came from the fracture of England the wherewithal to hold up the broken mirror of his country to his audience and scream like the Green Man from behind it.

Although one tends to think of mediaeval battles as taking place on vast plains, the Battle of St. Albans was fought in the cramped confines of the streets around the Town Square. Henry and his force of a few thousand men stopped in the city, so York placed his own army just outside whilst the two sides parleyed. The inexperienced Henry was not even present at the parley and sat in full armour on his horse by his Standard, alone in the middle of the Square. With a customary instinct for doing exactly the wrong thing at the wrong time, he then penned a hugely belligerent and intolerant letter to York.

On reading the letter, York simply ordered an immediate attack which it seems nobody on either side was suspecting. The whole thing lasted about half an hour. The Yorkist forces fell onto the makeshift defences to the east of the Square and were soon locked into a stalemate in the small, cowering streets. So Warwick led his forces around the side of the city and attacked the Lancastrians who were still putting their armour on and having a fag or whatever it was they were doing. Breaking into the Square, the Yorkists showered them with arrows and then cut them down mercilessly.

Henry never moved a muscle. Surrounded by a special guard, he sat on his, no doubt, rather twitchy horse, with arrows raining down around him and bouncing off his armour, until he got shot in the neck. He was bundled off to a blacksmith's to be treated. At least he and his father could share the fact that they'd both caught an arrow in the head at one stage of their lives. No wonder he lost his mind.

With the King struck down, everyone else fled and the swords fell silent. Two hundred of Henry's men and about seventy of York's force lay strewn around the cobbles, among them the Duke of Somerset – the reason York marched on the King in the first place. He was killed outside the Castle Inn, fulfilling a prophecy (Shakespeare makes it the witch Margery Jourdayne's prophecy) that he should beware of castles. Lord Clifford was also killed. Their two bereaved and angry sons, Young Clifford and Young Somerset, would form the backbone of the Lancastrian fight for the next twenty years.

St. Albans is a very lovely place in late afternoon in summer. The red buildings shimmer and glow in the old warmth of the sun and each building seems very particular if you lift your head up above the bland uniformity that has painted over our high streets in the last forty years or so. The old, old buildings that huddle in the Square are drenched in identikit coffee shops and the usual cack. Another battle is raging in the streets of St. Albans, as in every other town: that of the individual shopkeeper and fruit-stall holder against the imperial juggernaut of global commercialism. It's as insidious, whitewashing and all-encompassing as any Reformation, and is rapidly being shown to be as corrupt as any pre-Reformation Catholic Church. If Shakespeare was to walk past his own birthplace in Stratford-upon-Avon and see the empty shops on the High Street like broken teeth on a beautiful face, and witness the creeping monotony of chain stores wiping society cleaner than the walls of the Guild Chapel, he may have tossed away his quill and not bothered.

Yet there is release. As I walk down the hill through the small alleyways and sweet resistance of little shops selling jewellery and life, my spirits begin to soar with the sun that shines on the vast red and white bulk of the cathedral towering over this part of town.

It really is two-tone. It's as if the cathedral starts off in the East of England and ends up in the West. The tower is ancient red stone with flint and pebble, while the West front and the Lady Chapel is built with bright stone as if to signify the White of the patron saint from whom the city took its name, Saint Alban. He was the first martyr of these isles, who lived here in the Roman settlement of Verulanum and had his head lopped off for believing in Christianity. The colours and the sun render the whole building spectacular, whilst the archways as you enter are more redolent of the Moorish buildings in Spain than any Christian church. Its Evensong and the choir, like Coventry, are outnumbering the congregation but filling the walls with such beautiful music, I could weep. The notes wash through me. The mediaeval paintings and the blue figures of saints and knights that fill the altar screen somehow seem unusual and exotic compared to other Anglican cathedrals. How the place has survived is a mystery – earthquakes, the Dissolution and various crazy-minded architects have all done their best to ruin the place, but as a consequence it has an anarchic charm all of its own.

Which could be said of the late Humphrey, Duke of Gloucester, who is buried here and whose casket you can see down some steep little stairs in a crypt next to the shrine of Saint Alban. His casket is covered in a red cloth patterned with a golden cross and the coat of arms of the Fleur-de-Lys and the Three Lions. Its simplicity makes it very present. The chants of Evensong carry on around Humphrey and I, the colours in this extraordinary building fizzing and bleeding, coming to life. I find myself very moved, looking through this grill into Gloucester's crypt – lost in Agincourt, Greenwich and Bury St. Edmunds – moving through Time with the man who tried vainly to keep his brother's spirit alive.

Once more Time runs out on me because when I finally get back to the twenty-first century the singing has stopped. I hurry to the exit but the door is locked. I like to think I am not a superstitious man but I turn from the door in mild panic, envisaging an uncomfortable night with Humphrey and Saint Alban snoozing by the altar. I make my way back through what is the longest nave in Britain, further elongated by my sweating mind. Rounding one of the huge pillars I sigh audibly with relief when I see a woman approaching me with a mildly quizzical look on her face.

'Do you know how to get out?' she says, in a rich Canadian accent.

'Shit,' I think.

Then I see a Black Dog darting into the South Transept and I nearly fart with fright. With eyes darting anxiously from side to side, arms held alert in readiness for attack, myself and the Canadian follow the beast round the corner into the deserted shop, where suddenly a woman holding a dog lead pops up like a jack-in-the-box from behind the till.

'O, you startled me,' she says breezily. The Canadian and I could quite possibly have said the same had we not been metaphorically clinging to the roof, hair like a tuning fork.

'Ha ha ha hahaha ha hoo,' I say.

'Is…is there a way out?' stammers the Canadian.

'O yes,' cries the devil-beast-shop-counter woman, 'It's just through here. You're lucky. Ha. I was just about to lock up. I usually do a trawl to see if there are any stragglers and Sooty usually lets me know.'

'Ha,' I say. 'Sooty. Ha. Ha.'

Before we leave I take a last look back as the brilliant sunset is streaming through the West windows, turning the pillars to flame. Up above the shop, high on the roof of the transept, a White Rose and a Red Rose along with the flag of St. George shimmer and turn to blood.

Outside, as the sun goes down, I can feel for the first time this summer a slight chill in the air. I walk across the Close straight into the White Hart Hotel opposite and have a pint. I need it.

I have one last place to find in St. Albans, so after my pint I walk back up to the Market Square and stand on the corner of St. Peter's Street and Victoria Street where there is a wholly unremarkable branch of a Building Society. The Castle Inn once stood here and on the wall is a plaque commemorating where Somerset was killed... Having played him for over three years of my life, I doff my cap to the venal bastard.

Next to the plaque is a window which promises an affordable loan.

Shakespeare being Shakespeare, he places the furious sword that slew Somerset into the hands of Richard, the hunchbacked and withered youngest son of York. By winning his duel with Somerset and achieving his first kill amongst the carnage of St. Albans, young Richard starts his terrifying path – the chip on his shoulder as big as his hump.

With this in mind, I walk down George Street and go for another one in the Red Lion.

Wakefield

Wandering back and forth, uninvited, around a school car park in a suburb of Wakefield is not something I recommend doing on a daily basis. I'm sure it's illegal, but I am desperately looking for a stone, a plaque, a memorial that I've been told by a guy just a mile up the road is somewhere around here. Before I am arrested, I give up and walk back up the street past the school railings and the Victorian patina of studious red-brick buildings and boiled cabbage.

But then I see it sandwiched between the school and the fence. Gothic and blackened, it matches the nineteenth century uniformity of the school, but on closer inspection the small obelisk has a strange beauty that is topped off with the white cone and frills of a caring stonemason. An inscription reads:

> *Richard Plantagenet*
> *Duke of York*
> *Fighting for the cause of the White Rose*

Fell on this spot in the Battle of Wakefield
December 30th 1460.

Some say the actual place where he fell is just up the road where the school car park sweeps out onto the road, but that would be splitting hairs. The fact remains that here on Manygates Lane, next to Manygates Education Centre, by a small municipal park and the railway line, Richard Plantagenet lost his life. On the one hand it is an incredibly inauspicious place, but walk back up the hill which once gloried in the intriguing title Cock and Bottle Lane, and there between the farmland and the suburbs are the remains of Sandal Magna – the castle owned by York as a small foothold in the Lancastrian lands that smothered most of the North. This is where Richard Of York Gave Battle In Vain.

By the time he died, Richard Plantagenet had torn England in two once more. After St. Albans there had been a period of comparative quiet whilst the two sides tried to find a way to pull back from the brink. But each extended hand of peace was accompanied by the crossed fingers of the other, and England broke apart at the seams.

By the time York made his way to the Lancastrian heartlands of the North, Margaret was in charge of most of the King's armies. She had finally given birth to a son in 1453 thereby placing another obstacle to York achieving the throne if he so desired. There had been further skirmishes, most notably a battle at Blore Heath that reversed the Yorkist victory at St. Albans and scattered the rebellion to the four winds. However, in regrouping and getting himself named as heir apparent by Parliament – dramatically staged by Shakespeare in the first scene of *Henry VI Part 3* – York had at least achieved a legal means of gaining the throne and was not going to let Margaret, her son, or any of the Lancastrians, stand in his way.

The Queen was not going to accept her son's disinheritance and moved armies to defeat the Act of Parliament that had rendered him obsolete. When Margaret sent word north to the Earl of Westmorland and Young Clifford that they should mobilize their forces, York followed right into the heart of the enemy. With hindsight it was extreme folly to do so, although admittedly it turns out he was betrayed by one of Warwick's many cousins, Lord Neville, whom York was expecting to turn up with 8,000 men.

It may well be that he thought he could use his vast military experience gained in France to outwit his inexperienced foes, but York was hopelessly outnumbered and when he and his army of men eventually shot out of the castle like Butch Cassidy and the Sundance Kid, he was butchered without mercy alongside one of his sons, the Earl of Rutland.

Sandal Castle lies now amongst the quaint housing estates and farmland that, from the top of the hill, can be seen flowing into the distance. A little car park sits snugly like a cricket ground into the housing estate and from there, closer now, you can see the gummy banks with nothing on them that formed the walls of the castle.

This place is loved, however. With the houses nuzzling up to it, it feels like the town stopped and could not bear to paper over the place. Here and there are walls and piles of stones – but not a real castle shape like Pontefract most definitely boasts. But care has been taken. Stairs have been built to take you to the top of one of the banks and from there I see two school kids who climb over the fence and use the moat as a well-trodden shortcut home. My heart soars as they stop and look at the view. I hope they know of where they are treading. They leave the castle confines and walk across a cabbage field where the battle raged so long ago.

There is a Northern expression of 'Dickie's Meadow', which basically means you're up shit creek without a paddle, and many think it originates from here. Also, the expression of a situation being a bit 'dickie', meaning 'in trouble' or 'something not quite right about it' – comes from the same derivation. There is a visitor centre, although by the time I get there at half past three it is closing, so I knock on the window and am told that I can see the memorial down the road at the school if I want. So I find myself wandering through the cabbage patch and looking for the memorial round the back of the school. Which is a dickie situation.

Once you see the memorial you can't miss it. But because it is of the same brick as the school it somehow disappears into the background like the 'Perspective' paintings so favoured in the Tudor era which depicted one thing but if looked at from another angle depicted quite a different image – like the holograms one gets in a cereal packet today.

Many people have suggested that Shakespeare's plays may well be the literary equivalent of such devices, but here on Cock and Bottle Lane, or Manygates Lane, for a brief moment, I could almost see the same in History. It is spurious to think it, of course, but had York been victorious, in one glorious moment he could have stopped the Wars of the Roses stone dead. Henry would probably have been packed off to Bedlam or a Monastery. Had York ruled with anything like the sense that he did when made Protector (whilst Henry had had a nervous breakdown), the country would have been back on its feet twenty or thirty years later. The Tudors may never have happened and William Shakespeare would have been the son of a wealthy glover in Stratford-upon-Avon who had no cause to go to London to seek his fortune because his father may not have lost the lot through paying the fines of recusancy. And I would be out of a job.

The perspective shifted back again to the real world and left me standing outside the school. The broken-down Castle beyond the cabbage patch, instead of being the new Balmoral, is windswept and forlorn, a testament to what might have been. Opposite Manygates school there is a little park with a children's play area, and it is horrible to think a thousand people died here alongside the man who gave battle in vain.

For Richard there was no pot of gold at the end of the rainbow, just a sign saying 'No Dogs Allowed.'

Startlingly true in History is that after the battle Young Clifford came across his soldiers who had placed a garland of reeds over York's bloody head. Clifford ordered that York's head be cut off and onto it placed a paper crown. Such was the price of being a loser in those days.

Shakespeare's sources, Holinshead and Hall et al, all pick up on the story and report that York's head, alongside that of his son, Rutland, were taken to the City of York where the Queen was waiting in her hive. She gave the dead Duke a slap and then ordered the head to be placed on the city walls 'So that York may overlook the town of York.' Shakespeare cannot resist such a story and runs with it: making Margaret not only present at the battle but instrumental in the desecration of humanity that is York's death. She it is who places the crown on York's head and she it is who bids him wipe his tears with a napkin bearing his son's blood, thereby sealing England's slide into a Bosch-like layer of Hell, the fall-out of which Shakespeare and his contempories were still wrestling with.

Unfortunately, Margaret was actually in Scotland at the time cosying up to its Queen, trying to garner support and money. However, the heads of York, Rutland and Warwick's father, Salisbury, were indeed placed on the Mickelgate Bar on the walls of York. A gate under which York's eighteen-year-old son, Edward, was to ride in a few bloody months' time.

Mortimer's Cross

On the monument at Manygates School there is a small stone carving of York which is based on a statue placed on the Welsh Bridge at Shrewsbury a year before his death. That bridge statue now stands on the outside of the Market Hall in the Shrewsbury, looking out over the shoppers, cobbles and Ask Pizza, and is the only statue of the man anywhere in the country. The Marches, being the home of the Mortimers from whom York was descended through his mother, were the Yorkist heartlands. From the Trent across to the Severn at Shrewsbury and thence to Bristol, the land was flooded with the White Rose.

In the castle at Shrewsbury, York's eighteen-year-old eldest son, Edward, was still celebrating Christmas when news arrived of the death of his father and brother. He is reported to have been 'wonderfully amazed' with grief at the loss. However, from being the Earl of March he was now the Duke of York. What's more, if his father may have had understandable scruples about taking the Crown from an anointed King, Edward now had no such worries. He was bent on avenging his family and putting the Lancastrians to the sword. He quickly raised a huge army amongst his loyal supporters the length and breadth of the West, and resolved to march on London as quickly as possible before Margaret could head South.

Raising an army was getting easier. This was partly because cards were finally being laid on the table but mainly since the devastating Yorkist losses at Blore Heath, Ludford Bridge and Wakefield, the Lancastrian forces had gone wild. They raped, looted and tore apart the land held so dear by York. Ludlow Castle, his famous stronghold, had been stripped and set on fire. That meant huge swathes of society south of the River Trent were not just holding a grudge about the governance of the country, they were personally bent on revenge and the defence of their homes. They considered the people of the North nothing more than savages at the best of times, but now the conception was born that this Civil War was a battle between North and South.

When Edward was crossing the Severn near Gloucester and heard that Henry VI's half brother – Jasper Tudor, Earl of Pembroke – had raised an army in Wales and was marching to meet the Queen at York, he turned back to head them off. The hardened souls of the Marches had been fighting the Welsh since the Romans left, so by the time the two armies met on the banks of the River Lugg in a Herefordshire hamlet called Mortimer's Cross, Edward's men were champing at the bit.

Pembroke and his father, Owen Tudor – the man who had sired four children with Katherine, Henry V's wife – had wished to avoid battle, but they also had to get across the river and Edward's men, all 5,000 of them, were standing in front of it.

However, at dawn just before the battle, most of Edward's army looked east and fell to their knees in fear as what is known as a 'sun dog', 'mock sun', or in scientific circles a 'parhelion', appeared in the sky. This is a rare, natural phenomenon that happens when the light of the sun streams through ice crystals in the low-lying cloud and appears to be three suns shining in the sky. Edward, too, fell to his knees but encouraged his soldiers not to fear but pray, as he took it as a sign from God of the Holy Trinity and a symbol of the three remaining sons, or suns, of York. The magic of the old lands still lived on.

Contrary to Shakespeare's portrait of the three adult sons of York seeing the parhelion together, the other brothers – George and Richard – were actually twelve and nine respectively and tucked up with their mother in London at Baynard's Castle. So Edward was on his own, facing more experienced and hardened leaders. However the indignant and desperate Yorkist army smashed the Tudor Lancastrians. Pembroke fled and left his father, Owen Tudor, to the mercy of Edward who promptly took him to Hereford and beheaded him in the market square. Of the 9,000 that took part in the battle, it is said that 4,000 died and Edward only suffered light casualties. For the Tudors and the Welsh it was a disaster. It was not to be forgotten: Henry Tudor, Pembroke's young nephew who was under house arrest in Wales, was to tap this particular source of pain a quarter of a century later.

I used to play in these killing fields as a boy. I had a friend who lived in Kingsland, a small village a mile or so to the south of the battlefield. We would cycle everywhere around the country lanes, and just up by the old bridge we would skim stones on the Lugg and count the bounces. Miles farther downstream the river snaked close to my house and I would try to see if I threw a stick in at Mortimer's Cross, whether I could see it going past where I lived a day or so later. I never did.

I knew there had been a battle here because my father told me, but I'm not sure I would have played so freely had I known the true extent of the bloodshed. Besides the re-enactors and the battlefield enthusiasts, to most people the true cost of the battles in this Civil War seem to have been forgotten. Like my stick thrown into the Lugg, they have been lost in the river flowing endlessly to the sea.

The Battle of Towton Moor, just south of York, is the biggest tree trunk in this river of lost consciousness. Shakespeare never shows the battle at Mortimer's Cross because, sadly, there were greater horrors to come.

Ten

Towton

I see the cross in the distance.

It is hugely underwhelming as I drive along the road that sweeps out of Towton village onto the low moor that is the site of the battlefield. The fields are plump with harvest, burning russet and gold in the sun which seems harsher now that I have left the sanctuary of the low ground. The fields are wide and mostly unhedged but for an incongruous holly bush which stands by the road, defiant in the landscape, shielding the strange cross like an officious bouncer. It is a stone monolith topped by a small, almost Celtic, cross. Most probably it was just a parish boundary marker that, in a cursory afterthought a couple of hundred years ago, was made into a memorial for the thousands and thousands that were hacked to death here on Palm Sunday, 1461.

I stop the MG in a small lay-by and wretch as I am greeted with the terrible smell of rotting flesh. Momentarily confused, I begin to shudder at the thought that even after 550-odd years the carnage of bodies still lingers, but then I see a decomposing rabbit with its intestines, ears and putrid skin hidden in the verge. Even the crows don't come up here to scavenge.

I'm sure it's usually horizontal rain here, but today I can see for miles. Four mighty power stations linger in the distance. There's also Selby coalfield to the east – a site of another shameful battle that ripped through England and Wales in the early 1980s. On either side, a mile or so away from the moor – certainly close enough for the dead to be strewn across them – two golf courses wither away into the distance. I wonder how many Yorkshiremen know what's in their bunkers.

I can even see York Minster peaking over the horizon. Richard Plantagenet's head was congealing atop its spike on the walls of York when the two mighty armies of his son, Edward, and King Henry VI met here. The Lancastrian army was actually led by Young Somerset because Henry was off cowering with his wife in York, but the nineteen-year-old Edward was definitely here assuming his standard in front of the huge troops assembled with him.

Fresh from his victory in the Marches, Edward had hot-footed it to London and been welcomed with open arms. Warwick had thus declared Edward to be King, and the people of London heartily followed suit. He was crowned in Westminster Abbey on 4th March, 1461, his superior claim to the throne from the usurping Henry Bolingbroke finally acknowledged by the Lords in Parliament sixty-two years after the event.

However, what really made Edward King was the cold fact that he was not only in control of the capital but the South was turning to him. Margaret and Henry's forces had won another battle at St. Albans against Warwick, but she had no money to pay her soldiers and as a consequence swathes of Hertfordshire, Buckinghamshire and Berkshire were stripped bare by the marauding Northerners eager to make a fast buck before heading home. Margaret was suddenly very exposed. She dallied – not sure whether to descend on London and assume control, or wait for her army and public opinion to catch up with her.

She withdrew. When she and Henry reversed from the capital and went North to the Lancastrian heartlands, the newly crowned King Edward IV followed after them. As he did so people swarmed to him like iron filings, so that by the time he crossed the Trent his army measured a staggering 40,000. At the threat of such an imposing force, the Northerners consequently flocked to their Lancastrian masters who turned and faced the Yorkists just south of Tadcaster.

The purportedly 50,000 strong Lancastrians lined up pretty much directly level with the cross by which I am standing now, and faced south looking downhill, believing themselves to be in a good position. They had the steep gully of Towton Beck to their right, and to their left the land sloped away to the far-off fenland below. But, in true English fashion, they hadn't bargained for the weather.

A powerful south-west wind blew into the faces of the Lancastrians, and it was mind-numbingly cold. This was 29th March 1461, but the winter had been long and remained unseasonably harsh. Flurries of snow beat mercilessly into the faces, helmets and longbows of Somerset's force, so that as the two armies squared up neither could really see the other.

The Lancastrians, perhaps because they were freezing, or perhaps because they got itchy feet, fired first. Their arrows soared into the air but fell uselessly into the no-man's-land between the two forces as the wind drove them back. Lord Fauconberg, leader of the Yorkist centre, simply made his troops step out of the way of the ineffective barrage and when the Lancastrians couldn't see because of the snow, got his own soldiers to go and pick up the arrows lying on the ground and fire them back with interest. With the added force of a gale behind them, these arrows thudded and tore sickeningly into the front of the Lancastrians who soon grew weary of being strafed by their own weapons, so the order was given to charge down the hill and meet the enemy – thus giving away their strategic advantage.

I walk the hundred or so yards from the cross that stands so small in the landscape. Here the red and white armies thunderingly met, running towards each other. They fought for hours, hacking each other to pieces.

No one really knows how many were killed, how many fought. That it remained a scar on the nation's soul right up until the next Civil War superseded it 180 years later, is evident in Shakespeare's treatment of it in *Henry VI Part 3*. Almost an hour of his play is devoted to it and some of the most famous scenes and speeches are from this battle. He has the Yorkists losing, on the verge of defeat, which may have happened, but resolving to die for the cause and pitching themselves further into battle, which may also have happened.

It seems to have been generally accepted, enough for Shakespeare to know and write about, that, whatever happened, it was a long, drawn-out, horrible and bloodthirsty stalemate that lasted for hours. As Henry says:

> *This battle fares like to the morning's war*
> *When dying clouds contend with growing light*
> *What time the shepherd blowing of his nails*
> *Can neither call it perfect day nor night*
> *Now sways it this way like a mighty sea*
> *Forced by the tide to combat with the wind*
> *Now sways it that way like the self-same sea*
> *Forced to retire by the fury of the wind*
> *Sometime the flood prevails and then the wind*
> *Now one better then the other best*
> *Both tugging to be victors breast to breast*
> *Yet neither conqueror nor conquered*
> *So is the equal poise of this fell war.*
>
> (*Henry VI Part 3 Act 2 Sc. 5*)

The saintly Henry is placed firmly in the middle.

The tide of the battle finally swayed to the numerically smaller Yorkists when the Duke of Norfolk arrived later in the afternoon, having been delayed with his mass of soldiers, and immediately attacked the Lancastrian left flank. Fresh troops, not yet laden down with the blood of their brothers, quickly pushed their enemy back and the whole battle began to swivel on its axis so that the steep gully leading down to Towton Beck, which had been on the Lancastrian right, was now directly behind them.

Weakened by their new position and the passage of time, they began to fall off the hill. The Yorkists simply had to shove. Down went the Lancastrians into the small valley sodden with the rain, snow and floods of a terrible winter, and they just got stuck in the mud. With an awful, bloody inevitability the Yorkists ran down the hill and chopped them to pieces. Those Lancastrians that survived ran over the bodies of their compatriots and reached the Beck, which, in nightmarish fashion is just that little bit too far to jump: certainly too far to jump for men sodden and laden with heavy clothing, wearing bits of armour and carrying weapons. Just too far. So they turned and faced the axe, cut down astride their own boggy grave.

I go to the steep hill overlooking the Beck that glimmers brightly in the valley. In the distance a green field rises on the other side. The one cloud in the sky passes briefly over and, as it clears, the field bursts into a bright red weal of poppies. The field burns pastel. I have never seen a green field so red. It IS red. There must be blood in the springs around here. They say Towton Beck ran red for three days.

In his restaging of Towton, as Henry sits on his molehill contemplating his navel, Shakespeare brings on a Father who has killed his Son, and a Son who has killed his Father. In one of the most aching of all his scenes, overseen by an agonized King Henry, each realizes what they have done after first killing, then robbing their enemy. When performing this part of the play, I was employing all my experience and training in essaying the role of a dead body. I had to lie on stage motionless for a good twenty minutes, but it gave me the opportunity to watch the audience as they saw one of the most heartrending scenes ever written in the English language. It is an extraordinary choice for a writer depicting a battle. Yet every night the audiences' eyes filled with tears:

Son

I'll bear thee hence, where I may weep my fill.

Father

These arms of mine shall be thy winding-sheet;
My heart, sweet boy, shall be thy sepulchre,
For from my heart thine image ne'er shall go;
My sighing breast shall be thy funeral bell;

(Henry VI Part 3 Act 2 Sc. 5)

England has torn itself in two.

Twenty-eight thousand people died here. It is the largest single loss of blood on English soil. In fact, if all the skirmishes from the previous two days are taken into account, and the subsequent slaughter as the Lancastrians fled, the figure is more likely to be 40,000. That's roughly 2% of the male population. There were no bullets and each person could look their killer in the eye.

I try to jump across the Beck, but lose my nerve as I would just bellyflop like a dog. I picture the bodies piling up, a bridge of death upon death. For a moment, in the hot sun, a zephyr runs over the field and I fancy I see through it back in Time to the sudden snow, mist, and blood. I see a son hunched over his father, his back shaking with sobs. The image melts into air, back into the green field.

I head back up the hill to the car. There are small, bleached wooden crosses placed around the base of the monument, and the two wreaths placed there are brown, dried and blasted by the weather which must rip through this moor on any normal day. I can smell the dead rabbit, cooking in the sun by the car and I see another rabbit head a metre or so away.

Has some mythical beast been here? The Black Dog, feeding on the blood of England for centuries? But I think it is just a fox, a red and white dog. The poppies and daisies lining the wheat field beside me sway in the warm west wind.

A few yards further away on the other side of the road there is an empty can of cider, tossed into the verge. A McDonald's milkshake carton lies next to a bin bag of rubbish. In the hedge is a duvet, and the grass wilts around it.

In proportion to population, this battle killed more people than the Battle of the Somme in 1916. Where are the tablets of white stone that would fill these fields with memory and remorse? Instead, there is a fucking McDonald's carton and a wet duvet.

This place has become a backwater of history. Perhaps it was just too enormous, too vile even to think about: a collective blanking from the national consciousness. Judging by the way Shakespeare features it so much in his play, the Elizabethans remembered it in the same way that I remember my grandfather fought in the First World War. But the Tudor world was riven by so much division that it ultimately led to the tide of the Civil War and Cromwell covering the tracks. I suspect History is more like the bloodstream of the body than the river flowing to the sea.

The village of Saxton is about half a mile away down a small road. I sit outside the pub in the sun and read about Towton in a leaflet from the bar produced by The Towton Battlefield Society who desperately try to promote and preserve the spirit of place. They obviously have no money (three pounds for a leaflet?) but they give it their best shot. I try to think if a visitor centre, organised tours, coach parks, and some down-on-their-luck actors wandering about in mediaeval costume would be best for the place. I sigh and think that if it raised the memory of so many lost sons, then maybe it would be a good thing, and probably good for the local economy, I suppose. But maybe I rejoice more in my pint and solitary walk. They should just put a significant monument here – one that will chime rightly through time.

Richard III may have been found in a car park in Leicester, and it's extraordinary. Let him take all the limelight – why change the habit of more than a lifetime. But there are thousands here who fought against, and alongside, his brother that will never be so recognised.

So I decide, before I go, to pay small homage at a location about a mile away. I walk past a farm down a small incline where to my right are two humps in the field that are burial mounds of the battle. The bodies were thrown in and left to feed the soil of what is on the face of it a beautiful valley. It was reported in the eighteenth century that the grass here grew uncommonly well. No wonder. Inevitably these lumps have got smaller over the years but I can't believe how small they actually are. There is a huge mound at Marathon, in Greece, that comprises the dead of that famously influential battle, yet here there are two small rises in the folds of the earth. But at least they are still here.

Next to the mounds is a rusty corrugated pig hut. Old bits of metal and gates poke from the ground. Then, suddenly, on this track that is fit for nothing except tractors and animals, a blonde girl drives past me in a purple 1970's Mini. She flashes me a toothy smile and disappears over the hill in a cloud of dust.

I wonder if that did actually just happen or if, like the battle, I actually exist.

'The earth hath bubbles as the water hath,' I say.

I tip my hat to the mounds in the earth, walk to the MG, and drive to York.

Eleven

York

The killing went on long after the battle had finished. The routed Lancastrians that managed to escape the battlefield were chased far and wide in the pursuit of death, vengeance and hatred that only a civil war can generate. Raising Cain through their victorious nostrils, the Yorkists slew as they ran.

People fled to Tadcaster, five miles away, some even managing a small defensive rearguard, but were dispatched quickly in the streets. Others began to appear at the gates of York but were slaughtered in the alleyways whereupon Henry, Margaret and the somewhat sheepish Duke of Somerset left smartly out of the city's North Gate – the Bootham Bar – and fled to Scotland. Almost at the same time, the victorious Edward swept in under the Eastern Gate – the Mickelgate Bar – adorned with the head of his father. With such a victory, and such carnage, Edward could finally proclaim himself King in reality as well as name.

Edward ruled a country in desperate need of it. He re-established mercantile confidence and fostered prosperity not only through governance but by the creation of many lordships in place of those killed or torn asunder by the Wars. Most of what we now call the Wars of the Roses was a dynastic struggle that took place well above the heads of the majority of people in England, but Towton affected everyone because of the sheer numbers involved – even hardened observers sought to comment on just how bloody it was.

This was particularly felt in the City of York not only because of the proximity of the battle, but also because the greater losses had been on the Lancastrian side to whom the city up until now had largely showed allegiance. So when Edward rode underneath the rotting head of his father into York, it must have seemed a somewhat pyrrhic victory.

You can stand to this day on the Mickelgate Bar set within the walls of York. They stretch for two and a half miles around the City, the main body of which still lies nestled and protected within their compass. They circle unbroken but for a small gap that used to be a lake and is now filled with Homebase and the like. White and imposing, the walls shelter a housing estate, the castle and Minster in turn. They are wonderful.

I want to walk the walls not least because Richard Plantagenet's head spent some time adorning them, which Shakespeare dramatises, but they are also one of the great city walks. As H. V. Morton observed crisply:

> I walked round the wall of York... rejoicing in this peerless city. York is not conscious of its beauty like so many ancient towns; it is too old and too wise and too proud to trick itself out for the admiration of tourists. That is one of the many reasons why I love it...

He is right, and it remains the same, just about, to this day. It could teach Stratford-upon-Avon a thing or two.

There's always a touch of incongruity when there is a huge great traffic system throbbing right by a mediaeval gate, and the Bootham Bar is no different. I walk along the road for a while past the Yorkshire Museum where a burnt-out car smoulders from last night's excesses and a sign next to it reads 'Our bid to give York World Heritage Status'. Just by the river a woman lies bleeding on the pavement. A paramedic attends to her – she's been hit by a bicyclist, poor woman – her trail of blood stretching a little way to a bridge crested by the White Rose and Red Lion all the way along the balustrade. I cross the river and walk the walls to the Mickelgate Bar in a thoughtful daze. The sight of human blood always makes people go quiet, and she is certainly not the first to have shed it at this place.

Traditionally, monarchs have entered the City through the Mickelgate Bar ever since the new King Edward IV triumphantly came through here after Towton with his father, brother and uncle looking lifelessly down upon him. Edward immediately and solemnly declared that they be taken down and rejoined with their respective bodies that had been hastily buried at Pontefract, of all places. It was to be another five years before he could reinter his father's body at the Yorkist headquarters of Fotheringhay with due ceremony and honour. Standing on the Bar now it is surprisingly easy to picture the heads on their spikes, with the foul-smelling train of men on campaign passing underneath.

Walking the walls brings you into the Mickelgate Bar halfway up, high above the modern road which still passes through the gate below. There is a little shop in it with the obligatory rip-off museum. One of the two girls behind the counter is trying to explain English humour to the other, who is Dutch. Using Monty Python as an example, she starts quoting lines like 'I fart in your general direction', 'It's just a flesh wound' and 'He's not Brian, he's a very naughty boy'. It makes sense somehow of both the building and Monty Python. The Dutch girl looks blank and laughs with a panicked whimper.

The mediaeval walls of York were built upon the ramparts left by the Romans, so it is not only clear what the Romans did for us but they are huge as a consequence. Down in the South West corner they are so complete and perfect as to almost resemble a film set. There are no buildings cramming in on them as they stand in splendid isolation on the *limen* of History. The contrast with Towton is all the more marked.

That feeling of unremembered History is increased by the wall coming to an end at a mound which used to be the site of William the Conqueror's castle. Or perhaps he should be called William the Genocidal Maniac, as when the North rose up against his invasion he built this place as a base to stop the rebellion and ritually slaughter them. The Domesday Book states that 940 houses out of 1,400 in York were still derelict fifteen years after William had systematically wiped out large swathes of society in what is known as the Harrowing of the North. It is said not a village was left inhabited from York to Durham. No wonder it seems like a different country up here. Let us remember that the Kings of England after William the Conqueror spoke French as their first language for another 300 years, until Henry Bolingbroke spoke English at his coronation. It took a long time for those invaders not just to feed off the land they stole, but to become part of it.

In the end, of course, what was 'English' just adapted and became bigger, rounder and more complex. The same man that built much of Westminster Abbey, Henry of Reyns – a Frenchman – built Clifford's Tower which is the most memorable sight of York Castle that now sits by the River Ouse. Standing atop the Tower, the Minster can be seen on the other side of the City with its great West frontage turning red in the afternoon sun, and I certainly get the impression that York was such a powerhouse that monarchs gave it a wide berth for a very long time. Its Viking heritage and sense of identity – it is most definitely of the North – make it strong and therefore threatening. Yet the plastering of White Roses around the whole City is testament to the fact that once Edward had won Towton, this place took the Yorkists to their heart, which in turn became a strong, and belligerent, identity in itself. He was the Duke of York after all. After Henry VII, there should have been many a Tudor Rose on display here, but no – the White Rose and the Three Suns are emblazoned on the bridges and the walls.

Beyond Clifford's Tower I see a policeman telling off a woman for cycling on the pavement. She tries to explain that she had been unable to ride on the road as a lorry would have knocked her over, but he won't listen and drones on with the relish that only a jobsworth can quite pin down. He turns away, flicking his stupid hat with a satisfied smile, and both she, myself and three other people communally give him the finger behind his back.

Pressing on round the walls, past the Eshergate Bar, I suddenly feel as if I am in an inverted Historical Theme Park. I find myself walking on this wonderful turreted age-old wall and looking out at the exhibits of the modern world. To the right is the ring road and all the attendant trash that comes with it, and to the left is an '80s housing estate that brings the wall into a sharpened perspective. There's even a Travelodge. The houses and gardens lap the wall like a moat. How strange it must be to have this wall at the back of your garden and the tourists looking at you every day. In one exhibit, sorry-house, music blares from a top window. In a garden there's a couple having an argument. In another a White Rose flag flaps on the washing line.

At the Walmgate Bar, the barbican is very impressive but it's a bleak part of town and as I climb up to the other side three drunks are shouting, the fresh scars on their faces creasing moistly in the sun. Two fat men eating fish and chips squeeze past me on the wall, and I begin fervently to hope that this place becomes a World Heritage Site. It is not Venice or the Alhambra, but the walls are all of England and have a beauty all of their own. None of it is preserved in aspic – the walls are beautiful, wasteful, rich, poor, grand, fat and drunk. They are Falstaff.

If you want to see England, take a walk around the plump walls of York: you see every type of architecture from Roman to Mediaeval, Elizabethan to Georgian, Victorian to the '80s, finally to a building under construction. You see it in the people's faces, from the drunks and the priests that wander through the Close around the Minster, to the couple arguing and making up under the White Rose flag.

The wall runs out for a while where the King's Pool used to be. It lasted for 700 years but silted up and has been reclaimed by the corporations and the commerce desperately laying siege to your buck. But then the walls gloriously soar back through Jewbury where at the Monk Bar there is a Richard III museum in a portion of the building supposedly built by the man himself in 1484. On the wall, it sits firmly on the fence in portraying Richard as either the demonic killer or the good king defamed. It is full of quill pens and portcullis rubbers, succeeding in fleecing the tourists nicely. Away past the wall there is a row of Victorian houses at the end of which a 1940s advert reads: NIGHTLY BILE BEANS. KEEPS YOU HEALTHY BRIGHT EYED AND SLIM. I'd love it if they sold those in the museum.

By the time I got back full circle to the Bootham Bar the whole walk had taken me well over two hours. More drunks were arguing in the little room in the Bar, so I find it hard to picture Margaret, Henry and Somerset with a retinue of about 600 men fleeing underneath here. But through the window the Minster that holds two thirds of the mediaeval stained glass in England rises above the heavy-lidded buildings and my heart soars. This place, like H.V. Morton says, most certainly is 'too wise and too old and too proud to trick itself out for the admiration of tourists.'

I come down off the walls, one of the great *limens* of England, and get lost among the lanes.

Twelve

Berwick-upon-Tweed

The clouds break and in the distance Holy Island gleams white with ice like a fairy castle. The mediaeval walls of Berwick-upon-Tweed glitter for a while in the sun and then fall dark as another snowy squall barges in from the sea leaving me breathless. Like York, the walls can be walked around and span wonderfully across allotments and the High Street, from which you can see people huddled against the wind – bustling in the same way Lowry so loved when he painted matchstick men here on his holidays. I stop to take some notes next to the fortifications built by Elizabeth I that proved so important to keep Berwick the English side of the border, but my pen has frozen. It is a remarkable, strange and ethereal place – perhaps made all the more unusual by the force ten gale and cold that could shatter teeth, yet I think that's pretty usual up here. The constant sound of the sea, white from the wind, is imposing. From these turrets I can see the distant howl of storms crashing past the castles which litter the coast like stalagmites.

Henry, Margaret, and their son, Edward, plus a small army of supporters, stayed at Berwick on their flight from Towton, and for someone like Henry who seemed permanently on the edge of mental collapse it must have been a frightening place indeed. Margaret and Edward eventually left for Scotland and thereafter fled to France to raise funds for a retaliatory army. Meanwhile, according to Shakespeare, Henry disguised himself and went for a look at his country in a forest near Berwick and got caught. It seems his appetite for self-destruction, like a lot of potential saints, knew no bounds.

Before the Act of Union, Berwick was an important pawn in the battle between the English and the Scots. It was used by Margaret as a bargaining chip to procure funds from the Scottish Queen, and a hundred years later Elizabeth's defences were considered to be the most expensive undertaking of this kind during her reign.

They needed to be strong. Not only were the Scots making the occasional forays into England, but the families up here were old, gnarled and very pissed off. They had been marginalised by Elizabeth for their roles in the seesaw events of the Tudor era and the inept 'Rising

169

of the North! Thus the old Mediaeval Houses that had ruled so much of the country as a personal fiefdom were clinging on to existence like the castles they lived in.

But certain families quietly charted their way through very stormy waters. Berwickshire is Swinton country. Stemming from the Anglo-Saxon kings of Northumbria they have hovered just North of the border in Scotland for 1,500 years. Like the Ardens, Shakespeare's ancestors, they were one of the few landowning families to keep their prosperity when William the Conqueror arrived. They are very, very tough: in the fourteenth century, the Sir John Swinton that was lynched in London for wearing the livery collar of John of Gaunt was paid twice the usual pay to fight in Gaunt's army. This sounds cheap at the price when you consider he once famously attacked a town in France single-handedly and fought the entire attending French nobility on his own for an hour before his army caught up with him. Leaping to his horse, he is reported to have cried, 'Adieu, adieu, Seigneurs, grand mercis' and sped on his way. Another later Swinton, as you may imagine, was the inspiration for the Scarlet Pimpernel.

A further family member, Major General Sir Ernest Dunlop Swinton, came up with the idea of what we now call the tank and I can only imagine that he was thinking of his ancestors when inspiration struck. It is a wonderfully tough land that has bred a wonderfully tough people.

Typically for a man brought up in the Borders, Major General Swinton also coined the term 'No-Man's-Land' which is pretty much what this whole area itself became during the Wars of the Roses. The Lancastrians made a series of ultimately unsuccessful forays into England, and the many castles which exist there were taken and retaken by the Yorkists over the course of many years. Ultimately, at a battle in Hexham, the Duke of Somerset was killed and his small band of fighters routed, thereby effectively ending all Lancastrian resistance to King Edward IV's rule. Henry actually got caught after nearly a year of wandering about the north of England with one or two close companions. A monk betrayed him in Waddington, Lancashire, as he was receiving the hospitality of the monk's brother.

Henry was taken to London and put straight in the Tower by a joyous King Edward IV who could finally sit on his throne with a little more ease. Tall, strong and handsome, it is said that Edward's resemblance as a young man to his grandson, the future Henry VIII, was uncanny. He reinvigorated the Royal finances and also empowered the merchants who had been struggling under Henry's rule – so much so that they were prepared to put up with him squiring their wives and daughters provided they turned a profit. It was almost as if he was born to rule but, like his grandson, his penis got in the way. It was Edward's marriage to the beautiful Elizabeth Woodville, widow of Sir John Grey who had fought for the Lancastrians at St. Albans, that flew in the face of every political and sensible judgement at the time.

It incensed virtually every ally he had, most importantly the Earl of Warwick who had fought so diligently for power (and lost his own father, uncle and brother in the process), that he was not going to deliver it up lightly. For a few years Warwick had effectively ruled England, with Edward being happy to share power and the weight of government. Warwick was consolidating his vast estates, and looked to foster his and England's interests abroad by marrying Edward off to the sister-in-law of the King of France, Lady Bona. He had not catered for what Edward was thinking with.

The village of Grafton Regis, just off Watling Street in Northamptonshire, is remarkable not least for maintaining a semblance of peace and quiet only five miles from the Orwellian hellhole that is Milton Keynes, but was also, it is said, the place where Edward and Elizabeth Woodville met under an oak tree. The King was not used to women who refused his advances and he became obsessed by the beautiful, clever woman that wouldn't relent. A situation made for Shakespeare, who takes the horny king and drives a wedge between him and the rest of his family with glee.

Edward and Elizabeth were indeed married at Grafton Hermitage which can now be seen as little humps in the ground, sheep grazing happily, just off the main road opposite the White Hart pub in Grafton Regis. The landlord is a history enthusiast and the whole pub seems to be given over to the goings-on of various aristocratic wastrels in Grafton over the years.

The village was given its 'Regis' moniker by Henry VIII who spent most of his summers here and loved the Manor that so dominated the area, which then became part of Elizabeth's flock of houses. It is notable for its rather grand occupants in the shape of the Earls of Leicester and Essex and also William Cecil, aka Lord Burghley – the power behind Elizabeth's throne. Henry Wriothesley, Earl of Southampton, patron of Shakespeare, husband to a Vernon, was also known to have wanted to buy the place in the late 1500s. In fact, a portrait said to be of Shakespeare survived in a cottage in Grafton for 250 years having been rescued from the Manor house in the Civil War. It is known as the Grafton portrait and is almost certainly not Shakespeare but makes a pretty story.

There is no pretty story, however, throughout *Henry VI Part 3*. Like any good Morality Play, 'Vice' is waiting in the wings. The Lord of Misrule, weird little Richard, is waiting like Ridley Scott's Alien whilst the world goes on about him, the hump on his back getting bigger with every battle that he fights.

Let's be clear: in Shakespeare's plays, Richard, the newly made Duke of Gloucester, is no mediaeval figure. He is as Elizabethan and as contemporary to Shakespeare as any character he ever created: through Richard, Shakespeare drags the theatre from the Mediaeval into the spitting and fiery Modern. Richard talks of setting 'the murderous Machiavel to school' – the infamous political schemer having written his theories long after the historical Richard had died at Bosworth. He is a character that would be recognised by any Tudor audience as one of their own.

Robert Cecil was the son of William Cecil, Lord Burghley, who had run the Elizabethan Court with a rod of iron through the latter half of the sixteenth century. Burghley's was the final voice that had whispered in the ear of Elizabeth that her cousin, Mary, Queen of Scots, should be consigned to the block – a fact for which Elizabeth banned him from the Court whilst she reconciled her private grief with the Machiavellian need for the public good. As time went on, a new generation of Lords and Courtiers began to surround Elizabeth with their own machinations and chief among them was Robert who gradually assumed more and more of his father's duties. Schooled not only by his father but also by Sir Francis Walsingham – the Queen's spymaster – day by day Robert's influence grew until by the mid-1590s it was his voice that whispered into the Queen's ear when Lords grew restive, or the commons sought solace. Diminutive in stature, he walked with a limp and carried on his back a hunch that would grace any of the subsequent actors portraying Richard ever since. The Queen used to call him 'my elf' or 'my pygmy'. His nickname amongst his fellow Courtiers was 'The Toad'. Richard, amongst many other things, is called a 'poisonous bunch-backed toad' by Margaret. Spitting Image couldn't have done it better.

The Cecils were the family that could, in Elizabethan times, set the murderous Machiavelli to school, and whom Shakespeare could satirise under the disguise of a hunchback exaggerated by the Tudors themselves. Richard was the Lord (Burghley) of Misrule whom the audience could laugh at whilst within the confines of the theatre, but could be fearful of the moment they stepped out of bounds. No wonder Shakespeare kept a low profile.

So when Edward IV wanders off into the night with his highly inappropriate bride, Richard is the one left on stage to let the audience know that, just like his father, he wants the crown. Since Nature has made him repellant, he will take the crown instead.

Gloucester

…And yet I know not how to get the crown
For many lives stand between me and home,
And I – like one lost in a thorny wood,
That rents the thorns and is rent with the thorns,
Seeking a way and straying from the way,
Not knowing how to find the open air,
But toiling desperately to find it out –
Torment myself to catch the English crown:
And from that torment I will free myself,
Or hew my way out with a bloody axe.

(Henry VI Part 3 Act 3 Sc. 2)

The creature in the woods; the devil in our minds; the other face of the clown has come to life.

Edward IV was hampered by having to put down rebellion after rebellion and therefore waging taxes to pay for an army, so it is a surprise that he didn't quietly let Henry starve in the Tower the same way Bolingbroke did with Richard II at Pontefract. But Henry wasn't really his problem, Margaret was.

By the time Warwick was busying about the French Court furthering his ambitions, Margaret was seething around France living off the goodwill of others and throwing herself at the coast of England periodically in more and more desperate attempts to re-establish herself. But then it all changed when King Edward married for lust rather than politics. With Warwick's desire to see an alliance with France, the two old friends could go only one way – apart.

Over the course of the next few years Edward also spent his time promoting and ennobling a good deal of his new bride's extended family, which alienated most of the surviving aristocracy including his own brother George, now Duke of Clarence, thereby factionalising the Court once again. Both parties tried to step away from the brink but relations deteriorated so badly that war was inevitable.

The fortunes of both sides fluctuated – with Warwick winning a decisive battle at Edgecote Hill against Edward's forces, and Edward himself being imprisoned. But reluctant to kill another anointed King and place Clarence on the throne (which would make *three* potential Kings wandering about England), Warwick found himself releasing Edward in order to achieve some sort of Royal Authority. Within a year Warwick was back in France asking for money to raise an army against Edward in exactly the same way that Margaret had been doing for years. King Louis of France saw no harm in getting the two together and the scene was set for one of the iciest meetings ever to grace the corridors of History when Warwick and Margaret finally met in the palatial rooms of the French Court in the summer of 1470. He even agreed to give his daughter, Anne, to her son, Edward. His other daughter, Isabel, he gave to Clarence who had sped over to France to rebel against his own brother. From there he presumably couldn't hear his father, Richard Plantagenet, spinning in his grave at Fotheringhay.

Warwick and Clarence quickly raised an army and landed at Dartmouth. They marched North to meet King Edward who, knowing the odds were against him, promptly fled – taking with him his brother, Gloucester, and Sir William Hastings. Warwick swept imperiously to London, released Henry from the Tower, and set about running the country the way he wanted to do it.

It is a rather bemused Henry that Shakespeare gives us who totters from gaol, but is a soul that has found release through his confinement. The Tower has been his chrysalis and he is now in full-on saint mode, promising to repay his gaoler for his 'kindness' and giving over government to Warwick and Clarence. He also finds time for a spot of light divination when he espies the young Earl of Richmond, Henry Tudor, being shepherded by the new Earls of Somerset and Oxford.

King Henry VI

Come hither England's hope. If secret powers
Suggest but truth to my divining thoughts,
This pretty lad will prove our country's bliss…

Make much of him, my lords, for this is he
Must help you more than you are hurt by me.

(Henry VI Part 3 Act 4 Sc. 6)

What a good Tudor boy Shakespeare appears to be, and it's interesting to note that when Henry Tudor became King, he asked the Pope to make Henry VI a saint. It never happened, but by painting Henry VI as a divining saint Shakespeare was potentially portraying the Wars of the Roses as religious sectarianism, and playing a very dangerous game with the authorities. The hunchback was watching.

By fleeing the country, Edward wasn't finished. Having borne him two daughters, Elizabeth Woodville now gave birth to a son, Edward, whilst in sanctuary at Westminster Abbey. With an heir to his Yorkist throne, Edward resolved to retake his kingdom and in the spring of 1471 he landed at Ravenspurgh, the exact same place that Bolingbroke had landed seventy-two years earlier and which has since rather apologetically fallen into the sea. Edward only had a small group of ships and men, and the North was not his natural territory, so when he arrived at Hull the gates remained firmly shut to him – the Mediaeval equivalent of not answering the phone. But at Beverley they received him with open arms and by the time he got to York he was cheered in the streets.

Borrowing a trick from Bolingbroke, he maintained that he had come only to claim his dukedom, which few people actually heard let alone believed, and there then followed an extraordinary cat and mouse game where Warwick and Edward followed each other around the country with large armies seeing who might crack first. The answer was that neither of them did. Clarence did it for them.

Faced with the actuality of fighting his own brother, George, Duke of Clarence, just couldn't do it. He and his presumably very confused army of men defected to the Yorkists, where he was given a full pardon by Edward and allowed to stand at his brother's side. Now in full flow, Edward marched to Coventry where Warwick was holed up behind the city walls, and demanded to fight.

Even though he was in his heartlands – Warwick Castle is just a few miles down the road – Warwick knew he had the strategic weakness and refused to come out and play. So Edward merely ignored him and belted down Watling Street to London. By the time he got there the cowering Londoners were singing his praises and Henry was probably already walking to the Tower himself.

Edward just had time to meet his son for the first time before leaving London again to meet the fast-pursuing Warwick. The two sides met on the morning of the 14th April just outside the small town of Barnet, ten miles North of London.

Barnet

These days I always think of Barnet as a pretty unprepossessing place. Stuck on the end of the Northern Line, it is the outer reach of London. But get out of the Tube station and have a look around, and the money that seeps from the High Street is self-evident. Turn the corner to the common on which a large proportion of the battle was fought and the houses are wealthy and attractive, the gardens prim and neat, the net curtains replaced by a simpering Jag in the driveway. The obligatory golf course snaps away beyond the hedge.

Beyond the common, on a small grass clearing in between a fork in the road, a stone commemorates the battle that raged through what was fields but is now a cosy suburb. It was erected in 1740 – exactly the halfway point between the battle and today.

Having staged Clarence's *volte face* and the stand-off at Coventry, the hardest task when performing these plays was then to belt round the theatre ready for a full-on fight at Barnet. When we staged it, there were fifteen guys with broadswords fighting each other onstage while Clive Wood as the ghost of Richard Plantagenet, Duke of York, walked through them to watch his son, Edward, and his best friend, Warwick, fight to the death. Not easy at the best of times, but when you've just ran round the theatre and avoided impaling an old woman in the back row who has decided now is the time to go for a pee, it was a tricky fight. Yet it worked every time, not least because this is the end of a long story: Warwick and Edward fight each other to the death.

What Shakespeare can't show, of course, is the thousands of other people doing exactly the same thing in the cause of their masters. There was mist that day on 14th April in Barnet. Edward was actually hopelessly outnumbered, but the weather, as ever, seemed on his side. Warwick let loose a huge battery from the newly invented cannon that had swept aside earlier opponents in his recent battles, but their ammunition soared uselessly over the Yorkists who were actually much closer than they thought. Edward forbade any retaliatory fire as that would give away their position and then launched a stinging attack from close range. The Earl of Oxford, who led the Lancastrian right wing, immediately charged and easily broke the Yorkist left who fled back to Barnet and miles beyond. Oxford desperately tried to gather his pursuing troops to head back into the battle proper, but when they returned to the fray the Lancastrians thought Oxford's troops were Yorkist forces as they were coming from the wrong direction. So the Lancastrians were fighting each other without knowing it. Had it not been for the mist they would have been able to tell.

By the time the confusion was over, the Lancastrian centre was crumbling and Edward poured through. Warwick's men fled and the rout began as thousands ran for their lives. Warwick, having dismounted his horse to fight on foot, knew how close victory was and desperately exhorted his men to turn around, but eventually he knew the outcome. He was trying to run back to his horse to marshall the retreat when he was surrounded by Yorkist soldiers and hacked to death.

All the men that had picked a rose in Shakespeare's Garden were dead. Warwick's prediction that this faction would '*send a thousand souls to death and deadly night*' had proved true for themselves as well as the innocent blood of England. For what? Shakespeare, a man born into the great chasm of division whose fathers had seen the country sway first one way then the other, then back again, is pretty clear when he gives Warwick his final words:

Warwick

…Lo, now my glory smeared in dust and blood.
My parks, my walks, my manors that I had,
Even now forsake me: and of all my lands
Is nothing left me but my body's length.
Why, what is pomp, rule, reign, but earth and dust?
And live we how we can but die we must.

(*Henry VI Part 3 Act 5 Sc.2*)

Falstaff couldn't have said it better. Or, for that matter, Romeo and Juliet. Or Lear. Or Macbeth.

Behind the stone obelisk erected at Barnet, there is a sign to Hatfield House – the great symbol and symptom of the Cecils' power – whose descendants still live there today. Before their rise, here it was that the young Princess Elizabeth's Catholic sister, Mary, had been forced to wait on Elizabeth as penance for attending Mass by their Protestant brother King Edward VI. Here it was too that Elizabeth heard, after her own short sojourn in the Tower, that the same sister, now Queen Mary, had died and she herself was Queen. The pendulum of faith had swung back towards her and all those caught in the middle were all out of time.

Tewkesbury

So too was Queen Margaret. The day before Warwick was killed at Barnet, Margaret landed at Weymouth with her son and a small army, ready to fight. Intending to meet up with Jasper Tudor and the forces he could muster from Wales, she headed North but soon found out about Warwick's defeat when the bedraggled remnants of her Lancastrian aristocracy raced West to meet her. She at first despaired and wanted to head back to France, but was persuaded that there was still hope if the two forces could unite beyond the Severn and head north to Lancastrian territory.

Edward was also in despair at having to gird his loins for yet another campaign. No sooner had he returned to London in triumph with Warwick's body displayed in an open coffin at St. Paul's, Edward had to raise another army.

As Margaret went North and West, funneled up between the Cotswolds and the sea to Berkeley Castle, Edward headed towards them along what would now be considered the M4 corridor. Knowing that speed was of the essence in order to isolate Margaret from her Welsh contingent, Edward jumped over the Cotswolds in a thirty-mile route march in one day – an extraordinary achievement at any time let alone for an army of 5,000 worn-out men. He descended the hills at Cheltenham and made for Tewkesbury where the Avon would cut off Margaret's progress as she tried desperately to cross the Severn.

Had she been able to do so and met up with Jasper Tudor there is a very strong chance that with massively superior forces, Margaret would have smashed the Yorkist army. But cornered, tired and dehydrated in the unseasonably hot early May sun, the Lancastrians turned to face the Yorkists for one last time.

Tewkesbury Abbey glows white and gold in the winter afternoon, and the trees stand bald in the cold crisp sun. I have brought Miles Richardson with me, who played the Duke of Exeter in *Henry V*, Lord Clifford in *Henry VI Part 2* and the Bishop of Ely in *Richard III*. We eat across the road from the Abbey and then walk the 'Battle Trail' which takes us through what, for me, is yet another housing estate. Momentarily we are lost, as we find ourselves in a completely unconnected cemetery, but then through a gate the path broadens to playing fields crowned with a commemorative stone to the battle. From the memorial, the fields dotted with rugby posts and a small playground sweep down to the Abbey which after our long walk pulses now red and gold like fine cloth.

It is painfully obvious to see what happened here. The Lancastrians, led by Somerset and the battle-virginal Prince Edward – Margaret and Henry's son – shepherded by the experienced Lord Wenlock, took up their position on advantageous ground atop the hill where the stone now stands in their memory. With the Abbey behind them they were numerically superior, but the ground was inferior. Even Margaret was not sure about it, but Somerset prevailed and she rode in front of her troops exhorting them to greatness, then shot off to a Manor nearby to await the outcome.

Whilst having smaller numbers, Edward's men were by now an almost professional elite, having honed their fighting technique over many battles – none of which Edward had lost. He it was who gave the order to attack and the charge uphill through hedges, dykes and trees was almost impossible. But the cannon nicked from Warwick after Barnet came in very handy, softening the Lancastrians, who nevertheless stood their ground. Edward's brother, the wily Richard, Duke of Gloucester, sounded the retreat in a bid to entice the enemy from its advantageous position. Somerset, leading the Lancastrian right, was as green as the trees through which he saw a hallowed victory, and charged down the hill at what he thought was a defeated Yorkist army. He was quickly surrounded by hidden troops, and when Wenlock and the young Prince Edward sensibly preferred to keep their station on the hill, his men were annihilated.

Making his way back to them, Somerset lost no time in branding Wenlock an incompetent traitor, forgetting that he himself was the one who had fallen into a trap in the first place. Before Wenlock could even raise a finger in his defence, Somerset promptly planted an axe in his face, splitting his head in two. The no doubt somewhat shocked Prince Edward, and his troops, probably coughed and reminded Somerset which side he was on. But it was futile. Gloucester, seeing the advantage, descended on the broken Lancastrians with fury. It was over within an hour.

Standing on top of the hill looking down to the Abbey it is very clear to see where the Lancastrians fled. There is a small brook wending its way to the river just in front of the Abbey, and like Towton ten years before, the Lancastrians just couldn't cross it. It was merciless. Some of those that managed to cross sought sanctuary in the Abbey, but were dragged out and slaughtered on the spot.

Some say it was Clarence that did it; others say it was all three of the York brothers. What is certain is that the eighteen year-old Prince Edward, only son and heir of Henry VI, grandson of Henry V, died that day at Tewkesbury. There seem to be enough contemporary accounts that indicate it may well have been the brothers that finally did the deed, and certainly Shakespeare seizes on the drama of it with both hands.

He makes Edward's death crueller still by having Margaret present. Before the mother, the son is killed.

> **King Edward IV**
> *Take that, the likeness of this railer here.*
>
> **Gloucester**
> *Sprawl'st thou? Take that to end thy agony.*
>
> **Clarence**
> *And here's for twitting me with perjury.*
>
> **Queen Margaret**
> *O, kill me too.*
>
> **Gloucester**
> *Marry and shall.*
>
> **King Edward IV**
> *Hold, Richard, hold, for we have done too much.*
>
> (*Henry VI Part 3 Act 5 Sc. 5*)

I played Somerset in these plays and I was dragged off to my death just beforehand. From backstage, as I wiped the blood from my face, the howls of a mother's pain for her son's death left me numb every night.

The young Prince Edward is buried in the Abbey and I try to find his grave now. It is as glorious a nave as any in England despite its relative size to the more shouty cathedrals elsewhere. In the amount of monuments, tombs and repositories it is second only to Westminster Abbey – a treasure chest of History made all the more poignant by the horrors that took place inside and out after the battle. Above the altar is the most glorious depiction of the sun and white roses – so much a part of the Yorkist story. I look up to the roof and they explode in glorious white, gold and red. I look down to realise that I am standing on Edward's grave. I hurriedly step back in a gesture of apology and guilt – the poor lad has been through enough. A small diamond plaque of gold engraved with Latin is all that indicates the spot. Talk about subjugation. The White Rose clearly won. The inscription reads:

Here lies Edward Prince of Wales,
Cruelly slain while still a youth
Anno Domini 1471
Alas the savagery of men
Thou art the sole light of thy mother
The last hope of thy race

Too true. With Edward's death the last hope of the House of Lancaster went. Margaret was a broken woman. Told of the outcome of the battle she fainted and was taken by her ladies into hiding at Malvern Priory. Two days later she was found by Sir William Stanley and brought before King Edward at Coventry. Lucky to escape with her life, she was paraded before him and pelted with mud and stones as he entered London in triumph. She was sent to live with her one great friend, Alice Chaucer, the wife of Suffolk. When Alice died, Margaret was packed off to France and survived on a meagre pension provided by the French King. She died in 1482, aged 52, and is buried in Angers Cathedral, the woman who would be King.

There are so many dead people to look at in Tewkesbury. Isabel, Warwick's daughter, is here alongside her husband – the pinball that was Clarence. It's a fine monument and accompanied by Isabel's own small chapel. Clarence had gone over to Warwick in the hope that he himself would be made King – because he couldn't really believe that Warwick would side with Margaret. When Warwick did just that, Clarence was in an untenable position and his double defection was inevitable. He is forever painted as the hovering, indecisive fool, yet all he did was back the wrong horse and realise before it was too late. But the damage was done – he was never trusted again.

I cannot for the life of me find Somerset. He was buried here two days after the battle having been found guilty of treason by a military tribunal headed by Gloucester. Presumably they took his axe away from him, the nutter. I want to find him as I spent three years of my life portraying various different Somersets and I think it only right that I should at least acknowledge the old boy. Miles is also trying to find him and eventually asks in the shop. From where I am standing at Clarence's tomb, I can hear the exchange:

'Somerset?', the woman replies, 'Ooo, I don't know. We've got allsorts here. That chap Clarence is just down there, is that any good? And Prince Edward's at the altar, poor lad. We don't often get asked for Somerset. I'm pretty sure he's buried here, but I don't know where.'

My heart sinks.

'Hang on,' she says, 'Cathy'll know.' Her voice rises as she calls to another room. 'Cathy, where's Somerset? Is he…? O yes, that's right, he's the one… Of course he is. Yes, that's right.'

My ears prick up.

'He's under the till.'

'What?', says Miles. I hear his laugh beginning to ring round the hushed Abbey.

'What?', I say as I turn the corner into the shop.

'Yes,' she chuckles, 'Right underneath me just here. There's a carpet so it's keeping him nice and warm.'

For some reason – not least because the spirit of England is alive and well and living in this woman behind a till in Tewkesbury Abbey – I could have hugged her.

You can see Tewkesbury Abbey from miles around. If you're driving on the M5 it glints bright white amongst the green. It stands in the flood plain created by the confluence of the Avon and the Severn, so when the rivers burst, it enjoys splendid isolation whilst the rest of the town goes under. How is it still here when the Abbey at Bury St. Edmunds, or the hermitage at Grafton are gone? Or Bisham Abbey, where Warwick is buried, which is now underneath a leisure centre?

Tewkesbury is different, in that the town drowns every now and then, but then lies draped around the Abbey like a lifejacket. The two are inseparable. When the dogs of the Dissolution came to tear it down, the townspeople were able to claim that it was still their local parish church and not just a Monastery and Abbey. They somehow cobbled together enough money – £453 (a vast amount of money in the 1530s) – to cover the costs of the roof that would have been stripped from the building, leaving it a lifeless ruin.

So this place at the end of the Avon survived, throbbing gently in the aftermath of the Reformation, and acting as a beacon for the idea of an older England, catholic – of the land – England. I notice in the publicity and the prayer books, it calls itself 'Anglo-Catholic' – a hybrid of both what became the Anglican Church and Catholicism. It no longer had the Pope, the Mass, the chalices and chasubles – or the flaccid overbearances of too much money, land and power. But it still plugged into the ancient rites, rituals and superstitions of this land – the wherewithal that let people know who they were. The deep and unfathomable well of community. The magic of who we are, drawn from every blade of grass, tuft of trees, ritual dance or story told. An overriding sense of where we come from: the land. It trod the line, and still does.

To me, it mirrors what Shakespeare was. However corrupt and corpulent the monks had become, and however tyrannical the Protestant world ruled, it is the *land* that makes us breathe. Built on the banks of two rivers that have flowed from England and Wales, the Abbey, too, sits on the *limen*. With every boat that rowed up the Avon into the heart of England through Arden, or that wended up to Wales on the Severn – the message went out: No matter how you tell us to think, or misgovern us, or how corrupt you become, we – the land and the people – are still here.

Thirteen

London

Tewkesbury Abbey is built not of the yellow stone of the nearby Cotswolds, but of the white Caen stone so favoured by William the Conqueror. Westminster Abbey and Canterbury Cathedral are all quarried from the same hearth of Europe, as are bits of the Tower of London – the symbol of foreign domination which became the very notion of England.

From any playhouse in London in the late 1500s, be it The Rose in Southwark, or The Curtain in Shoreditch, you could walk to the Tower in a matter of minutes. Along with St. Paul's Cathedral, it was the predominant building in the City of London, and loomed large both physically and within the mind of England. If you go there now, it's still an impressive sight but the glassy bulk of the modern City seems to dwarf the place, huddling as it does by the river – almost pushed in by time. But it is built of sterner stuff. Apocryphally started by Julius Caesar in 54AD, William the Conqueror was the one who began what we see now – the facades clothed in his beloved Caen stone. Tall, monolithic and curiously unbeautiful it was at once the seat of power and the physical expression of it. That mantle eventually transferred up river to the Palaces at Westminster so the Tower became something much more useful to a feudal state: an armoury and prison.

The modern-day symbols of power, the Crown Jewels, still reside there alongside all the tomfoolery that comes with the accoutrements of History – beefeaters in costume, soldiers prancing about in silly hats, and the like. It is a sprawling complex lined with toothy walls, and lawns spreading luxuriously to the White Tower at its centre. Here it is that so many figures in English History come creeping down the catwalk. Bolingbroke kept Richard II in here whilst deciding what to do with him. Anne Boleyn was executed. Lady Jane Grey too. Sir Walter Raleigh spent so long shut up here that he had his own apartments and his family moved in. Strangely, Rudolph Hess, Hitler's deputy, was imprisoned for four days in 1941 – the last state prisoner to be held at the Tower.

Standing on the lawns, if you begin to think of all the people that have waited to die in this place, it is almost too much. Yet because The Tower is here – because it reaches an arm back to Caesar – it is breathtaking. The list of luminaries that have died here is a roll call of History that defines England as much as the Crown Jewels that shimmer in their bulletproof facades. It is one of the murkiest and most mixed symbols of England there is. As is Richard III.

There is every reason to suspect that Richard was indeed lurking about the Tower when Henry VI was killed. Most sources place him there on the fateful night. The official story was that Henry died of grief at losing his son and wife, but nobody believed it even then. You can stand in the small private chapel in the Wakefield Tower, part of the Tower complex, where he met his end. The tourists and the students pour through and don't notice – there's lots more showy things elsewhere than this room. Within the chapel there's even a window to the Thames, but all you can really see is the testicle of the Mayor's office over the river.

How must Henry have felt when the executioners came to call? He would have known about his son's death and his dynasty's disintegration. What more did he have to lose? This poor, poor man that came to the throne when he was but nine months old and blown like an autumn leaf, forever withered in the evening light. From the moment his father died, his violent death seemed almost inevitable. For Shakespeare, it is the final rite of passage for both Henry and Richard: one to be martyred, the other to descend to hell, yet a living version of it. Henry's invective against Richard is his final salvo against the injustices he has received and caused. There is substance in it, and he touches Richard with his words, not a sword.

Henry's last speech lists the many superstitious omens that presaged Richard's birth. Henry has achieved the role of seer, a prophet rooted in the ways of the old, lost world:

King Henry VI

And thus I prophesy, that many a thousand,
Which now mistrust no parcel of my fear,
And many an old man's sigh and many a widow's,
And many an orphan's water-standing eye –
Men for their sons, wives for their husbands,
And orphans for their parents timeless death –

Shall rue the hour that ever thou wast born.
The owl shriek'd at thy birth,– an evil sign –
The night-crow cried, aboding luckless time;
Dogs howl'd, and hideous tempest shook down trees;
And chattering pies in dismal discords sung.
Thy mother felt more than a mother's pain,
And, yet brought forth less than a mother's hope,
To wit, an indigested and deformed lump,
Not like the fruit of such a goodly tree.
Teeth hadst thou in thy head when thou wast born,
To signify thou camest to bite the world:
And, if the rest be true which I have heard,
Thou camest –
Gloucester
I'll hear no more: die, prophet in thy speech.
For this amongst the rest was I ordained.
King Henry VI
Ay, and for much more slaughter after this.
O, God, forgive my sins and pardon thee.

(Henry VI Part 3 Act 5 Sc. 6)

Machiavellian reason kills off the superstitious ways of the past. Drunk on his own power to kill for the better good, Richard has secured the House of York in a dynasty that will be his. He is set firmly on his road.

As ever in Shakespeare, the road of reason and Machiavel – not of magic and the soul – always leads to destruction.

With the demise of Henry, the source of rebellion was stopped. The deaths of the axe-wielding maniac Somerset and his brother, at Tewkesbury, wiped out the Beaufort line – so now all of John of Gaunt's male progeny from his many marriages lay in the ground. The Lancastrian cause was over.

There was, however, one Beaufort left behind. Margaret Beaufort, daughter of the Somerset who had killed himself thirty years earlier, was the only 'Lancastrian' to linger. Married at the age of twelve to Henry VI's half brother, Edmund Tudor, Earl of Richmond, she bore him a son, Henry, a year and a half later. Margaret subsequently married two more immensely wealthy members of the aristocracy, and so was ideally placed to further the interests of her first-born.

Henry VI was silenced before he could name the young Tudor boy as his heir but nobody really thought it was necessary anyway: Edward IV was sitting on the throne not only by right of inheritance but by force of arms, and had not one but two young sons – an heir and a spare – to lay the foundations for the great Yorkist Plantagenet dynasty to come. Margaret Beaufort, secretly scheming and weaving a tangled web, would have to wait fourteen years to guide her exiled son to power.

For twelve of those years, by all accounts, Edward ruled well. Until his death in 1483, England settled to a certain degree. Indeed, a lot of the success of Edward's reign is down to the circumstances in which it came about – namely the end of the mutual headlock with France. The bitter pill England swallowed with the loss of France ultimately freed the economy and social structure to flower without the enormous drains put upon it by war and absent men. This was more by accident than design, as the very notion of being English required some sort of belligerence to the French, and Edward was always trying to plot an invasion or some form of destabilisation. He even raised an army and invaded France, but was met by the French King on a bridge in Picquigny who paid him a fortune to leave, thus securing Edward a tidy profit – the spirit of war for profit, rather than honour or survival, was thus confirmed.

There was still restiveness amongst the nobility, however, as once more the Woodvilles – the family of the Queen – were preferred, and the age-old aristocracy that had survived the swinging axe of the battlefield now found themselves crowded out of Court by what they saw as cuckoos.

As a consequence Clarence was committed to the Tower for treason in 1478 and it is thought he may well have even chosen the manner of his death – most probably drowned in a barrel of wine, or 'butt of malmsey'. What a way to go. Or he may have just been drowned in his bath which was usually made from half a wine barrel. In Shakespeare's new play, *Richard III*, Clarence's only crime, according to Richard, was that of thought. No truer word was spoken in the Elizabethan Court.

Of course the real truth and history got blurred. It seems that Richard had a slight curvature of the spine – as a Leicester car park has shown. This probably came about because of the incessant sword training he went through, as a slightly runty adolescent, which enlarged his right arm and shoulder. Contemporary accounts describe Richard as being the brother who looked most like his father, the Duke of York, who himself was a small man, and in no way physically imposing like most of the Plantagenets. Other facts have got blurred too: it may well be that Richard had something to do with the Princes in the Tower getting killed. It may well be that he managed skillfully to get Edward to issue Clarence's death warrant. He may not have done any of these things. The interesting thing is the debate and the identity it brings in itself: the most committed 'Ricardians' who passionately claim that Richard is much maligned behave as if they have been wronged themselves, and are as intractable as the dyed-in-the-wool traditionalists who say otherwise. The truth, as ever in England, and as we are beginning to find out because of a car park in Leicester, lies somewhere in between.

Much like Shakespeare. Whilst most might associate Richard III with clambering about *sans* horse at Bosworth, *Richard III* is essentially a London play. Plotting his way to the throne, Richard creeps about the walls of the Tower for most of the first act and schemes amongst the streets in the next, having fun in his anti-Morality Play: The 'bunch-backed' joker with white face and red lips is amongst us and we love him. There's a reason why clowns are creepy. It's fun as we watch him slap his brother Clarence on the back and into the Tower, and then pay money for his murder; then we witness a bare-faced Richard woo Warwick's daughter, Lady Anne Neville – whose first husband, Edward, we saw being killed by Richard at Tewkesbury. We exhort him as he manipulates the nobility or toys with the Woodvilles; and plays with the Church that sit like lambs to the slaughter of the Machiavellian genius limping about the stage. The Toad is centre stage, and loving it.

Henry VI's death may have made him a saint in many people's eyes, but another saint is ever present in *Richard III*. Sir Thomas More, canonised in 1935, wrote *The History of Richard III* and in one stroke ostensibly did more than any other man to create the Tudor myth that Richard was a hunchbacked psychopath. In a neat hand-me-down of history, More lived in the same house as Richard: Crosby House in Bishopsgate. From the same rooms in which Richard paced and perhaps plotted, More wrote his *History* from 1512 to 1519, but it remained an unfinished work. He never published it. There seems no doubt that he was writing to keep his master Henry Tudor pleased, but given how Henry had tortured More's father, and his subsequent handling at the hands of Henry VIII, the work can be seen not only as a Tudor rewriting of History but a book theorizing on the effect of tyranny and power – much like the one Machiavelli was working on from a different perspective at the same time in Florence. The Tudors were being commented on, not Richard III. Like any History, the time in which it is written frames the view.

After More was executed by Henry VIII for refusing to take the Oath of Supremacy in 1535, Crosby House subsequently fell into the hands of More's son-in-law, William Roper, who famously became ardently Protestant, but then recanted thanks to the prayers of his father-in-law, he said, and avowed his Catholicism to the end. Roper's wife, Margaret, was considered to be one of the finest minds of her generation next to her father. More had believed strongly in women's education and all his daughters had received tutoring in the great Humanist subjects of Classics, Music and Languages that were later to hold Elizabeth I in such good stead. It was to Margaret that More wrote his final 'prison letters' detailing his conviction in the Catholic faith and the heresy of Protestantism. It was also Margaret that bribed somebody on London Bridge to retrieve the head of her father after he had lost it in the Tower, and brought it back for safe-keeping to Crosby House.

Amid the cacophony of the Cade rebellion in *Henry VI Part 2* there is an extraordinary little scene where Queen Margaret cradles the separated head of the Duke of Suffolk. It is the most surreal image and throughout all The Histories there is nothing to compare to it. But to have a 'Margaret' standing there cradling a head, lamenting, is truly remarkable:

> **Queen Margaret**
> *Ah, barbarous villains! Hath this lovely face*
> *Ruled like a wandering planet over me,*
> *And could it not enforce them to relent,*
> *That were unworthy to behold the same?*
>
> *(Henry VI Part 2 Act 4 Sc. 4)*

Margaret Roper is perhaps the woman in the picture here.

Crosby House, in Bishopsgate, was more than just Richard's House. To the broken Catholics of England it was a shrine to a lost, Moreish, world. One of the few facts known about Shakespeare is that when he first moved to London, on receiving a demand for taxes owed in the 1590s, he lived in Bishopsgate.

St Helen's, the church which was once attached to Crosby House, is still there and survived the Great Fire and the Blitz but ultimately fell victim to the forces of violence, the causes of which it had been witness to. When I first moved to London the whole of Bishopsgate had just been blown apart by a bomb. The IRA was aiming at the heart of the English economy, but little did they know they were pinpointing one of the many hearts of the schism of which they, and their enemies, are the most prominently unfortunate inheritors. The bomb blew the roof off St. Helen's and destroyed many of the monuments that exist there. It has since been rebuilt and boasts that it is second only to Westminster Abbey within London in housing so many artefacts.

Bishopsgate is always a landmark for me – from the bus I watched it being rebuilt every day, the temples to a new religion now bathed in such a saturation of money and glacéd buildings that it seems an island. Just a few hundred yards down the road the City runs out and the teeming interest of Shoreditch begins. The site of Crosby House itself is now a bank.

In another quirk of fate, the house was moved in 1910 and rebuilt brick by brick at Cheyne Walk on the Embankment in Chelsea, on land that used to be an orchard owned by More himself. There is a statue to More on the road by Cheyne Walk and I have lost track of the amount of times I have driven past it with never a glance. But if the traffic knew it was an orchard, a little slice of Eden, and that the apples still grew here after the fall of More, then perhaps they might slow down and see with glittering eyes what Magic lies about.

Meanwhile, the hunchback is getting closer to the throne. Edward IV died. Having survived the battlefields and plots of his youth, at the age of forty-one, he simply died after a short illness. Whatever the cause of his death, it was a disaster. His son was only fourteen and the country had only just begun to heal from the wounds inflicted when a similarly strong King – Henry V – had died prematurely leaving behind an infant son and an empty space. Edward had appointed his loyal servant and brother, Richard, to be Protector of the Realm should anything happen, and Richard set about his duties with severe glee.

His power base was the North where he had either inherited or assumed massive tracts of land that spread from coast to coast across the Pennines and further South to the Trent. He had governed well, with York and Middleham Castle – where he had been brought up by the Earl of Warwick – as his principle residences. Even now it is these areas that bridle at the portrayal of Richard as a murdering schemer.

He at first sought to dampen the family that had so benefited from Edward's patronage. The Woodvilles had risen to such an extent through Elizabeth's marriage to the King that they posed a serious threat to the old aristocracy that chuntered in the corners of the Court. One of those old families, the Staffords, had at its head the young and charismatic Duke of Buckingham, who now joined forces with Richard in a spectacular closing of the old guard. If they could control the fourteen-year-old Edward V, then not only would the Queen's party be in a weakened position, the aristocracy could fight back. The days of a factional Court were back.

Lord Rivers, the Queen's brother, and his nephew, Richard Grey, were told by the Queen to bring her son, the young Edward V, post-haste to London from Ludlow Castle where he had been under their stewardship. The boy was a ball in a game in which Richard made the rules. Firstly, Richard wrote a conciliatory note to the Queen assuring her of harmony, which had the effect of lessening the armed force that accompanied Rivers and the boy on their journey to the capital. Richard and Buckingham simply marched from the North with a much bigger force of men and by the time Rivers and young Edward stayed in Stony Stratford on their way down Watling Street, the old guard just happened to be ten miles away in Northampton, polishing their nails.

Hopelessly outnumbered, Rivers and Grey were arrested by Richard and sent North to Pontefract where within a few days, along with another Woodville acolyte, Sir Thomas Vaughan, they were beheaded without trial. With the boy King now in their charge, Richard and Buckingham came to London where the Queen and her other son, the Duke of York, had taken sanctuary on hearing of her brother's death. Richard acted fast and decisively, flooding the City with his troops. The threat of civil war was once more looming.

There then followed a masterpiece of civil deception that rivals anything modern newspaper moguls could dream up. Richard and Buckingham denounced the sons of the late King as bastards because Edward's marriage to Elizabeth was unlawful, as he had been contracted to marry Eleanor Talbot beforehand. Lady Talbot never produced proof of such an alliance even years after the event, but thanks to the skilful oratory of Buckingham on the streets of the City – most probably in front of some beefy Northerners brought in for the event – Richard won out.

There is still much argument as to whether the illegitimacy was true or not. To me, it seems counter-intuitive that the two Princes should suddenly be declared illegitimate although no apparent talk of it for the previous twelve years should surface. But then Richard may well have been acting on what he thought was right. It seems that far from being the evil hunchback of History, he was an extraordinarily religious man. His thoughts may well have stemmed from a disapprovingly pious stance on his brother's rampant life – not least the marrying for love and lust that had seen the Woodvilles so advanced. But the fact remained that with Clarence's children attainted from inheritance because of their father's treason, the way was clear for Richard to be pronounced King.

Within the space of a few short weeks Richard was about to assume power. At a council meeting in the Tower, Sir William Hastings complained vociferously that Richard had gone too far. It was one thing to curb the Woodvilles, quite another to usurp the throne from Edward's son. Richard and Buckingham instantly arrested him and he was taken outside to the grounds and beheaded, once again without trial. John Morton, the Bishop of Ely, was lucky to escape with his life and fled.

Edward's two young sons, Edward V and the Duke of York, were forever consigned to be called the Princes in the Tower, more famous for their mysterious disappearance and probable deaths than any spark of life.

Richard, Duke of Gloucester, the younger brother who had served his family for so long in search of the Crown, was now sitting on the throne himself.

The tracing-paper image Shakespeare places over History for this play is surprisingly faithful to events. One of his most remarkable feats, though, is to resurrect the dead. Completely unprompted by any of his Tudor sources, Shakespeare brings back Queen Margaret. Now not only is there Vice, but there's a witch too. As preternatural as any weird sister, Margaret proceeds to use her bitter experience of having her son killed in front of her to divine the evil of the *bunch-backed toad* that so hobbles about the stage.

It's clear that the wronged past will be present on stage. Nowhere is this clearer than in a scene set on the streets of London between three frightened citizens who simply discuss the passage of events. They are not just catching up on the news; they are covertly assessing one another and guardedly stating their point. It very often gets cut from the play but to me it is as important a scene as any in The Histories.

> **First Citizen**
>
> *Come, come, we fear the worst. All will be well.*
>
> **Third Citizen**
>
> *When clouds are seen wise men put on their cloaks...*
>
> **Second Citizen**
>
> *Truly the hearts of men are full of fear.*
>
> *You cannot reason with a man*
>
> *That looks not heavily and full of dread.*
>
> **Third Citizen**
>
> *Before the days of change still is it so.*
>
> *By a divine extinct men's minds mistrust*
>
> *Ensuing danger as by proof we see*
>
> *The water swell before a boist'rous storm.*
>
> *But leave it all to God. Whither away?*
>
> **Second Citizen**
>
> *Marry we were sent for to the justices.*
>
> **Third Citizen**
>
> *And so was I. I'll bear you company.*
>
> *(Richard III Act 2 Sc. 3)*

Off they go to the justices – we never see them again – and one wonders what will happen. Is one an informer? Does somebody know something? Is the King/Queen dead? If so, who's going take over? Whose side will they be on?

It is as if Shakespeare is taking a scene that is happening outside the theatre as the play is going on, and directly putting it on stage. This play was written sometime around 1594 – they had another nine years to go before the old Queen went. The long, bony arm of an insecure, frightened and intolerant Queen and State reached everywhere. Long gone were the days of the religiously tolerant Virgin Queen giving birth to Britannia. She had been worn down by plots, wars and intrigue. Thought was now a crime. It was only on her deathbed that she affirmed that the Protestant James VI of Scotland, Mary Queen of Scots' son, would be King. Until then, walking the streets of London and talking to the wrong people could land you in the 'Justices'. Turning from the setting to the rising sun was treason.

Walk east from the Royal Courts of Justice now and you are on Fleet Street where some people have felt a similar chill of fear in more modern times. The great buildings of the old newspapers still reach out in faded stone, but the journalists have gone now to be replaced by the suited regimen of workaday London. William Caxton's apprentice set up the first printing press here in 1550 and by Shakespeare's day there were printers and publishers stretching all across Fleet Street and the bridge over the fetid river of the same name.

The Word was now not just with God. In the middle of depicting Buckingham and Richard's arch persuasion of the Mayor and the populace, Shakespeare has a man wander onto the stage on his own and speak directly to the audience. Again it is a small scene which is often cut, but he speaks of how he had been told to create the indictment of Hastings the night *before* Hastings was killed.

> **Scrivener**
> *... Here's a good world the while. Who is so gross*
> *That cannot see this palpable device?*
> *Yet who so bold but says he sees it not?*
> *Bad is the world and all will come to nought*
> *When such ill dealing must be seen in thought.*
>
> *(Richard III Act 3 Sc. 6)*

The manipulation of the Word, as Lord Leveson can testify today, is not a new phenomenon.

Go to the eastern end of Fleet Street, turn right, and you will be walking above the old Fleet River that flows into the Thames just a hundred yards away underneath what is now Blackfriars Bridge. On especially rainy days when the tide is low, you can see the filthy water spewing out from a hole in the wall. It was on these banks of the Fleet and the Thames that Baynard's Castle was built. Once held by the weak-willed Edmund Mortimer, Earl of March, and inherited by Richard Plantagenet, Duke of York, it had been the place where Edward IV was crowned by Warwick in 1461 and in 1483 was home to York's wife, Cecily Neville – mother to three dead sons and a hunchbacked one still very much alive. This extraordinary woman was born five months before the Battle of Agincourt and lived to see all but two of her thirteen children die. She finally died in 1495 at the age of eighty, her granddaughter having married Henry VII – a union from which all the subsequent Kings and Queens of England have descended.

Her presence is very strong in the play acting as a conduit for the history to be told and a scolding influence on the venality of Richard. As ever in Shakespeare, it is the women who mostly speak sense. The Duchess of York and Elizabeth Woodville ultimately unite to bring some sanity to the proceedings and open the way for Henry Tudor not only to seize the throne but tie the two Houses of York and Lancaster together by marrying Edward's daughter, Elizabeth of York, the sister of the two Princes in the Tower.

Like her youngest son, the Duchess of York is a divisive figure. Far from the compliant and quietly supportive wife that mediaeval chivalry decreed, she was an important heiress in her own right, so by the time her husband York had fallen at Wakefield she it was who became the cement in the Yorkist cause to rally her son to the throne. Labelled an adulteress during her lifetime when Edward IV himself was accused of being illegitimate, she was far from being spotlessly clean and these seem to be the key divisive points. Did she or didn't she? The fact that she seems to have been one of the most politically savvy and skilled survivors of her time is forgotten amongst the usual male preoccupations over whether she was unfaithful or not. She it was who stayed with Clarence and Warwick before they departed for France – some say to try and fend off the impending schism with Edward and keep her boys together, others to make sure her second son got hitched to Warwick's daughter, the most eligible girl in the land, and thereby giving her a win-win situation – especially as Edward, so they say, was indeed illegitimate. Some even suggest it was she who engineered Richard's rise to power after Edward's death because Edward had condemned her legitimate son in Clarence, and she could finally have a non-bastard on the throne.

Again, she may or may not have done any of these things. She was probably flintily political in allowing Richard his head even if it meant the probable destruction of her two grandsons. She had known all her life the consequences for a country run by a boy King and may have thought it better that her personal grief, already considerable, would be outweighed by the public good. On that she could have taught Machiavelli a thing or two. The truth lies buried between the stones under the Fleet that washes to the sea.

Walk from Baynard's Castle at Blackfriars back up past Fleet Street and you are walking the line of the river which once formed the boundary of the City. It is why Holborn Viaduct goes over nothing but a road, as there used to be a small gorge here where the Fleet cut through on its way to the Thames.

This time I walk up the steps of the Viaduct back onto High Holborn and there in front of me is Ely House and the Mitre pub that I first sat in to witness the fictional death of John of Gaunt. In *Richard III*, when Hastings is duped and cast aside by Buckingham and Richard, the Bishop of Ely is sent out to get some strawberries from his garden at Ely House. It was indeed famed for its garden, and is why the street that is now so famous for its jewellery is called Hatton Gardens.

Sir Christopher Hatton, as well as being indicative of the earlier parts of Elizabeth's reign in that he was tolerant to religious division and sought a way through the fundamentalism of both sides, had also sat on the councils that condemned first the conspirators of the Babington plot and then sent Mary, Queen of Scots to her death. It is even said that he was the one who encouraged William Davison to carry the order for Mary's death to Fotheringhay, even though Elizabeth was against it. It seems that the public good, and his own self-interest, weighed against the desire of his faith. Interestingly, his nephew bought New Place in Stratford-upon-Avon and that nephew's son was to sell it to Shakespeare.

Sitting in the Mitre pub again with its small rooms and wonderfully cozy beer, I can almost feel the taut wire of England that Hatton so delicately trod.

The taut wire – the path in between – had been negotiated long before, of course. None had walked it more successfully than the man who owned Ely House and who was sent to fetch the strawberries by Richard. The Bishop of Ely, John Morton, was one who trod the line of the Wars of the Roses with a finesse all of his own. He had fled with the Lancastrians to France, was present at both Towton and Barnet, but was ultimately pardoned by Edward and survived to thrive in the Yorkist era. He backed the right horse in Henry Tudor and eventually became Archbishop of Canterbury and Lord Chancellor – effectively running the country alongside Henry VII, inaugurating a tax system that revolutionised the finances of the King. He died at the age of eighty in 1500. Serving him as page boy was the young Thomas More, and there seems no doubt that for *The History of Richard III*, More mined the household of his youth and knew about the strawberries his master had been sent to fetch when Richard killed Hastings and made his bid for the throne.

It is difficult to imagine the Garden at Ely House now, standing by the smokers in the grey of the street outside the Mitre. The jewellery shines gold and silver, replacing the lost apples and strawberries that once glowed red in the sun. A window dresser has laced the floor of one shop with red rose petals which somehow chime with my thoughts, as I stand once again looking for colour in the grey.

When Hatton lived here in the 1580s, the Fleet River would have sludged past, flowing to the Thames a few hundred yards away, with Baynard's Castle looming large on its banks. By that time the castle was owned by Henry Herbert, 2nd Earl of Pembroke, whose wife, Mary Sidney, also lived in Crosby House. From the solitary red petals under the rings and trinkets of Hatton Gardens, I decide it is time to go to Arcadia.

Fourteen

Wilton

Wilton is a small town a few miles from Salisbury that squeezes the A30 into a single lane – a sure sign that some serious landowners will not be compromised by the demands of modern transport. In this case they are the Earls of Pembroke who own the remarkable Wilton House and Estate that used to sweep for eighty square miles up the Downs to Shaftesbury. The House used to be home to the 'Wilton Diptych' which was commissioned by Richard II and portrays him and his beloved White Harts, and a sprig of rosemary, being presented to the Virgin Mary by John the Baptist, St. Edmund of Bury, and Edward the Confessor. England.

But here in these privileged environs of folded valleys and sweeping hillsides of the Wilton Estate, the foundations were laid for one of the very tenets of a poetic England.

I'm also in Salisbury because it is here that Buckingham met his end. Richard had been crowned on 6 July 1483. Exactly fifty-two years later, to the day, Thomas More would be executed. The new King Richard processed through the streets from the Tower with his wife, Anne Neville, to the rather dubious cheers of a confused England. Legally Edward's marriage had been declared null and void by Parliament, so the way was clear. Edward's children, the Princes in the Tower, were last seen playing on the lawns of the Tower that summer. After the Restoration, the bodies of two small children were found in a staircase in the White Tower. They were declared by Charles II to be the two Princes and reinterred with full honours in Westminster Abbey, thereby sealing up the greatest mystery, and one of the greatest crimes, in English Royal history.

Buckingham himself was confused. No one really knows why he revolted against the newly crowned King Richard III. Buckingham had many grievances against Edward IV – not least for making him, the Duke of Buckingham no less, a member of the ancient aristocracy, marry one of the Woodville parvenus at a young age. He also felt that he had a right over vast areas of the Marches which Edward had steadfastly refused to give to him. He was duly promised the estates by Richard who, in turn, never gave them to him. Shakespeare seems to indicate that this, alongside a growing unease, is why Buckingham left him, but the counter-argument goes that Richard never had time to give them as Buckingham was already up in arms. Perhaps Buckingham wished to throw in his lot behind the boy King, Edward V, become the power behind the throne, and get his lands that way. He may well have risen up against Richard when he found out that the young Edward V had been murdered. Or he may have wanted the Crown for himself – his claim was just as valid as Henry Tudor's, if not more so, as his paternal line stemmed from Thomas of Woodstock.

What is certain is that England south of the Thames and west of the Severn rose up against the new King Richard straight away. From the depths of Herefordshire, in the land once ruled by Glendower and his magic, Buckingham coordinated his forces. His uncle had married the indefatigable Margaret Beaufort, the other great matriarch of England, and it was probably her that did most during Edward's reign to keep the Lancastrian flame alive. She was finally able to contact her son, whom she hadn't seen in twelve years, with hope for rebellion. Henry Tudor, last of the Lancastrians in exile, raised an army and set sail.

Yet once again the weather got in the way. All but two of Henry's ships launched at the English coast were driven back by the storm that raged for days. Some of the forces in the South jumped the gun and became bogged down in such bad weather that Richard was easily able to identify the rebellion and crush it mercilessly. There are even reports Henry's ship was encouraged to come ashore by waving English soldiers that in fact were Richard's men in disguise – but Henry smelt a rat and departed back to France. By the time Buckingham's forces had heard of the disasters in the South they were wet, tired and bedraggled and simply wandered off into the ether. Whatever Buckingham was, it appears he was no leader. All the wavering lords of the North West who may have helped were conspicuous by their absence. Buckingham was betrayed whilst in hiding near Leominster and taken to Salisbury where Richard was mopping up the rest of the rebellion.

Refusing to see him, or place him on trial, Richard had Buckingham executed in the Market Square. In what appears to be a running theme with Richard III, nobody knows what happened to the body. Even Richard suffered that fate himself for 500 years. A headless skeleton was found in the Blue Boar Inn on the market square during the Georgian era, but neither the skeleton nor the pub survive.

The market still churns wonderfully away in the square – selling everything from watercress to underpants – and one side of it is Blue Boar Row which is perhaps the only marker to what took place here in 1483. It was All Souls' Day – the great Catholic celebration of, and communion with, the dead – when Buckingham lost his head, an irony that Shakespeare doesn't forget.

> **Buckingham**
> *This is All Souls' day is it not?*
> **Sheriff**
> *It is.*
> **Buckingham**
> *Why then All Souls' Day is my body's doomsday...*
> *This, this All-Souls' day to my fearful soul*
> *Is the determined respite of my wrongs:*
> *That high All-Seer that I dallied with*
> *Hath turn'd my feigned prayer on my head*
>
> (*Richard III Act 5 Sc. 1*)

On All Souls' Day the community would pray for the souls in Purgatory that had not yet reached Heaven. The Reformation initially tried to stamp it out, as Purgatory was a 'popish' invention and incompatible with God's will, but the celebrations of All Souls', and especially All Hallows the day before, remained in Scotland and Ireland where they had been celebrating Samhain and Halloween for centuries. The Puritans that went to America were initially resistant to such superstitions but with the mass Celtic and Catholic immigration from both countries in the nineteenth century, alongside that of the Italians, came the inevitable celebrations and beliefs.

It is Halloween when I visit the Market in Salisbury. Everywhere there are rubber skeletons and witch hats that have accompanied Halloween in its great migration back from America in the new church of consumerism over the last twenty years. In England there is now a rather unique and wonderful combination of a superstitious, Catholic, Halloween allied to the Protestant celebration of 5th November. In Lewes, Sussex, for example, they wander around in witch costumes one night and then a week later burn an effigy of the Pope through the streets. Still, it is always nice to know we have fire to ward off the devils in the dark of winter – whatever form those devils take. The fireworks and bonfires that light up the night sky still do so with magic in our hearts as well as hot dogs.

Salisbury Cathedral is said to have been built at the place where a magical White Hart, shot with an arrow from the ancient settlement of Old Sarum, had finally stumbled and died. It might explain why the monks built the place there, as it's a terrible place to build anything – let alone a cathedral. Its foundations are about four feet deep and it has the largest spire in England. How the place has remained standing is a testament not only to ingenuity but sheer luck.

Five small rivers meet at Salisbury and the place regularly floods. But all of them flow through the enormous Wilton Estate just a few miles away.

One of the arguable results of Humanism, the Renaissance, and the Reformation, was to bring a form of heaven (and happiness) to earth. For some, no longer did we have to suffer in this life to achieve a Heavenly joy. By the mid-1500s, life in all its sweaty glory could actually be enjoyed to a certain extent, and a social hierarchy achieved whereby the ancient order of things could create a fullness and proportion in life. Christened 'Arcadia' by the Tudor poet and adventurer Sir Philip Sidney, the centre of this ideal in England was Wilton House – the palatial home of the 2nd Earl of Pembroke.

Pembroke had studied at Douai – the great Catholic finishing school on the Continent. Yet he married Mary Sidney – niece of Robert Dudley, Earl of Leicester – and henceforth became close to the cherished inner circle of Elizabeth I, and sat alongside Hatton on the board that prosecuted Mary, Queen of Scots.

His wife, Mary, set about creating at Wilton a vibrant artistic community led by her brother Philip, whose book *Arcadia* is dedicated to his sister and did much to establish the literary explosions that took place soon after. It was *Arcadia*, not Shakespeare or Marlowe, that Charles I quoted on the scaffold. The Petrarchan tradition of blank verse espoused by Henry Howard in his sonnets, the strictures of poetry and the soft romantic joy of the rural idyll, were all funnelled into this new expression of Heaven on Earth, Arcadia, as was the landscape and community of Wilton itself.

Whilst being ostensibly Protestant, it harked back to a pre-Reformation era of chivalry, shepherds and damsels in distress that evoked a somehow purer, less cynical time. Arcadia was full of pastoral pleasure and a world in which everyone knew their place – Lords looked after the peasants, who in turn looked after and worked hard for their Lords. The earth, landscape and human endeavour were united as one. It was, of course, an elitist, pie-in-the-sky morality that would not take into account human nature in the harsh labourings of the peasant or the casual domination of an uncaring master. But this didn't stop the minds of a privileged few who dreamt of the high ideals of honour, a natural life in Edenic bliss, and a Muse to inspire them. Through the sheep-nibbled Downs and the stream-washed valleys around Wilton, Sir Philip Sidney sieved this ideal of a new England for his own Muse, his sister.

Sidney died in typically dramatic fashion at the Battle of Zutphen in 1586 fighting for his uncle, the Earl of Leicester, and the Protestant cause. He had become more fundamental after witnessing unparalleled Spanish cruelty when present at the St. Bartholomew Massacre in Paris, and was vocal in his support for an all-out attack on Catholic Spain. Yet his writings reveal a more subversive, complicated yearning for an undivided, tolerant world. His circle of Arcadia was much more dissident in its condemnation of division. He was as confused, or double-sided, as Buckingham. It was only after his death that his sister Mary finished his work and began disseminating copies of *The Countess of Pembroke's Arcadia* around the cognoscenti of London. His passing caused much hand wringing of the ruling aristocracy with whom he was closely woven. His wife was Walsingham's daughter who went on to marry the Earl of Essex, and his family had been part of the governing class for generations. His funeral at St. Paul's was such a lavish affair that it nearly bankrupted Walsingham. Eight days after he died, Mary, Queen of Scots was sentenced to death at Fotheringhay by a council of thirty-six noblemen including Walsingham and William Cecil.

All of which increased the pressure in the bottle and eventually the cork popped with the Spanish Armada a year and a half later. All Catholic hopes of a redemption seemed to be tossed to pieces like the Spanish ships on the rocks of a new-found England – this sceptered isle. Yet the events of 1588 merely gave fresh impetus to Jesuits like Robert Southwell and Robert Parsons who used the persecution of Catholics to spur on sympathy for their counter-reformation. This was the reality of Shakespeare's England not the mythical, honour-filled world of Arcadia.

There seems little doubt that Shakespeare was hugely influenced by the 'Arcadian' principles of the pastoral idyll. Both Henry V and Henry

VI, for example, wistfully talk of the life of a shepherd being the true one. The regal destiny is shaped by the wish for the peace of a better England. A return to Arcadia. But Falstaff, for example, is no ideal warrior, or shepherd, and scoffs honour as much as he scoffs his food.

Many scholars place a performance of *As You Like It* staged for James I at Wilton in 1603. In the play Duke Senior casts off his regal slough in the Forest of Arden(nes) and professes himself happy to endure the seasons: '*Hath not old custom made this life more sweet/ Than that of painted pomp?*' Arden is a word that combines the mythical paradise of Arcadia with the biblical paradise of Eden. Shakespeare strode the two and within it he helped define England.

The old Wilton estate that stretched to Shaftesbury is no more, but the remote villages still nestle in the bosom of the hills, so nowadays you can drive around Arcadia. The roads follow the rivers in the valleys, and on either side the land rises to the hillside in delicate marks across an old, folded body. This is ancient country. It *feels* old here. The last ice age didn't come this far south so it was never wiped clean and reshaped like the more shouty places of the North or Snowdonia. There are no sharp crevices or crags here – no wonder Sidney found in its folds the mythical, pastoral wonder of Arkady in Greece.

It is an event indeed when a car comes past in these villages, so hidden and discreet, that I'm sure they still think of me and the MG as I potter through them. Drive through Fovant and the 'Pembroke Arms' is boarded up and desolate, but the valley opposite opens out to reveal a glorious array of chalk hillside carvings etched not by prehistoric man but by soldiers going to the trenches in World War I. The badges of the Wiltshire Regiment, the Post Office rifles, the London Rifle Brigade and many more proudly light up the Downs as memorials to a lost generation. Even on a dull day in late October the white chalk of the badges seems to light up the landscape. I think of all the bodies Geoffrey and I stood over at Agincourt, and the nearby ranks of white graves that awaited the men that carved these proud signs. Sir Philip Sidney died in battle at Zutphen, near Arnhem, 300 miles north of where all these boys found themselves in an earthly hell – as far removed from any paradise as humans could dream.

I drive to a pub a few miles away at Dinton where the landlady greets me warmly and offers me the choice of a long handle or straight glass for my pint. She says she is going to be busy with the shoot that afternoon when they finish with the pheasants and come for a drink. An old, old man coughs and shudders over his pint in the corner.

'It's getting colder, Mary', he says in the deepest West Country burr I have heard in a long while. She agrees, and I say it is cold, yes. I tell him I could feel the temperature dropping outside. 'Aye', he says, 'It's getting colder in here'. It isn't.

Five minutes later he says, 'It's getting colder, Mary' and she replies with the same thing, so I can't work out whether this ritual takes place every few minutes or he is genuinely getting colder. Anyway, he seems happy enough.

Then a boy walks in dressed in a check shirt, tie and plus fours. My pint stops on the way to my lips. Behind him comes his father dressed in exactly the same way. Exactly. His face is redder then Christmas, his hair as white. In a voice that could cut glass he orders a pint for himself and a lemonade for his son. Then he says loudly, and with no hint of embarrassment, 'I need to MAKE SOME ROOM. Where do I go?'

'The toilet's just through there', points Mary. His son eats some crisps at the bar, looking a fool. Now the beaters come in and sit around – more fathers and sons, this time in jeans and coats. When I get up to leave, Estragon says 'It's getting colder, Mary' and Pozzo and Lucky are at the bar eating their crisps.

Arcadia is alive and well.

Fifteen

The old kingdom of Wessex, of which Wilton was the capital, and who championed the cause of St. Edmund into the idea of England, can almost lay claim to have bypassed the Wars of the Roses. There is no doubt that people were swept up by their Lords to fight but most of the carnage took place elsewhere. It was the seething differences in the North and Wales compared to the South East, especially London, that fuelled the fire – as well as the dynastic squabbles and personal ambitions of two families. The West Country, as it does today, kept a low profile. It doesn't have to shout to make its presence felt.

Another of the areas that managed to avoid having too much to do with it all was the North West. This was chiefly because it was almost an autonomous state owned by one family that exercised such power and authority, and played such a canny political game, that the whole region could rest easy. The Stanleys were supreme.

Having grown from being Master-Foresters in the Wirral, they prospered through the wars in France under Edward III and still provide Prime Ministers and Tory politicians as much as the Cecils do today. What really marked their rise to power, however, was their uncanny ability to pick the right side at the right time. Sir John Stanley, for example, was in Ireland with Richard II when Bolingbroke was busy marching his juggernaut through England. Showing a chameleon-like talent for survival inherited by his descendants, he managed to switch sides successfully under the new regime and when most of the Northern magnates were siding with the Percies at Shrewsbury he remained loyal to Henry IV – getting an arrow in the throat for his pains. Yet he had picked the winner and thrived accordingly, being created titular 'King of Mann' and hoovering up lands all over Cheshire and Lancashire. His son quietly became a Baron through the minority of Henry VI and his brood disseminated all over the North West, ruling by the family name and the massive income of land, trade and astute marriages.

By the time Shakespeare was writing they had become the Earls of Derby and were as closely woven into the old English aristocracy as any Neville, Talbot or, indeed, Tudor. Many felt their claim to the throne was a viable one and for some they also had an added advantage because they were closet Catholics. Or, at least, they didn't say anything to the contrary. As a consequence most of Lancashire and Cheshire remained a hotbed of recusancy while the rest of England began to roll over. The Jesuits Robert Parsons and Edward Campion both used the area as a safe haven and there is an increasingly loud school of thought that Shakespeare had many connections here and may even have spent part of his 'missing' years at Hoghton Tower, near Preston.

The Stanleys were extremely adept at hiding anything that could be construed as intention – which is perhaps why they have spawned many a subsequent politician. They simply came across as having 'no' religion which, in the fevered Court of Elizabeth, could mean everything and nothing. Even Parsons wrote that their religion was 'doubtful.' To be opaque of religion was bad enough in the Elizabethan Court, but to be in potential line of succession was even worse. It took all of their famed ingenuity to stay alive. Henry Stanley, 4th Earl of Derby, was married to Margaret Clifford who felt she herself should be Queen and as a consequence fell in and out of intrigue with Elizabeth for most of her life – not least in trying to predict the Queen's death and thence being accused of witchcraft. A course of action that Dame Eleanor Cobham could have advised her upon. Derby himself fell in and out of relations with his wife whom he eventually divorced complaining that she had virtually bankrupted him. Yet that had almost been achieved by Elizabeth herself when she kept insisting on visiting him and procuring the lavish hospitality expected. The Tudor monarchs had been doing a good job of trying to curb the Stanley power for the best part of a century, as their vast wealth had been a serious threat to them all.

But Derby proved loyal to his sovereign. He, too, sat on the panel that convicted Mary, Queen of Scots, and was trusted enough by Elizabeth to become Lord High Steward in the trial of his own relative, Philip Howard, Earl of Arundel, who was eventually made a saint in 1970.

Even if Derby did a fine job of playing the good Elizabethan he was always accompanied by the whiff of treason either from connections with his fellow Northerners, or from others in his restive family. Foremost among these was his cousin, Sir William Stanley. Fighting alongside Sir Philip Sidney in the Battle of Zutphen in 1586, Sir William had been an exemplary warrior for Elizabeth's cause but had subsequently, and famously, defected to the forces of Philip II of Spain. He spent the rest of his life wandering about Europe sheltering in the lee of the Spanish Court. His right-hand man was a certain Captain Jacques, and the two men became the meeting point for various military plots to place a potentially Catholic Stanley on the English throne. Sir William's defection caused huge consternation at home, and his name became a byword for treachery amongst a Court and populace faced with the growing Armada of Philip II.

Despite all this, Derby clung on. Philip II even stated Derby was 'most fit to be proclaimed King... so as to gain the hearts of the people'. Philip did the same disservice to Derby's son who was perhaps the biggest enigma of them all. The interestingly monikered Ferdinando Stanley, Lord Strange, heir to the earldom of Derby, was named after the Holy Roman Emperor and lauded as a gifted poet and quicksilver intellect. He kept his cards very close to his chest, yet he remained one of the greatest benefactors of arts and theatre in his era.

The Stanleys were heroes to the performers, tumblers, actors and impresarios that had leapt from the tireless merry-go-round of travelling theatre to the more stationary delights of performing in one place and solely putting on plays. The cultural shift that had allowed theatre to thrive was financed not only by the Reformation but by the families of the wealthy keen to see the spirit of the 'Plays' survive. Troupes of actors, named after their benefactor, would perform at their various grand houses – or go on tour in times of plague and hardship. They would eventually vie with each other in the theatres of London to pull in the punters. This meant that the great Stanley houses at Knowsley, Chester or Bickerstaffe rivalled any royal palace with courtly entertainment, theatrical innovation and intellectual endeavour. There is considerable debate about whether Shakespeare was part of 'Lord Strange's Men' but it seems certain that his *Henry VI* plays were staged by them in London in the early 1590s, and there is no doubt that the Earl of Southampton, Shakespeare's principal benefactor, was both a relative and acolyte of the Stanleys.

All of which goes to explain Shakespeare's depiction of Thomas, Lord Stanley who changed the course of history at Bosworth in 1485. Like Richard III, Shakespeare's Stanley is a Renaissance man in mediaeval clothing. For a start, Shakespeare calls him the Earl of Derby which he wasn't at all until the newly crowned Henry VII created him Earl in gratitude for his deeds at Bosworth. Other Shakespearean grafts to the story include how Queen Elizabeth Woodville, Edward IV's wife, was in conflict with Stanley's wife – but there is no known record of any such fractiousness although it was certainly true of Elizabeth I and Margaret Clifford, Derby's portentous wife.

All of the sources Shakespeare used for his play depict Stanley as a mere husband of the main player in the saga, Margaret Beaufort. Shakespeare doesn't even let her in to his play. It's all about Stanley and he it is that liaises with Henry Tudor, still lowly Earl of Richmond at this stage. He proposes the union between the two houses and is the man treading the precarious boundary between loyalty and treason.

Shakespeare also merges two Stanleys together. The mediaeval Thomas, Lord Stanley, was the head of the family but his younger brother, Sir William, proved to be the real spy. He was the one who actually plotted with the Earl of Richmond and Margaret Beaufort to launch an invasion.

Thomas, whether he knew of his brother's plans or not, was meanwhile sitting elusively on the fence in Richard's Court: he had been one of the lucky lords to escape with his life from the infamous meeting in the Tower in which Hastings lost his head.

As a Northerner, the new King Richard III had perhaps known which side his bread was buttered, and felt it better to keep Stanley sweet – he was, after all, a man who presided over nearly half of England. So after Buckingham's rebellion, Richard toured England and introduced a fleet of reforms that were later to be commended by both Wolsey and Bacon even through the gritted teeth of Tudor propaganda. But he suffered personal tragedy in quick succession when his ten-year-old son, Edward, died at Middleham in August 1484. His wife, Anne Neville, soon followed in March 1485. There is no evidence to suggest that Richard, as the chronicles rumoured and Shakespeare suggests, had poisoned Anne in order to marry his niece Elizabeth of York. Indeed, contemporary reports tell of Richard weeping openly at his wife's funeral. She lies in Westminster Abbey a few feet from Richard II and the shrine of Edward the Confessor. Thus swirled the final eddies of the powerful oar that was the Earl of Warwick.

But by the time the Stanleys were busy plotting, Richard was a lonely man suffering private grief for not much public good – so he was desperate to ensure his throne and a strong succession. He made enquiries as to new wives amongst the royalty of France and named John de la Pole, his nephew and Suffolk's grandson, as his successor. He also strongly suspected the Stanleys of treason, so he interrogated Thomas's son, George, who revealed the liaison of Sir William Stanley with Richmond. Richard declared William a traitor and placed George under house arrest, on pain of death, to ensure good behaviour from the Stanley faction.

But this time the winds of rebellion were on Richmond's side and whether or not he was bolstered by the secret news of Stanley's support – or at least neutrality – he managed to land on the coast of his native Wales at Milford Haven in the summer of 1485.

Except that South Wales wasn't that bothered. The few men Henry Tudor had with him were not joined by a tearful multitude greeting the prodigal son. It was only when he headed north to Mid Wales that he began to reopen the wounds of Mortimer's Cross and garner support. By the time he got to Shrewsbury he had a few thousand men at his disposal and set off to London.

On hearing the news of Henry's march through Wales, Richard issued a Royal call to arms from London and promptly left with an army up Watling Street, the great curved spine of England, to head off the traitor before he could get any stronger.

The scene was set for them to meet in the middle.

Bosworth

Just north of Coventry, Watling Street begins to curve westwards and it is here that the two armies began to circle each other, eventually settling a few miles over the Warwickshire border, near Market Bosworth in Leicestershire. No one can be more specific than that, as the Battle was given many names once fought, and no one really knows the exact spot. Important finds have been discovered in a field a mile or so away from what was thought to be the battlefield, so it seems likely that it took place here and not further back up the hill. It was *somewhere* around here – a fact about which the Bosworth Visitor's Centre is refreshingly honest. It was built in 1974 and only in 2009 did it realise it was in the wrong place, but at least there is a Centre, I suppose, and at least it is in the general environs. There has to be some way of marking it: ask anybody to name an English battle and they will probably say Hastings or Bosworth. We still live in an age of Tudor propaganda (a word first used by Jesuits in the early sixteenth century) and this is a battle imprinted on the national consciousness, unlike Towton, or the rest of the far bloodier battles that have scarred the land.

Beside the obligatory 'mediaeval' houses and various coats-of-arms dotted about, considering what it could have been, the Centre is not so bad. The most striking thing is a beautiful sundial on top of the hill which seems to double as a memorial and from here you can see across the whole shallow valley where the battle was probably fought and also the hill where they thought it had been fought. There seems little doubt that where the Centre sits, Ambion Hill, was where Richard's troops lay up to rest and reflect the night before the battle.

Richard himself spent the night rather famously at the Blue Boar Inn in Leicester, which is now a Travelodge. The old building was knocked down in the nineteenth century and according to local legend had changed its name from the White Boar, Richard's insignia, to the Blue Boar once the outcome of Bosworth became clear. Whichever way, the security grills of an overpriced car park and the conformity of faceless windows do perhaps chime with the Purgatorial Richard tossing uncomfortably in his bed, as Shakespeare portrays him. Plagued by the ghosts of those he has killed in his past, he is seen as a demonic dreamer finally confronting his conscience. I wonder if the architect of the present-day building feels the same.

But on this wind-blown winter day in the Bosworth Visitor Centre, I see no ghosts – just the silver sundial that marks out time. I walk the 'Battlefield' trail to get a feel of the land. It is the dead of winter and the hedges are brown and leafless. In the summer someone has obviously carefully picked up their dog's shit in little plastic bags, and then summarily thrown it all into the hedge only for it to be exposed by winter. So every few hundred yards I come across another little parcel of joy hanging on a branch. If you fancy a good game in summer, go to Bosworth, hide behind the hedge and fling it back at them.

I dutifully take in the information boards dotted around the site, but in truth it's not very inspiring countryside and the main thing that made a difference in the battle is no longer there: the entire battle was fought around a marsh which has now been drained. The two armies had to avoid the area at all costs – so Richard III's forces were ranged across the hill looking south over the marsh, with the Duke of Norfolk leading his right flank away from it. The left flank, guarding the area behind, was headed by yet another Henry Percy, Earl of Northumberland.

Henry Tudor had never fought in combat before and somewhat sensibly gave the running of his battle to the Earl of Oxford who, when Richard ordered Norfolk to avoid the marsh and attack Henry's left, instructed his men to huddle together rather than widening to fight, so the rampaging Yorkists just couldn't find a way through.

Seeing Norfolk's attack foundering, Richard gave the order for Northumberland to attack on the left. Northumberland didn't move a muscle. Whether this was the act of a traitor we shall never know, but it may have been a militarily sensible move as he either had a marsh in front of him or another sizable force in the body of men that constituted Lord Stanley's army. Stanley and his brother were waiting in the wings to see what would happen. True to their blood, they hovered on the line and bade their time.

Perhaps in a bid to persuade the Stanleys, Henry Tudor broke from the main battle to head round the marsh towards them, and Richard seized his chance. Taking only his most prized fighters and trusted Lords with him, he launched a daring cavalry charge straight for Henry in a bid to finish the battle once and for all. It was the last charge of Chivalry and mediaeval passion. Honour, death or glory, and a victory to sing through the ages were all at stake as Richard spurred on his horse towards his enemy, sword outstretched.

He sank. The marsh put pay to his ambitions and the mediaeval era went with him. Considering the circumstances, he did pretty well in taking out Henry's standard-bearer and managing to get within a few feet of the no-doubt perturbed and sweating Henry, whose bodyguard formed a circle around him that proved impenetrable.

But Richard's horse, laden with an armour-clad man, simply disappeared into the mud. Forced to fight on the boggy ground, Richard began to lose his footing. Stanley, seeing that Richard's gamble was failing, launched an attack on the small band of men that had got so close to the Lancastrian leader, and it was over within minutes as Richard was borne down by mud and the cloying pull of treason. The skeleton they have found in the car park in Leicester has a stab wound in the back – there is no finer allegory for his death. Six days after Bosworth, William Caxton published Malory's 'Le Morte D'Arthur' – which may have been in response to the final Plantagenet's death, and sealed the Age of Chivalry and Arthurian Britain as a mediaeval conceit forever.

When Shakespeare shows Richard scrabbling around in the mud shouting for his horse, it seems he is simply recording fact. But the ensuing showbiz fight between Richard and Henry is a complete fabrication. However it neatly rounds things off and leaves the way for Henry Tudor to be crowned by Stanley, his step-father. To Shakespeare, this glorious honour of Henry Tudor keeps the authorities sweet whilst the allegorical killing of Cecil remains.

Cecil's death was all a fantasy, of course. Robert Cecil, the 'Toad', survived to ease the Protestant transition from Elizabeth to James I, and also to foster a Cecil line that continues to this day. So do the Stanleys, but not through the eldest son, Ferdinando. He died in mysterious circumstances in 1594, just as he inherited the Derby title. It is thought he may even have been poisoned by Jesuits when he refused to countenance Catholic plans for another plot against the Queen. Whichever way, with him went another hope of salvation for a tolerant society most Catholics so craved.

Crown Hill, where Henry Tudor was crowned, is not far away in Stoke Goulding which advertises itself on the sign on the way into the village as 'the birthplace of the Tudor dynasty' – which seems a tad boastful, but looking at the village, it is perhaps the only thing they can cling on to. On this weekday afternoon both the pubs are shut, but the 'Dog and Hedgehog' in Dadlington a mile or so away is packed, and offers a much better view of the battleground than even the Visitor's Centre. I sip a pint of 'Henry Tudor' ordered from the bar and look over the wintry fields, drained of the water that so bogged down the last mediaeval King. The Plantagenets – chivalric, insane, honour-laden and the Roses of England – have turned to dust.

Or have they? After the battle Richard's body was paraded naked by Henry for three days, and we now know that he had a dagger shoved up his arse and was buried with little ceremony in the quire of the Greyfriars' Chapel. This was subsequently torn down in the Reformation and lay forgotten and undiscovered for 500 years. A quarter of a mile from the Travelodge that adorns the Leicester ring road, an exhibition has sprung up in the Guildhall to celebrate finding King Richard III in a council car park.

Whatever I may think of the more important 20-40,000 dead of Towton, it's a wonderful archaeological discovery and I find myself standing in the queue next to two middle-aged women who are firmly in the 'Ricardian' camp. A man who works for the Exhibition plies the queue with flyers and is dressed in a stupid mediaevalesque costume that sports a fine white T-shirt underneath. He says to one of the ladies that a woman came into the Guildhall four years ago and came over all funny. Apparently she pointed to the wall beyond the cathedral and said Richard was over there in the car park. The ladies' eyes widen with delight and disbelief.

But these two know their stuff and their excited and warm chatter is infectious, talking about all the books they had read and who was right and who was wrong.

'I've always loved him', says the one on my right. 'For me, it was always Richard III. And then Prince Rupert.'

'Richard III and Prince Rupert' says the other. 'And Bruce.'

Pause.

'Bruce?' I say.

'Springsteen, of course.'

'Of course.'

'Richard, Rupert and Bruce.' They sigh together.

When they discover I am an actor who has appeared in *Richard III* they tut with dismay and proceed to throw facts and figures at me with the zeal of the wronged. The discovery has led their rebellious, almost underground, cause to be wrenched out into the open alongside his bones. And what wonderful, curved, bones they are – nicely muddying the argument that many Ricardians posed that he didn't have a hunchback. It seems the Tudors started from a small acorn of truth and grew it into their own oak. Aside from that, whatever arguments reasonable Ricardians make seem decent and well-founded, although until someone comes up with a definitive answer as to what happened to the Princes in the Tower, and why he made a bid for power, we can only ever make a judgement. If Richard had won the Battle of Bosworth, the children of Edward IV might always have been declared illegitimate and we would have excused his accession on the grounds that he acted decisively, perhaps even piously, and saved the country from yet more civil war. Henry Tudor would have been a footnote alongside all the other pretenders to the throne that he himself subsequently crushed with an iron will. Our modern-day sensibilities obscure not only mediaeval moralities but hard facts, and those hard facts about Richard are only just beginning to come to light. With his body being discovered it will be interesting to see how 'The Richard III Society' copes with toleration.

The Society used to write to every actor that played Richard III at the RSC to let them know they were pedalling a lie. Perhaps now they won't feel the need to anymore, and we can all appreciate the play for being one of the greatest artistic expressions of human venality, national culpability and social commentary that will ever be created – as pertinent now as it ever was.

Sixteen

Fotheringhay

From Bosworth, head back down Watling Street then turn left and follow the River Nene – the artery from the heart of England to the fat belly of the East – and, like Tewkesbury, you can see the aspiring and gracious tower of Fotheringhay shimmer proudly on the riverside. This huge, mighty church sits wonderfully, incongruously, in the landscape. Such an ornate church might be found in the confines of a lofty city but here there is no other building for miles that approaches anything like it – in fact, there is no place like it at all. Tewkesbury has a town around it, but Fotheringhay has nothing but a couple of farms and a gaggle of houses. From the bridge over the River Nene, looking at the church I see a vision of power and majesty that fleets along the riverside before closing once more on a solid lump in the ground that was the castle. It is as eloquent a piece of landscape as I have seen on my journey.

It was once owned by King David I of Scotland in the twelfth century – the man who was mythically charged at by a magical White Hart, and built the Palace of Holyrood in Edinburgh at the spot. But this church at Fotheringhay is all that is left of the great headquarters of the Yorkist movement that so boldly made its bloody mark on England. In the soaring altar lie the boiled-down bones of Edmund, Duke of York – Aumerle of Shakespeare's *Richard II* – who died fat, sweating and untouched at Agincourt. On the other side lie his nephew Richard Plantagenet, Duke of York, and Richard's wife, the long-suffering and formidable Cecily Neville. Their son, the Earl of Rutland, killed alongside his father at Wakefield, also shelters in these arches.

Richard III was born here and christened in the font that stands underneath the York family crest of the fetterlock and falcon. I stand open-mouthed as I look upwards and see the more intimate signs of a family. These are not the conquering, dynastic White Rose and golden suns of Tewkesbury where one of York's other sons, Clarence, lies buried, but here the family crest and the calm of the soaring arches belie the violent notes of its founding family. Had history been different this place would have been as grand, important and revered as St George's Chapel at Windsor, or Buckingham Palace. Because it became a tributary of History not the river itself, it feels intimate – like a lost family photo album.

There is an organist playing as I wander through the past, and I try to make some sort of a noise so as not to give him a heart attack, but it is no use – he is lost in the reverie of music that provides an extraordinary soundtrack to the marbled tombs of the Dukes of York.

Edward IV built a huge Chantry chapel here to house the bodies of his father and brother when they were brought back from Pontefract by the young Richard, still only Duke of Gloucester, in 1476. However, Henry Tudor was understandably not too keen to lavish funds upon the Yorkist headquarters once he became King and later, during the Dissolution, the whole building fell into disrepair so that by the time Elizabeth visited in 1566 she was horrified to discover the resting place of her great-great grandfather so abused. She ordered the Chantry to be knocked down, the church cleaned up and the bodies of her ancestors re-interred in shining new tombs. These are the tombs that flank the altar, and the bricked up archways to the non-existent chantry behind can clearly be seen.

I stand swathed in music and think back to these tombs' progenitor – the hovering, equivocating first Duke of York, buried at King's Langley, that roundly admonished Bolingbroke and yet sided with him. I think of his rebellious son Aumerle, who lies to my right, that so wanted Richard II back on the throne but who finally straddled the divide and ended up fighting for the usurper's son, Henry V. I think of the mud of Agincourt into which Aumerle fell from his no doubt relieved horse. I am taken to the Temple Garden where Richard Plantagenet, who lies to my left, had the fictional argument that kicked off the ensuing carnage. I think of Cecily Neville, who lies with him, mothering her brood by the river in Baynard's Castle as the hounds closed in. Beside me is a magnificent pulpit built by Edward IV that seemingly winds all the colours of the rainbow up to the lectern. I remember how his father gave battle in vain and yet three months later, at Towton, Edward gained a crown swimming in the blood of thousands upon thousands upon thousands.

'SHIT.'

'Woah,' I say.

'Oh Jesus. Sorry. You startled me.' As if wrenched from a record player the organist has noticed me and now clutches his heart. The silence.

'Sorry, I was trying not to.' I say.

'That's alright, it's a bloody tricky piece this anyway.'

'It sounds lovely.'

'Hmm,' he says, 'Still haven't got it yet. I'll try it again later.'

'Don't let me stop you.'

'No, it's fine. My wife has a pork pie.'

'What?'

'A pork pie.'

'Really?'

'Yes. I'm late for it.'

'Ah.' I say. 'Enjoy.'

'I will. Goodbye.'

He gathers his music, rubbing his heart, leaving me to the silence of the tombs.

Outside, the octagonal tower rises to the heavens and the whole place is thrumming with bees and rosemary. A huge bush of it lies where the bodies once lay in the long-gone chantry. I think of the Wilton Diptych where Richard II is depicted as the divine majesty of England in a cloth of red and gold bearing White Harts and sprigs of rosemary.

Along the northern roof of the church are gargoyles of the man who fought for that majesty – Richard, Duke of York, his wife Cecily Neville, and the man who built the church, William Harwood and his dog, Buster. In between the man who would be King and the artisan and his dog sits a Green Man – the man in the forest who, like Shakespeare, unites them all. Standing in the graveyard, once again I get lost in time. The smell of rosemary, the sound of the bees, the tingle of the Wars of the Roses and the man in the forest, wash England over me like cider from the orchards of my youth.

Such hopeless romanticism doesn't last long when you walk to the castle. There is nothing there other than a big lump in the ground and a ditch. Looking like a pillow under the jumper of the land, the whole place seems to be returning from whence it came. One lone piece of masonry forlornly sits by the river, like the final prow of a sinking ship.

Or a poodle under the dress of a Queen. When Mary, Queen of Scots was beheaded here in 1587, not only did her wig fall off to reveal a grey-haired woman who had aged before her time, but a small dog was discovered hiding in the now lifeless red dress of her mistress. The faded hopes of the old world could not have been better represented. Shakespeare was twenty-three and the divided world he had been born into could not have reached wider. Her death did give fresh impetus to the covert priests, recusant writers and treasonous Lords that so defined the era, to counter the likes of Cecil and Walsingham in what they saw as the tyranny of England, yet the head was off in more ways than one. Although Catholic hopes shifted to other candidates, not least Lord Strange, the focus seemed to have gone. The potentially Catholic aristocracy like Derby, Pembroke and Sir Christopher Hatton had sat on their hands and watched Mary's head depart her body. The spirit of old England was seeping away with a Scotswoman's blood back into the land. The wringing hands of the nobility were tied by heroic failure, quivering inaction and the passage of time. Their followers could only stare and pretend to believe in the church they were forced to attend.

Yet the smoking timbers of society the Reformation left behind became the scaffolding of the new theatre: ritual, community, magic and belief were now used to build a New World of the imagination. From the friction, the Chaos, grew one of the greatest artistic expressions of what it is to be human: to be or not to be – that was the question. Whether it was nobler in the mind to suffer the slings and arrows of outrageous fortune or by opposing, end them.

Shakespeare wrote *Hamlet* in 1599 – the same year he completed *Henry V*. Elizabeth was STILL in power. He would go on to complete his Histories with *Henry VIII* once James I was on the throne and the Elizabethan Court was safely swept away. The Earl of Essex, whom Shakespeare so eulogises in *Henry V*, was yet to have his ineffective rebellion on the eve of which *Richard II* was performed for the conspirators. Essex was the last in a long line of aristocratic subversion that many Catholics backed, as he represented a case for tolerance and freedom. The Earl of Southampton, Shakespeare's earliest benefactor, would languish in the Tower for two years afterwards. Honour, chivalry and decency were no longer enough to survive in the New World. Combine them with commerce, ingenuity and not a little venality and it would get you a lot further. The stage was set for Britannia – born between Mary Stuart, Queen of Scots, in red, and the white brilliance of Elizabeth the Virgin.

Sitting atop the mound of earth that is Fotheringhay Castle one can see so much of this green and very pleasant land. It feels like sitting on the past: a plug stopped into History. It feels as if at any moment if it were removed a whole different swathe of reality would come exploding out, like a burst appendix in the historical bloodstream.

But that would be Magic.

The rolling hills in the distance still roll. They are split by the lilt of the Nene heading back upstream to the heart of England.

Deep beneath me is the blood of a woman whose grave personified the schism of these islands. After the death of Richard III, this place was given to the successive wives of Henry VIII and so became the bounty of lust, folly and power. For a while it became the barometer of England. But Mary's son, the Protestant King James I, rather understandably allowed the place of his mother's execution to fall into disrepair.

I go and stand by the river, flowing gently to the sea, near the lone piece of masonry surrounded by a metal fence upon which a plaque reads that Richard III was born here and that Mary, Queen of Scots was beheaded. Beside the plaque is a freshly cut thistle from which hangs her picture. There is also a piece of tartan and attached to it, wound in its folds, is a White Rose. The unfolding history of the dispossessed, the Pretenders, carries on.

History, as Shakespeare knew, is not history at all.

If you head west from here on the modern A14, it pretty much follows the River Nene back to its source near Watling Street in the small hills of Northamptonshire. Another river rises in the same hills only separated by a small valley – the Watford Gap. Instead of heading East into The Wash like the Nene, this river instead travels West and flows into the Bristol Channel. It is the Avon.

These two rivers form a cross from which North, South, East and West can be drawn – there is still a saying of Southerners that 'anything North of the Watford Gap' is a mystery to them. But it also forms a boundary in History as well as Geography, for it was on these fields that James I's son, Charles I, finally saw his Royal power defeated. The village of Naseby sits almost equidistant between the rivers.

The Civil War battle of Naseby in 1645 was the turning point for the Parliamentarians against the Royalist forces. The King's power, and that of Prince Rupert for that matter, was smashed and he turned to the Catholic nations of Europe and Ireland for help. History had come full circle. Four years later, Charles lost his head. It was the culmination of all the social, political and religious upheavals Shakespeare and his contempories had been documenting. Eleven years later the King was restored and England, later Great Britain, proved itself capable of living above a chasm, a *limen*, that still exists today. We now view History through the prism of Britannia and the carnage of the Civil War, so places like Towton and Barnet are forgotten.

Walk from the grave of Henry V in Westminster Abbey, through the magnificent Lady Chapel, stand behind the tombs of Henry VII and Elizabeth of York, and you will find yourself where Cromwell was buried and then disinterred. Through the window, across the road, you can see his statue standing guard by Parliament and Westminster Hall. Back in the Abbey, walk to your right and you see the extraordinary white marble of Elizabeth I, lying with orb and sceptre, whose body was actually placed *on top* of her Catholic sister, Mary I, in their tomb. Close by, in a magnificent tomb created by her son, Mary, Queen of Scots lies with the red, Scottish, lion at her feet. These are the prisms through which most of the English view their History – Agincourt, Bosworth, Britannia and the Civil War – not Towton, Barnet or back at the bloodied and bruised shrine of Edward the Confessor, the soul of England. The damp squib that is St. George's Day compared to the heady celebrations of the Scots, Welsh and the Irish on their national days is a testament to this. Those nations have all fought bloody and serious battles against the forces of Westminster imperialism, but strangely, so have the English. It's just forgotten under the patchwork quilt, golf clubs and twitching suburbia of Great Britain. The dubious trident of Britannia.

The soul of England, however, lived on in the people. Once the Church became a place of individual worship and mandatory thought, the Church-ales and Parish-ales that had fed the community migrated straight to the pub. Anti-temperance, Falstaff, was born. The authorities and priests charged with making sure that people attended Service during the Elizabethan era noted with increasing desperation that most of their flock found it better, and more non-committal, simply to go down the pub than make a statement by going to Church. The 'authorities' have been wagging their finger from the other side ever since.

James I's insistence on his Red Lion insignia being placed on public buildings sealed forever the names of so many pubs that had changed their name from the White Hart two hundred years before. But James had more to contend with than pissed parishioners, and Shakespeare was on hand to comment upon it. James, the son of Mary, Queen of Scots, proved a disappointment to the more fervent Catholic extremists, some of whom decided to take up arms against a sea of troubles and launched a 'Plot' to end all plots from their heartlands in Warwickshire. The very idea of it, let alone its failure on 5th November, 1605, succeeded in putting toleration back a hundred years. Robert Catesby, a distant relation of Shakespeare, was the ringleader and Guy Fawkes's hung, drawn and quartered body was barely cold before Shakespeare performed his new 'Scottish Play' about an increasingly insane Scottish King, Witches and Equivocators.

Likewise, a few years later as Shakespeare wrote *Coriolanus* with its depictions of a hungry population rioting for bread, so the Midlands Uprising was rocking James's administration to the core.

The uprising was born from the frustration in these very fields of Northamptonshire in 1607. Driving through the lanes and fields of Naseby now, I stop the MG in a lay-by where I can see a red and white flag fluttering through the trees. It hangs above a memorial to the battle, between a field of newly harvested corn and another of cabbage. I walk to the top of the hill. From here the water seeps to the Nene one way and the Avon the other. It is normal, lovely countryside. I can almost feel Shakespeare's vision that the Cathedral of Nature didn't need to be Catholic or Protestant to show the hand of his God. The A14 main road is shouting nearby, but Naseby Church sits peeking from the plump bounty of oaks and pasture. A man in a silly helmet even drives past on a Triumph motorcycle.

For a breath, a little scene, if you want it to be, it could be this other Eden, demi-paradise.

Of course it's not. There's too much life in England for that. Every place I have visited shows the gap that Shakespeare was born into and which he filled with humanity, magic and wonder. England would not be England without him and, standing at Naseby, I realise why The Histories which I performed every night for three years were so successful.

Thanks to time and the incessant plots against her, in the last ten years of her reign – when Shakespeare was writing his History Plays – Elizabeth lurched to a much stricter form of control. Her power came not through devotion to her but by enforcement. Through the machinations of the Cecils and her toiling Archbishop of Canterbury, Thomas Whitgift, the push for Conformity was ruthlessly increased. Thus the walls of both sides of the divide were pushed ever higher so the extremism that led the Puritans to America and the Catholics to ever more violent acts of terrorism was fostered. Shakespeare, the 'interior exile' who saw the change from his father's religion to the Protestant London ways, was putting his hand up through these History Plays for tolerance and freedom of thought in a troubled world. Through the telling of one History he was able to comment on another and it is why they are as pertinent today as ever. Conformity, extremism, tolerance and freedom of thought are sadly no less topical today as they were then.

When we watch these Histories we are watching ourselves. It becomes a little clearer here in the place which was such a watershed in History, where two rivers flow to the sea – one past Fotheringhay to the East, the other past Stratford-upon-Avon to the West.

During the writing of this book a White Hart was spotted in Exmoor – the hills that look out over the Bristol Channel and the sea. Perhaps this magical creature, at once a talisman of luck and also a harbinger of doom, is looking out over History. Perhaps it is not of an age but for all time. Perhaps it looks up the river, through time, past Tewkesbury, Stratford-upon-Avon and over Watling Street to where I stand at its source with glittering eyes, watching the world around me. I turn and go for a drink in the pub a mile or so away across the battlefield.

It's called the Red Lion.

Index

BY THE SAME AUTHOR

EXIT PURSUED BY A BADGER:
An Actor's Journey
through History with Shakespeare

9781840028928

WWW.OBERONBOOKS.COM